A
Storyboard
Life

A
Storyboard
Life

From $20 to Two Hundred
Documentary Film
Adventures, the Journey
of a Creative Person

A MEMOIR

Kristin Fellows

*This book is dedicated to every woman who has dared to dream,
often against the odds.*

And for Karen

*An artist who did things her own way.
You will always be with me.*

In the journey of a creative person,
every decision you take is what makes you who you are. . . .
You have to be true to yourself for every
moment of that process . . .
because following your dreams is to try to find yourself.

ROLAND MOURET, FRENCH DESIGNER

CONTENTS

Part I: Another World

Part II: Metamorphosis

Part IV: Saving Room for the Unimaginable

Part V: Wherever You Are

THE WOMAN ON THE PARK BENCH

A YOUNG WOMAN, just thirty years old, sits weeping alone on a park bench in the middle of Washington, DC. Her blonde hair partially obscures her tear-streaked face as she wraps her arms protectively around her large belly. She is six months pregnant. She shivers. It is the week before Christmas and she has just lost her job in a career she loved.

That young woman crying on the park bench back in 1986 was me. This was not how I had envisioned my life. I was a professional. I had a brilliant career. But after seven post-college years working for a creative genius in the world of international design—a job that took me to Europe and all over the U.S.—a corporate takeover had terminated my position.

I'd married in April, gotten pregnant in May and then, just six months later, found myself laid off without warning.

Life being what it is, this would not be the only situation to take me by surprise in the years to come. But I learned to navigate the upsets with two unlikely partners: a steady stream of documentary film projects and a quirky knack for sideways thinking. Time after time, these two partners would help me dance around obstacles and phoenix myself out of yet another pile of ashes.

If I could go back in time to that park bench, I would whisper into that young woman's ear:

> *"You won't believe the pivots and plot twists that await you. Hang in there, you'll be astonished by what you will make out of them."*

PART I

ANOTHER WORLD

I move throughout the world without a plan,
guided by instinct, connecting through trust,
and constantly watching for serendipitous opportunities.

RITA GOLDEN GELMAN,

TALES OF A FEMALE NOMAD: LIVING AT LARGE IN THE WORLD

WHAT IS A STORYBOARD?

SIMILAR TO GRAPHIC novels or comic books, a storyboard is a set of sequential drawings that tells a story in individual frames while also illustrating the passage of time. The linear direction of the story cells makes it perfect for layout and visualizing shoot sequences when making films.

This is how my own career in documentary film has unfolded—frame by frame—over a span of nearly three decades. I was not the artist of my own storyboard. I did not do the planning or lay out the scenes and I was only able to see it once the frames were behind me. And yet the linear sequence of film projects I found myself involved with over the years drove my own narrative forward in a way that seemed almost to have an intelligence of its own.

I was in my early thirties and climbing through the emotional fallout of losing a job I loved. My husband, Steve, worked in construction. Eventually he quit working for others to start his own plumbing business, the third generation in his family to work in that trade. We had a baby. When our little girl Zoë was two-and-a-half, Steve had a banner month, which we optimistically thought was a sure sign of good things to come. On the strength of that, we decided to have a second child. We bought a small wreck of a house from an elderly, and often inebriated, airport architect with half a dozen cats, which we renovated ourselves with the help of friends.

But the financial high didn't last and by the time our son was born the following spring, we could no longer afford daycare, or our house due to the costs of running Steve's business. We lost everything.

Steve had been orphaned at an early age and I was the youngest child of parents who prized an independent spirit in their offspring, so there was nowhere to turn for help. We were completely on our own financially.

After our son Leif was born, I used my background in design to work part-time for an architecture firm, while also freelancing for artists, illustrators, and musicians, and trying—at the encouragement of another author—to get a children's book I'd written and illustrated with my own whimsical hand-cut collages published. Most often I was hired to find gigs or fundraise because someone once told me artists would rather chew off their right arm than ask people for money.

My contractor husband was a generous soul who sometimes had a difficult time asking customers to pay him for his work. And I had more clients for whom I worked on commission than on salary. Together, we earned just enough to barely get by.

The career in documentary film and television that sprang to life from this precarious lifestyle was not planned. I didn't have a degree in film, or any experience. There was nothing in my life up to that moment to even hint I might be headed in that direction. Thinking back, however, if we *hadn't* been so broke, it might not have happened at all.

But broke, we were.

As luck and strange circumstance would have it, the career I would never have imagined for myself began with Mikhail Baryshnikov, a set of bedsheets Sophia Loren had once slept in, and a deserted island.

Pondering these random items, like jigsaw pieces from different puzzles, it seems so unlikely they would launch a decades-long career. But somehow, I found a way to put them together into a paying gig that sustained me and my children. Had any one of them been missing, I likely would not have wandered into this astonishing career at all.

Over the coming years, working with documentary films would upend my life, and then upend it a second time. But working with films would also put my life back together again and again, and in ways I could never have imagined or foreseen. It was a storyboard created on the fly, a storyboard that revealed itself just one frame at a time as the future sketched itself out for me.

I've now worked in one capacity or another on close to two hundred films, a number that never fails to astonish me. I have traveled via documentary films to London, Istanbul, various locations in Germany and Italy, as well as many cities across the U.S.

I've worked with dozens and dozens of visionary storytellers, many of whom are now friends. I've had my eyes opened, my mind expanded, and my heart filled many times over.

Normally, story frames begin with a title slate. But in my case, mine began with twenty dollars.

The Night Baryshnikov Opened the Door into Another World

I WAS BORN in a rural farming community in New Jersey, an hour by train from New York City, where we lived in a very old stone house known as Round Ends. According to local lore, it had been built with rounded corners so the devil couldn't get in. My father loved that and laughed each time he told the story.

When I was five, my mother saw an advertisement in the *New York Times* for what was called a mid-century modern house, one with glass walls. She ordered the architectural plans, engaged contractors, and over the following year, "the New House" was built on the other side of the woods on our fifty acres of land.

Modern as it was, we still lived on a dirt road in farm country. My mother taught third grade at the local school and my father, a vice president for Eastern Airlines, worked in New York City.

Each December, my mother and I would take the train into the city to marvel at the big department store Christmas-themed window displays, visit my father at his office, watch the skaters at Rockefeller Center, have lunch and then see a matinée performance of *The Nutcracker*. The Hoffmann fantasy about a little girl who befriends a nutcracker that comes to life on Christmas Eve never failed to thrill me. Tchaikovsky's score has always been the soundtrack of the Christmas season for me.

Once I became a mother myself, I wanted to relive those happy memories by taking my own daughter to see *The Nutcracker* at Christmas in New York City. By then, however, my world and circumstances had altered dramatically. My husband and I were both self-employed. Our little family of four lived precariously, month to month, in the suburbs of Washington, DC. We had just lost the house of my dreams, a little mid-century modern glass-walled house in the woods that we'd renovated ourselves, similar to the one I'd lived in as a child, but much smaller.

Always short on money, Steve and I took turns avoiding phone calls, dodging bill collectors and threatening notices in the mail, trying to earn more while trying to make the rent each month. Financially, there was no possible way for me to take my daughter to New York City.

One dark December evening, when Zoë was six years old, I happened to notice our local PBS station was airing Mikhail Baryshnikov's *Nutcracker* that night. *If I can't get her to New York,* I thought, *we can at least watch it together from our sofa and I can make believe we are there.*

What I didn't realize at first was that WNVT was showing this performance as part of their on-air pledge drive. So I was a bit thrown when it stopped midway and a young woman with long, dark hair appeared on the screen to ask for money.

Irritated, my first thought was to ignore it. That was just about the last thing I could afford to do. But then it occurred to me—here I was being offered the opportunity to see *The Nutcracker* with my daughter, after all. Surely, I could part with a few dollars in appreciation?

I thought about it for a moment. Then, slightly misty with memories and gratitude, I called the station and offered them $20 from our weekly food budget.

A pleasant voice on the other end of the line tried to talk me up to a $30 donation, promising their monthly guide as part of the deal. I told her quite honestly that I didn't even have the money I was offering. She took my debit card number, then asked if she could mention my name on the air in appreciation.

"Sure," I said, wondering why on earth they would bother over such a small amount. I hung up and went back to Zoë and *The Nutcracker*.

The next pledge break came about twenty minutes later. Once again, the young woman's face appeared on the screen.

"I'd like to thank everyone who's called in tonight to support the station," she said, rattling off a handful of names. She ended with, "And thanks to Kristin in Mount Vernon for her generous donation!"

Speechless, I stared at the television screen. For most people, $20 was not a generous amount. But at that time, it was to me. My thoughts quickly spiraled—perhaps they'd made a mistake and thought I was donating $200? If so, they might try to charge my card for that amount, and it would bounce. There would be bank fees to pay. I'd have to spend an entire day, perhaps more, trying to untangle this.

On and on they went, these nightmare thoughts. After what felt like hours, Clara's dream world vanished, and she awakened at the foot of the Christmas tree. Once again, the smiling young woman was back on the screen.

"Thank you all so much for tonight's pledges!" she said with a big smile. "Thanks to you, we've raised $265!"

Two hundred and sixty-five dollars? I stared at the screen in disbelief. *That was all?!*

No longer worried they'd charged the wrong amount to my debit card, I went to bed that night, puzzling over what I considered to be their lackluster results.

The following morning, I picked up the phone and called the station.

A PBS Mind in an MTV World *

"HELLO, YOU DON'T know me, and I don't know anything about fundraising for television," I said, in what I hoped was a bright and confident tone. "But would it be possible for me to come in and talk with you? I think I might be able to help."

I was speaking to the receptionist at WNVT. Having just witnessed what I thought was a rather meager pledge drive the night before around Baryshnikov's *Nutcracker*, and even though I had no idea what I was doing, I thought surely I could help them raise more than $265.00.

I had no way of knowing this simple phone call would launch a whole new set of adventures that would involve a set of Sophia Loren's bedsheets and a private island owned by nudists somewhere off the coast of Bermuda.

The receptionist put me through to someone named Andy, who—to my great surprise—invited me to come over to the station and talk to him.

I showed up on the appointed day wearing what I hoped was a professional-enough-looking outfit, hastily cobbled together from recent finds at Goodwill. I felt an anticipatory thrill of excitement just walking into the television station, dwarfed as it was by the enormous telecommunications tower that loomed over it with its colorful twinkling lights reaching far up into the sky.

Andy, a tall and affable young guy with blonde hair, turned out to be the person in charge of fundraising for the station. He glanced over my résumé: former vice president of a Danish furniture and textiles importer; director of development for two architectural firms; and independent fundraising consultant for MENC, a national children's music education non-profit. After a few questions and pleasantries, he offered me freelance work raising money for the station on commission, mainly for their annual televised auction which would be coming up in a few months.

I can work from home, watch the kids, and still earn money—and I'll be working in television! I tried to mask my internal state of euphoric disbelief. This was 1992 and working from home was unusual back then. But there was still more to come.

"If you have a minute," Andy said with a smile, "there's someone else I'd like you to meet."

Andy led me through a warren of offices filled with people talking quietly in small clusters or gazing at computer screens, past rooms filled with lighting apparatus, camera gear and equipment, past edit suites, across the floor of a darkened television studio, and past the glass-enclosed room filled with computers, knobs, dials and switches I would soon learn was called master control—the heartbeat of a broadcast station. I had no idea how all of this worked. I just knew I really wanted to be here, in the midst of it all.

We eventually reached the office of the station's vice president for operations. Once there, he paused just long enough to hand me off to Dave Gallagher, a gray-haired, robust, Scottish-looking man of indeterminate age with a well-groomed beard and piercing blue eyes. Gallagher greeted me, grasping my small hand in his enormous paw, and pulled me into his office.

Less than an hour later, I emerged with a *second* freelance contract, this time to bring in sponsorship money—underwriting—for the station's regular programs as well as some of their specials.

Shaking with excitement that I would suddenly be working at a television station, while trying to ignore the voice in my head that kept reminding me I had absolutely no idea what I was doing, I drove home to share the good news with Steve.

* title by Jimmy Buffett

SOPHIA LOREN'S BEDSHEETS

"LET ME SHOW you how to approach public television fundraising," Dave Gallagher said to me on my first day of work. "Suppose I came to you with a special about hunting? Where would you go for funding?"

Busy fending off a barrage of flashing images of rifles, bows and arrows, blood, and dead animals, I didn't reply.

A veteran of KQED, the powerhouse PBS station in San Francisco, Gallagher was a burly human treasure chest of ideas for how to creatively acquire sponsorship money for public television shows. He made it fun and interesting, as well as intellectually challenging. An adventure each time.

"You might think of a gun manufacturer," he continued, not waiting to hear my thoughts. "But *anyone* could think of that. Instead, think about the tangential aspects of that hobby. For example, what about a freezer manufacturer? Hunters need to store their meat somewhere, right?!"

Taken by surprise, I recognized a kindred spirit. Right away I understood and appreciated Gallagher's thinking. I identified with it from my own life experiences of what I thought of as my quirky sideways thinking—solving problems, obstacles and challenges not in linear, logical or conventional ways, but from unusual angles.

"Here's another example," Gallagher went on. "When I was at KQED, somebody there knew somebody who worked at a luxury hotel in San Francisco where Sophia Loren had just spent a few nights. We were able to get the set of bed linens she'd slept in!"

My thoughts veered abruptly from bloody animal carcasses to rumpled, post-shagging sheets. *And do what with them?* I wondered, not sure I wanted to know.

"Now, we could have sold the sheets off during our on-air auction," Gallagher rattled on, ignoring the expression on my face. Clearly in his element, he seemed to be thoroughly enjoying this teachable moment. "But that would have resulted in only *one* donation."

"So instead . . ." and here he paused for effect, leaning towards me, "we dyed the sheets burgundy. Then we sent them to a seamstress who cut them into dozens of small pieces and stitched the edges. And then we auctioned them all off to viewers!

"Men *loved* having a pocket square that some part of Sophia Loren's skin may have brushed up against," he recalled, leaning back in his office chair, arms raised behind him, cradling his head. He grinned happily at the memory. "They made a bundle for us!"

I had to admit, I *was* impressed. An hour later, I left with a list of programs he wanted funding for.

I was unable to duplicate the celebrity sheets stunt, of course, but using the Gallagher thought process over the following weeks, I lined up the largest regional plumbing business to underwrite a season of *This Old House* and found an out-of-state supplier of vintage car parts to sponsor a thirteen-part series on restoring Mustangs. Project by project, I eventually found a funder for just about everything he gave me. Thousands of dollars, altogether. The big guy was delighted.

At the end of February, Gallagher called me back into his office for a special meeting.

"I have a new assignment for you," he said, skipping pleasantries. "The station's annual on-air auction is in April."

I waited, uncertain how this news pertained to me.

"We need donations," he said. "And I need *you* to get some for us. Unusual ones, big ticket ones!"

He grabbed a magazine from a pile of papers on his cluttered desk—a recent issue of *Washingtonian*. Puzzled, I watched as he flipped to the back, to the "Great Escapes" section—three columns of small advertisements on each page—and began reading out loud.

"Adventures Aloft, hot air ballooning flights over Maryland countryside . . . a farmstead B&B in Rappahannock County . . . a spectacular cottage with a fireplace at the beach in Chincoteague . . . a rustic lodge near Blackwater Wildlife Refuge . . . Harley Davidson motorcycle rides . . . a secret mountain hideaway, walking distance to the Appalachian Trail," he intoned, running a sturdy finger down the listings as he spoke.

"All these are possible! And, in return for their donations, tell them they'll get on-air publicity!" Gallagher spoke with confidence and enthusiasm. It all made perfect sense to him. He continued scanning the small advertisements.

"Aha! Here's a good one!" he said, his trademark grin lighting up his face as he took his eyes off the magazine long enough to see if I was paying attention—a grin I already knew to be just a little wary of. He was about to ask me to do something a bit out of my comfort zone—nothing illegal, but nothing I would have thought of myself. He picked up a red pen, then handed me the magazine so I could read what he had just drawn a big circle around with three exclamation points.

"Let's see if you can get this one!" he said to me, laughing.

For those seeking the ultimate island experience, rent your own deserted island in Bermuda, enjoying complete privacy while surrounding yourself with our crystal-clear waters. We'll

*take you out there by boat and come back for you a week
later. Enjoy fishing, our collection of books and games, our
well-stocked kitchen, and scavenger hunt maps we've created
to lead you around the island, looking for buried treasure—all
in complete privacy*!

Did I get the deserted island? Of course I did. There was simply
no way I could report back empty-handed to Dave Gallagher. The
owners of the island generously donated a week-long stay to WNVT's
on-air auction.

Working with Gallagher showed me how I might be able to make
good use of my non-linear mind and use it as a secret little superpower
working in television.

FOLLOWING A STRANGER'S SHOES

I GOT MANY other interesting donations, including the hot air balloon rides. But the island was, by far, the best one.

That island would come back to haunt me in the years to come when I reached out to the owners for a fundraiser to benefit the Washington, DC chapter of Women in Film and Video (WIFV). This time the owners sent a few homemade promotional videos for us to use during our auction. I screened them alongside the president of our WIFV chapter and watched in horror as the footage showed the middle-aged owners frolicking on the island and casting their fishing reels into the ocean—stark naked.

As we gasped in shock and tried to muffle our laughs, others gathered around to see what was entertaining us. Normally, a quick glimpse or two could be pixelated, but for a black-tie gala fundraiser, we couldn't use footage that showed any above the knee nakedness. That left us with a few beauty shots of the island, some of the ocean, and one of the cabin—about two minutes total (down from the original eight minutes).

A sweet young couple won the week-long vacation there. They planned to use it for their honeymoon but as luck would have it, a typhoon came along the week of their wedding, stripping the island of its trees and the little cabin, leaving nothing but a sandpile in the ocean.

A few weeks before WNVT's auction, Jim Moran, our Virginia congressman at the time, was scheduled to host a town hall meeting at the local high school. Not able to spare money for babysitters, Steve and I took turns getting out for the evening every so often, especially for civic events like this. This night was my turn.

Having never been to the school before, I had no idea where to locate the auditorium in what seemed like a vast complex of buildings. Wandering through the halls, I noticed a tall man, perhaps in his mid-forties, also looking around tentatively.

"Do you by chance know where the auditorium is?" I asked him. He shook his head no, and after a moment, disappeared down one of the hallways, like a lanky human version of Alice in Wonderland's white rabbit. He looked relatively harmless. I'd noticed he was wearing a nice pair of shoes, so I decided it was safe to follow him.

Eventually, he found the right door. As we entered the auditorium, someone asked us to sign in. The tall stranger with the nice shoes went first, then handed the clipboard to me. I read his name, which I immediately forgot because the two words next to his name caught my attention: documentary filmmaker.

What are the chances?! I thought. *He works in documentary film and I'm working for a PBS station.* That seemed more than just a coincidence. I followed him down the steps and, uninvited, sat in the empty seat next to him.

He listened attentively throughout the town hall meeting as Moran—a liberal, opinionated, and fiery Irishman from the Boston area with a reputation for getting into fisticuffs on Capitol Hill—easily held the audience in his sway.

"I noticed you signed in as a documentary filmmaker," I said as the event came to an end. He nodded.

"I work at the local PBS station," I said. "Would you like to be my guest at our VIP auction reception in a few weeks?"

I filled him in on the details and he politely said he would try to be there. We parted ways and I went home to my husband and kids.

That simple invitation, which I didn't expect him to take me up on, changed my life. Which was a good thing, as I was once again about to lose my job.

WHEN ONE DOOR . . .

"KRISTIN, THE VP of Development role at the station is open," Gallagher said. "I think you should apply."

He held my gaze across his cluttered desk.

His words surprised me but thinking it over, I realized I was more than qualified. In my previous career, I'd been vice president for an international importer, so it wasn't really a reach. And having raised over $65,000 for the station in just a few months, I already had a track record with them. Based upon this, I hoped to land the security of a steady job. I enjoyed working at the television station and was excited about the prospect of a permanent position there.

Weeks passed during which dozens of applications came in. In the end, there were nearly one hundred people from all over the country interested in the position.

I made the short list, and then the even shorter list. The station's general manager invited me out for an interview lunch, which was initially to be at a sweet little French restaurant nearby. But as we left in his car, he changed his mind. He confessed he was scared to make left turns out of the station across the lanes of traffic. He apologized, turned right, and took me to a nearby Wendy's instead.

That turn proved to be foreshadowing. Of the one hundred applicants, I was told the following week I had come in second. A woman from Rochester, New York—a stranger to the Washington, DC area, someone with no local connections—was hired instead.

I was bitterly disappointed and vented with my husband about the irrationality and injustice of it all over a bottle of wine that night after the kids were in bed.

The following day, my phone rang. It was the stranger with the nice shoes.

At my invitation, he'd shown up at the station for the VIP cocktail party the night before the auction started. At the end of the evening, we'd exchanged contact information. I assumed it was just a polite way to end our conversation, never thinking I'd hear back from him. But here he was, on the other end of the line.

"I've spoken with my colleagues about you," he said politely. "We're wondering if you'd like to come have lunch with us next week. I think we might be able to hire you on a freelance basis."

And that is how I came to find myself discussing the craft of making documentary films over bowls of steaming hot chili at a dingy joint called the Hard Times Cafe with a nun from New Orleans, a Franciscan friar, and the stranger with nice shoes whose name turned out to be Martin.

My life was about to take another unexpected turn.

ON A (B-)ROLL

A HANDFUL OF days later, Martin was sitting in my kitchen. Over mugs of hot black coffee, he described the work he was offering me as a freelancer.

He was in the process of making a film on Thomas Jefferson. But the problem with making a documentary about someone who'd lived in the 1700s and 1800s, he explained, was the scarcity of images in those pre-photography days. Known in film and television production as "B-roll," these are supplemental or alternative visuals that are intercut with the main shot to cover or illustrate narration and on-camera interviews.

Having earned enough college credits in Art History to have had a minor in the subject, I was excited at this new prospect. I got to work immediately.

Back then, doing art research meant spending hours at the library poring over catalogs, art books and other reference materials—all of which I was able to do with the kids in tow, or while they were in preschool or school.

Martin and I met every week or two at his documentary workshop or at my kitchen table and always over cups of hot coffee. Each time, I'd show him photocopies of the images I'd been able to find at art museums and universities in various collections in the U.S. and Europe. And each time, he'd bring me a new list of sections of the documentary he needed covered, along with a paycheck.

It wasn't grand pay, but I was acquiring a new skill set and I loved it. I especially enjoyed dealing with history and art museums in Europe. I couldn't believe this good fortune had come about from getting lost and taking a chance on speaking to someone who had on a pair of nice shoes.

One hundred and ten images later, the work came to an end. I had been dreading that moment.

Fortunately, Martin had another idea.

"Would you be interested in doing storyline development for another film we're working on, one that's already funded?" Martin asked the next time we saw one another. I wasn't quite sure what storyline development was, but I liked the sound of it so I said yes, hoping I'd be able to figure it out along the way.

That weekend, still high on the possibilities of what storyline development might entail, I bundled the kids into the car and headed off as usual to see what was available in the surrounding neighborhood yard sales.

"Which way shall we go?" I asked them. It was Zoë's turn to ride shotgun that morning.

"I know," she said, with all the confidence of her six years on this earth. "I'll follow my nose to the right and you follow your nose to the left."

I laughed out loud. It sounded just like how I was trying to navigate my new career.

CINDERELLA AT THE PRESIDENT'S BALL

IN THE WORLD of documentary film—as I was to learn over and over—fundraisers rarely get paid a salary for their efforts. Filmmakers don't have a lot of cash on hand and if they do, it's considered risky to spend it on fundraisers, even though they desperately need them. On the other side of the coin, it's considered risky to spend your hours and days trying to bring money in to fund projects with no compensation for your time or efforts. Ninety-nine percent of the time, it's a lose/lose situation. Despite the odds, I was optimistic about the one percent.

The art research assignments Martin had provided me were just a way to pay me small amounts periodically and keep me, at least tangentially, on the documentary team. As a filmmaker, what he was most interested in were my fundraising skills. During the night of the WNVT auction, I'd told him how much money I'd raised for the station. I once read that documentary film-makers spend as much as 80 percent of their time trying to fund their projects, and 20 percent of their time actually making them—a statistic that made Martin wince when I shared it.

His film on Thomas Jefferson was mostly funded. But Martin had another idea that he needed financial support for—the history of news in America, from the first colonial newspapers to present day. He was a passionate collector of vintage newspapers, periodically going to conventions and picking up archival documents of interest.

We brainstormed ideas for where and how to raise money for what he envisioned as his first series.

Mostly because I still wanted to be part of the documentary workshop, I agreed to try to find funding for the news series, on what the British might refer to as "the never never."

The series didn't have a working title yet. I suggested *News & The American Character*, which Martin liked, and which made it easier to catch people's attention. It was a story that needed to be told and a perfect fit for PBS. With his degree in broadcast journalism from Boston University, Martin would be a good person to tell it.

Anxious to get results (and get paid), I set to work. Lots of leads, but no funding. I even arranged a meeting with Peter Prichard, director of the Newseum, an exciting new museum dedicated to news and journalism that promoted free expression and the First Amendment while tracing the evolution of communication. A perfect fit, I thought. Peter gave us a great tour of their facilities but as his organization was also in fundraising mode, he was unable to help us financially. Over the course of the following year, Martin compensated me for my phone bills but lacked the funds (since I hadn't raised any) to compensate me for my time.

Meanwhile, Steve and I continued to limp along financially, which was stressful for both of us. Steve continued plumbing, along with half a dozen other side ventures, while I tried to raise money and procure paid gigs for a small roster of artists, illustrators, musicians, and arts organizations, working from home to be with the kids. MENC, the Music Educators National Conference, a national organization of music teachers, was my best client and only actual income at the time. The director and I got along well. I designed some clever and innovative corporate strategies for them, all of which he loved, but none of which resulted in hard cash over the course of the next year. Eventually, he was pressured by his board to end our contract, which he reluctantly did, and with the loveliest and most gracious termination letter ever.

In the course of my efforts on the money trail, I'd heard about a new organization called Business for Social Responsibility—a group of socially minded entrepreneurs formed in 1991 to represent the voice of progressive businesses in policy formation in Washington, DC.

In 1993, BSR held its first annual conference in Washington, DC, featuring Ben Cohen of Ben & Jerry's; Anita Roddick, founder of The Body Shop; and Gary Hirshberg, cofounder of Stonyfield Farms, the first dairy processor to pay farmers *not* to treat their cows with synthetic growth hormones. (In the years to come, Stonyfield would go on to help create the Oscar-nominated documentary *Food, Inc.*, a staggering look at what really goes on inside America's corporate food industry.)

Three hundred people attended the first BSR conference, and I was one of them.

Another attendee was keynote speaker, Bill Clinton—just a few months into his first term as President of the United States.

It was my third time being in the same room as Clinton. Steve, a passionate Democrat, had campaigned for him partly because of Clinton's ideas and partly because they shared the same birthday, August 19th. Steve took that to be a sign of some sort and dedicated quite a few (unpaid) hours to the Clinton campaign.

When Clinton won, Steve managed to get tickets to one of the Inaugural Balls in town. I remember being surprised to learn there was more than one; I think there were at least a dozen of them in 1993. Embassies, organizations, high-donors, and special interest groups all wanted to host one in celebration of Clinton's victory. We went to the one held at Union Station.

It was a Cinderella night for me. I'd found a sexy,

brand-new-with-tags, sequined evening dress in my size at a second-hand store in Old Town in Alexandria for just $45. Having secured a trade-out with a babysitter, Steve and I dressed up and hit the town.

Bill and Hillary Clinton spent their celebratory evening racing around to make a personal appearance at as many of the Presidential Inaugural Balls as they could manage—something else I'd never been aware presidents had to do. When Clinton finally appeared at ours, it was late in the evening. He thanked everyone, danced briefly with Hillary, then played saxophone with the band on stage, much to the crowd's ecstatic delight.

Through his volunteering efforts, Steve also scored tickets to the coolest party in DC—the "Absolutely Unofficial Blue Jeans Bash for Arkansas," Clinton's thank-you party for Arkansas residents, which was a lot more fun.

"When Bill Clinton was elected President in 1992," wrote *Paste* journalist Loren DiBlasi, "after 12 years of Republican rule, [people] just wanted to watch the totally chill former Governor of Arkansas jam on saxophone." Looking back on that night, she later wrote the Blue Jeans Bash was "one of the more Clinton-esque events of the era."

Held at the National Building Museum, it featured a Southern feast of catfish and hush puppies with music by Bob Dylan, Dr. John, Ronnie Hawkins, Levon Helm, and Clarence Clemens. Stephen Stills was there. Actors Don Johnson and Melanie Griffith served as the evening's hosts. Ben and Jerry, dressed in jeans and tie-dyed T-shirts, served up scoops of ice cream for dessert.

"The whole state of Arkansas, it seemed, had turned up at the 'Absolutely Unofficial Blue Jean Bash,'" wrote Martha Sherrill in the *Washington Post*. "Even Bill Clinton's mother, who was hugging everyone in sight." (I'm pretty sure Steve got one of those hugs.)

It was easy to tell who was from where. Everyone from Arkansas came dressed to the nines in rhinestones, sequins, makeup, and big hair. They were the glitzy party animals, exuberantly happy, drinking, laughing, and dancing. Then there was the quiet Capitol Hill crowd tentatively hovering on the sidelines, dressed in polo shirts, khakis, and loafers. Steve and I avoided the locals and had a blast hanging out with the Arkansas crowd.

In addition to Bill Clinton, the other big-name guest that night was Bob Dylan. Steve and I planted ourselves by the rails and ropes security guards had put out to hold guests sequestered away from the stage, impatiently waiting for Clinton to make his appearance. To pass the time, I attempted to chat with a middle-aged man from Texas standing next to me. Wearing a business suit and cowboy hat, he looked like he regularly enjoyed meals at expensive restaurants.

"Aren't you happy he won?" I said in my naïve little buzz of happiness, somewhat starstruck by the whole event.

"Not really," he drawled nonchalantly, taking me by surprise. "Ahh give equal amounts to both campaigns, so it doesn't really matter to me who wins, as long as Ahh bet on the horse. And, Ahh always bet on *both* horses, so Ahh *always* win."

End of conversation and a mind-jarring lesson in the realities of politics in Washington, DC.

Bob Dylan stalled backstage as the crowd grew restless. When he finally appeared, it was anticlimactic. He performed "To Be Alone with You," a rollicking little dance tune from his album *Nashville Skyline*.

But that night, most of us were there to hear a little saxophone by the new president-elect. And we eventually did, much to the delight of the entire rhinestoned crowd, who whooped and hollered for their hometown boy.

What I remember most about that first BSR conference was watching Bill Clinton address the attendees, his comfort speaking to a crowded room and his incredible memory for numbers and statistics. When someone from the back interrupted him with a question, Clinton stopped mid-speech.

"*Hey*, now that's a good question!" he called out, acknowledging the person. He paused, sucking on his bottom lip for just a moment.

He answered the question thoughtfully, complete with backup statistics before resuming seamlessly with his prepared remarks. Both his reaction and his response were impressive.

With only three hundred attendees at the conference, it wasn't hard to meet interesting people. One of them was Will Spencer, a mediator and advocate for peace. Will headed up Pangaea International, a network of organizations working with conflict resolution and social change.

When I told him about Martin's *News & the American Character* project, he invited us both down to spend a day with him at The Carter Center at Emory University. A few weeks later, Martin and I did just that, flying down to Atlanta for a tour and talks.

While there, we met briefly with the twinkly eyed and delightful Jimmy Carter. I still have a photo from the day. In it, Martin and I are smiling for the camera, me in my best secondhand business dress—a tailored classic black and ivory light wool in a houndstooth pattern. Standing next to me is Jimmy Carter, his arm around my waist. I still remember the gentle little squeeze he gave me to ease my nerves.

Although I ultimately did not raise any production funds for *News & the American Character*, I would in short order raise over half a million dollars for Martin for a different documentary film—a project neither of us even saw coming.

Made of Stars: On Location with Madeleine L'Engle

"WE ARE ALL made of the same stuff as stars, you know," said author Madeleine L'Engle calmly.

Her words caught me by surprise. Although the stars, the sky, and the universe are all characters in a number of Ms. L'Engle's books—especially *A Wrinkle in Time*, her world-famous fantasy fiction novel from the early 1960s—I'd never heard this before.

Distracted as I was by the surreal astonishment of finding myself sitting *in her kitchen*, listening to *her* talk to us over a bowl of soup *her* son had made from scratch—that comment still caught my attention.

How had this all come about? In the weeks after saying "yes" to Martin when he asked if I'd like to work on storyline development for his latest documentary about the intersection of creativity and religion, I'd segued from our initial meetings over coffee in my kitchen to having a little workspace of my very own at the documentary workshop, along with a small but regular paycheck.

When he asked if I'd like to go with the crew on a road trip to Litchfield, Connecticut to interview Madeleine L'Engle for his documentary *Creativity: Touching the Divine,* I said yes again, beyond excited at the opportunity to meet the legendary author.

In the days leading up to the interview, my head filled with tingling anticipation as I reread *A Wrinkle in Time.*

The morning of our departure, the crew piled into a large white rented van—Martin; Bertch, our gaffer and lighting guy; Tim, the shooter; and Ellen, the woman who'd helped with a grant to fund the documentary and who was every bit as smitten as me with Madeleine L'Engle's stories. In addition to the five of us, there was also all the production gear, which occupied the space of several passengers. Sister Gretchen, the nun from New Orleans, stayed behind to run the documentary workshop in our absence.

After eleven hours on the road in the cramped production van, we pulled into Litchfield late in the afternoon the day before the shoot, checked into the Tollgate Hill Inn, then headed over to the on-site tavern to shake off the road over dinner and a few cold beers.

The following morning, we made our way slowly down the long road that leads to the old farmhouse Madeleine L'Engle and her husband bought and renovated back in the early 1950s. As we rounded a corner, suddenly there she was, standing at the open door, smiling and ready to welcome us in.

We parked and, one by one, tumbled out of the van to meet her. Nearly five feet ten inches tall with closely cropped hair, a wide-collared flowing white blouse and dark skirt, Ms. L'Engle towered over me. Her half-moon dark eyes and arched eyebrows had a slightly surprised but friendly look. She greeted us all enthusiastically, then she and Martin discussed possible locations for the interview while the rest of us unloaded the gear.

After considering the options, Martin chose the attic—a small space up under the eaves where Ms. L'Engle did most of her writing. Built-in shelves sagged under the weight of haphazardly stacked books.

Flowered curtains hung from the windows. An L-shaped workspace was cluttered with nests of papers and an old typewriter. An old keyboard was lodged behind them. This was the place where all the magic of her many stories had been concocted, the secret space where her writings went from her mind onto the paper.

We tucked, wedged, and squeezed ourselves along with the lighting setups, the audio recording gear, the tripod and video camera into the available nooks and crannies. With no other space available, I sat cross-legged on the floor, notepad in my lap, waiting to write down whatever she shared with us.

Martin posed the questions he'd prepared and Ms. L'Engle responded easily and openly. She'd done this many times before.

"I've been a writer ever since I could hold a pencil!" she said when he asked her how it all began. She wrote her first story, she told us, when she was just five years old. The only child of two loving but neglectful artists, she'd had a lonely and awkward childhood but grew up with an appreciation for creative responses to life's confusion, especially writing.

"Our truest response to the irrationality of the world is to paint or sing or write, for that's where we find truth," she told us. "Stories make us more alive, more human, more courageous, more loving."

Madeleine L'Engle was a devout Episcopalian. She explained how she loved to interweave faith with science and the universe throughout her writings, creating her own unique way of looking at the world.

"Some things have to be *believed* to be seen!" she quipped.

When she wrote *A Wrinkle in Time*, the story of a young girl and her younger brother transported through time and space in search of their father, a gifted scientist, she knew she had something special.

The two children are aided in their quest by the whimsical trio of Mrs. Whatsit, Mrs. Who, and Mrs. Which—all of whom conspire to help rescue the children's father from the evil forces holding him prisoner on another planet. Described as a mix of Christian-inspired themes and loosely conceived quantum physics, populated with supernatural characters and told in her own quirky writing style, *A Wrinkle in Time* was turned down by publishers twenty-six times.

With each rejection letter, Ms. L'Engle told us, she took her frustrations out at night, when she walked her dogs down her long farmhouse driveway.

"Why, God?!" she told us she would shout up to the stars. "You know it's good! Why can't anyone else see that?!"

Imagine the audacity of telling God that He knows something you wrote is good, I thought. That's confidence.

"You have to write the book that wants to be written," she said. "And if the book is too difficult for grown-ups, then you write it for children."

For children!? It seemed counterintuitive, but pondering it, I realized she was right.

In her writings, Ms. L'Engle drew upon Albert Einstein's theory of relativity; German theoretical physicist Max Planck, who'd received the Nobel Prize for his discovery of energy quanta; and Werner Heisenberg, one of the main pioneers of the theory of quantum mechanics. Their writings, she said, reminded her of staring into the night sky as a child which had given her an appreciation for the vastness of the universe.

But she knew her audience. That's why many of her novels have the same central theme: that it's okay to be different. Sometimes being different is a superpower. In her case, it was.

Eventually, someone did take a chance on *A Wrinkle in Time* and published it. It went on to win the Newbery Medal for Excellence in Children's Literature—among other awards—and has since sold more than six million copies worldwide.

After the interview, Ms. L'Engle invited all of us to join her for a bowl of soup in her big old farmhouse kitchen. With the camera and gear packed away, the conversation became folksier and more casual. She told us she used to show her husband early drafts of her books and his response would often be a list of the small changes he thought needed to be made.

"Don't tell me the mistakes!" she told us she would shout at him in frustration. "First, tell me it's good! After that, *then* you can tell me what's wrong. But first, *tell me it's good!*"

That this hugely successful author admitted her husband's approval was important to her was charmingly revealing. As the crew shuffled out to begin loading the gear back into the van, I lingered in the kitchen for a few minutes to ask if she had any advice for a shy but aspiring writer.

"I *do* have advice for people who want to write," she said. "There are three things that are important. First, you need to keep an *honest* journal that nobody reads, nobody but you. Write what you think about life, and what you think about everything. Second, you need to *read*. You can't be a writer if you're *not* a reader. It's the great writers who teach us *how* to write. The third thing is to *write*. Just write a little bit every day. Even if it's for only half an hour—*write, write, write!*"

I resolved to do all three. Before we left, Martin took a photograph of Ms. L'Engle and me standing together in her kitchen. In the photo, she towers over me, beaming. I'm standing beside her, looking shyly excited, with Martin's jacket draped over my shoulders as I hadn't dressed warmly enough for the cool Connecticut weather.

I left Litchfield with a head filled with more thoughts about writing than of filmmaking, while also appreciating that I would not have had this opportunity to visit with Madeline L'Engle were it not for this documentary.

As we made our way south on the highway for the long journey home, my thoughts once again played with the tenuous chain of what-if's that had brought me to this moment: *if* my mother hadn't taken me to see the *Nutcracker* when I was a child . . . *if I* hadn't wanted to duplicate that experience for my own daughter . . . *if* the PBS station hadn't been in pledge that evening . . . *if* I hadn't picked up the phone the following morning to call them about it . . . and *if* I hadn't spoken to the stranger with nice shoes at the local town hall meeting—well, this magical afternoon would have happened for somebody else, not me.

But this new career was only just getting started and the road ahead would soon be filled with potholes and plot twists I could not have imagined.

> *Don't try to comprehend with your mind.*
> *Our minds are very limited.*
> *Use your intuition.*
>
> MADELINE L'ENGLE

THE HOUSE OF MANY COLORS: ON LOCATION IN SAN ANTONIO

ANOTHER DAY, ANOTHER rental van.

This time it was just Martin, Tim the cameraman, and me, driving through a humble neighborhood in West San Antonio, tracking down my first idea for a storyline for the documentary *Creativity: Touching the Divine.*

We were here to interview Enedina Cásarez Vasquez, a Mexican American folk artist who, along with her husband Arturo, created hand-crafted, hand painted *nichos*—charming three-dimensional shadow boxes used as portable altars or shrines to a deity or loved one. Adapted from Roman Catholic *retablos*—paintings of a patron saint on wood or tin—these *nichos* often also featured little hinged doors that opened to reveal a meaningful image or tableau inside.

Enedina and Arturo's folk art, a synthesis of their Catholic faith and Native American-Chicano culture, was displayed and sold in art galleries and museum gift shops throughout the U.S. I'd come across them in my research and thought they'd be perfect for the film. I was looking forward to meeting them at their home studio.

But there was silence in the van as we drove into their neighborhood, getting our first look at the tumbledown, pieced-together little houses hovering between despair and optimism that scrolled past our windows like faded footage from the wrong film.

Here was another new lesson for me: The thrill of thinking up ideas for possible inclusion in a documentary can so easily be offset by the consequences of wasted time and the very real costs of making a bad choice. It's one thing to pick an interview with Madeleine L'Engle (really, what could go wrong?) but it's quite another, I realized, to track down a possible story with unknown characters in another part of the country.

With mounting anxiety, I calculated the cost to fly the three of us—with film gear—to Texas for this interview. If this was a bad choice, I would appear inept and might lose the responsibilities I'd been given to do storyline development.

"Don't worry, I'm sure it will be fine," Martin said as he scanned the street looking for the right address. He eventually spotted the number on an old mailbox and turned the van into the driveway.

"This is it," he said quietly.

It can't be, I thought, taking in the jumble of small buildings scattered in and among overgrown trees and scrawny shrubbery, the yard filled with discarded odds and ends. Whatever I'd been expecting, it certainly wasn't this.

Martin got out of the van, telling us to wait. Tim and I watched anxiously as he walked over to the door and knocked. A moment later, the door opened to reveal an older Mexican American man with a broad smile of welcome. After they exchanged greetings, Martin turned and gestured for us to join him. Tim and I got out of the van and made our way to the front door and into the house.

To my great surprise, we walked into a multi-roomed, dazzling jewel box. We followed Arturo through a jumble of rooms in vibrant colors, each filled with exuberant blazes of art. It was like walking into a life-size series of *nichos*, each room more fascinating than the previous one. We were walking into the eyes, heart, and soul of the artist herself.

I'd never seen anything like it. Everything everywhere was color. Every inch of wall space in each of the small rooms was covered with art—hanging from, nailed to, or painted directly onto the walls which were themselves various bright colors. In the spaces left between the pieces of art, there were writings in script painted on the walls. Strands of Christmas lights, prayer flags, and still more art hung from the ceilings.

In the middle of it all, there was Enedina herself, beaming at us. She hugged me, welcoming me to her home. I'm not sure what I said in response, buzzed as I was by the crazy abundance of color and happiness that surrounded me.

We quickly set up for the interview in the only space available that could accommodate the lights, the camera and tripod, and the three of us. Once camera was rolling, Martin began his questions, asking her how she came to express herself, and her faith, through art.

"I was born with a paintbrush in my hand," Enedina said with a charming accent. "Before speech, before walking, before everything! I work with paint and canvas and with a pen. I paint with words."

She gave a belly laugh. "Art is who I am, and I am what art is!"

While painting or writing poetry, she told us she carries on a conversation with God, calling what she does "prayer art."

At first, she said, she painted family portraits and moments she recalled from her experiences as a migrant worker.

"I wanted to capture the beauty of family, of working in the fields. My paintings were colorful, none were sad or depressing."

She then went on to paint what she called her *Mujer Grande* paintings series—colorful paintings depicting large women who seem to break out of the boundaries of the canvas.

Dazzled and distracted, I looked from wall to wall. Everything she thought and felt, everything she loved and believed in— it was all around us.

Afterwards, Arturo took us out back to his woodworking shop to show us where and how he crafts the little wooden *nichos* his wife will paint in many colors. I bought one for Zoë and Leif—to watch over them, I told Enedina.

I had also seen a small, hand-painted wooden cross in bright colors that completely charmed me. I pointed it out to her, but Enedina said it had already been sold to someone else. She told me she would make a similar one—one she would paint especially for me.

Before parting ways, Enedina told me she could feel I was *una mujer grande*—a big woman. I'm barely 5'4" and weigh 124 pounds. I must have had a puzzled expression on my face, for she laughed, her whole broad friendly face lighting up, and told me she meant big in a very positive way. Too big for my own canvas, I guessed.

On our way out, Arturo and Enedina took us through yet another little room in their home. Here, the walls were covered with outlines of hands. Each visitor to their home had left a message inside the shape of their own hand—an impossibly charming idea that revealed a lot about this artist couple. Enedina wanted ours there, too. She brought out a Sharpie, somehow found some space on the wall, and traced the outline of our fingers and palms. Then she asked us to write a message to them inside our hands, which we did.

On the way back to the airport, I looked down at the carefully wrapped little *nicho* I was holding. There were smudges of Sharpie still on my fingers, but I made no effort to rub them off.

A few weeks later, a small package arrived for me at the workspace. Inside, I found the brightly colored, hand-painted cross I'd ordered from Enedina—a charming, simple vine with green leaves and little red and pink embellishments against the aqua background I'd found so irresistible. A hand-illustrated letter was enclosed:

Dear Mujer Grande Kristin, It was such a treat to meet you and share some time together, even for just a while. I do hope that you will return to San Antonio one of these days so you can come home for a visit. . . . Enclosed is the cross, it was a pleasure working on it and thinking of you as I worked—all my thoughts, wishes, and prayers travel with it to your home.

Regards to all and know you have friends and a home here in beautiful San Antonio!

Enedina & Arturo

"Why didn't I get a thank-you letter from her?" Martin asked. "Because you're not a *mujer grande*," I said, teasing him.

THE MAN BEHIND THE MASK

MEANWHILE, ESCALATING TENSIONS on the home front over our financial insecurities had turned my fragile marriage into an emotional fault plane, exposing the deepening cracks and widening crevices between me and my husband.

A friend suggested I see a therapist to help manage the stress—something I'd never done before and could not really afford to do. She persisted, suggesting Dr. Paul Peckar, a psychiatrist whose children went to the same local school as ours. I yielded and booked a single, one-hour consultation.

There's no mistaking him. Paul Peckar is quickly recognizable for his badly scarred and disfigured face and hands, resulting from a horrendous incident a few years earlier.

"Paul Peckar was about to start a psychiatric session with a patient when the mystery package arrived at his Fairfax County office.

Peckar joked with his patient that 'it's probably a bomb.'

As the patient relaxed in a brown leather

recliner, the psychiatrist opened the package and peeked inside. Then the room exploded."

Knowing I only had enough money for a single session, Paul moved quickly through my background bio, work, and my family life, like a counseling version of speed dating. He was curious, interested, and empathetic. He even laughed occasionally—but only at the right places. Then he got serious and asked about my marriage.

I told him about a recurring dream I'd been having in which I was trying to keep from drowning in swirls of black water while carrying what felt like the weight of my husband on my back. When I was able to look up, I could see the sun shining on a beautiful jungle of thriving plants on a distant mountaintop.

"I wish I could paint," I said, "so I could put that dream down on canvas and get it out of my head."

Paul listened intently, asking the occasional perceptive question and taking a lot of notes with his damaged hand curving awkwardly around his notepad. As I was talking, my mind wondered, is he even able to read his own writing?

"Peckar, his clothes on fire, followed the voice of his patient, whose leg was broken—past the missing walls, under the collapsed ceiling, through the warped front door 15 feet away.

'I can't tell you what it was like, except it was a flash,' Peckar said. 'I knew I was burned. I knew my life had changed.'"

My life was about to change, too. Fortunately, not so dramatically. But for me, the kids, and Steve, it would still be a seismic shift.

Eventually Paul looked at me intently through his glasses and said, "So why don't you get a divorce?"

The room was quiet as his words hung in the air.

"It's okay to do that?" I asked tentatively, eventually breaking the silence.

"The blast . . . left burns over nearly 60 percent of his body, flaps on his scalp and face, a gaping hole in his abdomen and a three-inch chunk of pipe bomb just a heartbeat from his aorta. The scars on his arms look and feel like raw chicken skin. Because of severe nerve damage, his wrists flop and require splints for support."

"Why not?" he said.

He didn't tell me what to do, he just asked questions. But something in my head recognized the thought of being on my own again as the right next step for me. Perhaps the idea needed to come from someone who barely knew either of us. I don't know. But what I *did* know is that at that moment, light seemed to flood into my head, chasing out the sharp edges of the bad dreams. I can wear this, I thought.

"After a year's worth of hospitals and rehabilitation, Peckar, 51, looks at life differently through his hard plastic face mask.

What he sees is something positive emerging from all the pain. He says he is closer to his family now, more aware of how little of his life truly is under his control."

I left Paul's office, knowing there were more difficult times ahead of me, but also mindful that my troubles paled in comparison to what he'd been through. That helped me find a new perspective and—to use a film term—pull focus.

I also left unaware that the time I had just spent with Paul would bring a new documentary film into my life, one that would take it in a whole new direction—like a runaway horse bolting across the landscape with me clinging to its back, watching what unfolded with amazement.

Quoted passages are excerpts from https://www.washingtonpost.com/archive/politics/1991/06/02/piecing-together-a-shattered-life/9249ae58-1a68-4da0-9086-a2c1fcc19b5d/ by Patricia Davis, 1991.

Mrs. Doubtfire and The Man with the Key

THE SPLIT WITH Steve happened. It wasn't perfect or simple or easy. Were there difficult and painful times? Yes, of course there were. But there's no need to rehash or relive them here. Like underwear, you know it's there, hidden and held close to the body. But does everyone need to know the details? Probably not.

Despite our differences, Steve and I did agree on one thing as we prepared to go our separate ways: The kids would always come first. This simple mantra kept the untangling of joined lives (mostly) civil. We presented the new arrangement to the kids by telling them that they would now be living in *two* houses.

"Does that mean *two Christmases*?" one of them asked immediately.

Sort of, we said.

To distract and ease them through the transition, I rented a copy of *Mrs. Doubtfire* from Blockbuster. I didn't have the money to pay for cable television, which was disproportionately expensive back then, but Zoë and Leif could watch VHS tapes whenever they wanted.

The 1993 film, directed by Chris Columbus

and starring Robin Williams and Sally Field, addressed themes of divorce, separation, and their effect on a family. Based on the 1987 novel *Madame Doubtfire* by Anne Fine, the film tells the story of an actor who disguises himself as an elderly female housekeeper in order to spend time with his children who are in his ex-wife's custody. I'll admit there may have been a few similarities between Miranda—the hard-working, neatness-obsessed interior designer who considered her husband (much as he was devoted to his kids) a bit immature and unreliable—and me.

At the end of the film, Mrs. Doubtfire responds to a letter from a little girl named Katie whose parents have separated, telling her that no matter what arrangements families have, love will prevail.

It was the perfect film at the time. Mesmerized, Zoë and Leif watched it over and over—so many times, in fact, I eventually bought them a copy. It still sits in a box of their old childhood treasures.

Fortunately, there was no money to pay a lawyer to set up the arrangements, saving us thousands of dollars neither of us had. Having heard horror stories from friends about divorces costing up to six figures, I checked out a book on separation agreements from the library. I cherry-picked the examples I liked, then wrote up my own agreement. I showed it to Steve who didn't object. Through a friend of a friend, I was able to find an empathetic female lawyer who notarized and legalized it for a grand total of $500.

Throughout, Steve and I stayed involved with Zoë and Leif's micro soccer teams as volunteers. Steve coached one of their teams and I refereed their matches. Saturday mornings would find all four of us together out on the soccer fields. It was nearly always a peaceful place for us to be together as a family, even one that lived in two separate homes. I remember walking off the soccer pitch with Steve one afternoon when a friend came up from behind, slipping in between us.

"You guys are amazing," she said, putting an arm around each of us. "Tell me how you do divorce, Heflin-style!"

We hugged her back, catching one another's surprised eyes over the top of her head. Things weren't perfect, but it was nice that others thought so.

When our first post-separation wedding anniversary rolled around, Steve called to ask me what we should do. We'd celebrated that date for ten years and it would seem weird not to. Together we came up with the idea that instead of celebrating *us*, we would celebrate our favorite result of the marriage: the kids. We took them out for dinner at their favorite place to eat. We did that each year, drinking a toast to Zoë and Leif, then sharing a meal together—until Steve's next wife put an end to it.

As they didn't have a say in the going of separate ways, we told the kids they would have a room in each place we were renting and asked them how they might like to arrange their time with us.

"I know," Leif said immediately. "We'll do every other night at Mom's house and then, the every other, other nights at Dad's."

For some reason, both adults agreed to this plan.

(Fortunately, the kids would eventually tire of changing houses every other day and proposed changing every other *two* days instead. But it was still problematic keeping track of which house on which day, so I eventually suggested Mondays and Tuesdays with me and Wednesdays and Thursdays with their dad. On the weekends, Zoë and Leif could decide for themselves where they felt like being. And that arrangement stuck.)

When we parted ways, Steve found a small flat nearby. And I fell madly in love with a charming little house available for rent in an older neighborhood of smaller homes. It was white with cornflower blue shutters and was surrounded by large trees and huge azaleas. It even had a tire swing hanging from a big old tree in the yard. The house had a quirky layout, the result of random add-ons over the years. I was pretty sure nobody designed a house this way on purpose, and that appealed to me.

Completely smitten, I began stalking the house, taking every opportunity to detour past it. Fortunately, it was only a ten-minute drive away from the documentary film workspace. The more I drove past the house, the more perfect it became for me and the kids in my imagination. Mentally, I'd moved us in, painted the living room lavender, hung the children's art, and put pots of brightly blooming flowers out on the front steps.

I made an inquiry to see if I could rent it, but the property manager was difficult and obstructionist. And to be honest, my credit wasn't in great shape at the time; I wasn't sure I would even qualify for the reasonable rent they were asking. Documentary filmmaking is rarely a steady or well-paid job and I was still recovering from the financial mess of the marriage years.

After picking up Leif from kindergarten one day, I detoured as usual past the house, driving slowly and gazing at it longingly. There was an old Mercedes parked in the driveway. I pulled over and stopped across the street.

"Who do you think is here?" I said to Leif.

He gave a five-year-old shrug. *How should I know?*

We waited. I stared at the house anxiously, almost forgetting to breathe, worried someone else had moved in. Leif fidgeted, looking around for his Gameboy.

Fortunately, it wasn't long before an elderly man, slight of build with tufts of white hair on his nearly bald pate, emerged from the house. He closed the front door behind him, then turned to lock it.

"I think that might be the owner," I whispered to Leif. "What should I do?!"

"Why don't you say *hello*?" he suggested calmly, not taking his eyes off his player.

A brilliant idea in its simplicity. Here was the opportunity to make my case directly to the owner who might, hopefully, like me enough to put in a good word with the property manager.

I got out of the car, crossed the street and walked up the cracked concrete driveway to introduce myself. The man was indeed the 80-year-old owner of the house, Jules Renaud. His blue eyes peered at me curiously from behind his wire-framed glasses. The wisps of untamed white hair on his head puffed about in the breeze.

Friendly and delightful, he immediately put me at ease. He no longer lived here, he explained. He'd met his new wife, Mary Janet, at a yard sale and moved into her house in a much posher neighborhood.

I told him I worked for a documentarian making films for public television, hoping those words might somehow establish my credibility and trustworthiness. To my relief, his face lit up.

"Really!" he exclaimed. "Well, I'm an old TV man myself! I worked for the USDA's radio and television division! And my wife, Mary Janet, is a retired television writer and producer!"

What were the chances?

He beamed at me through his spectacles.

I told him how much I loved the house and hoped his property manager would approve my application to rent it. A moment passed in silence during which I hoped I hadn't overstepped. And then, a small miracle happened.

"Well, since you're here," he said, reaching into his vest pocket, "why don't I just give you the key to the front door?"

I stared in disbelief as he placed a small brass key into the palm of my hand.

I'm in!

TULIPS AND GARGOYLES: ON THE ROAD TO SINGLEDOM WITH DESMOND TUTU AND DAVE BRUBECK

THE KIDS AND I moved into the little house in early April. I painted the living room lavender, hung their art on the walls, and put out big pots of bright flowers on the front steps, just as I'd planned in my daydreams.

A few days after we took up residence, I got out of bed one morning and wandered through the house toward the kitchen in search of coffee. Zoë was sitting on the sofa in the living room.

"Look outside!" she said as soon as she saw me.

"Why?" I asked.

"*Just look!*" she said in that special child's tone of voice, the one that must be obeyed without question.

I glanced out the window in the direction of her pointing finger, to the side of the house where the big tree was with the tire swing and gasped in astonishment. The yard, which I had thought was just tall weeds and grass, had erupted overnight in long-stemmed tulips! All over the lawn, slender green shoots and colorful buds were reaching to the sky as if they were giving us—the new cottage dwellers—a botanical standing ovation.

"They're everywhere!" I gasped.

Zoë nodded with an eight-year old's smug satisfaction, very pleased to be the one who saw them first.

I made coffee, then walked outside, cup in hand, to wander through the flowers and admire them up close. Their colorful exuberance felt like a celebration of my newly single life.

In addition to the tulips, there were other colorful shoots of new experiences and adventures popping up in my life now that I was working at the documentary workshop full time as an associate producer. We occasionally shot interviews at Washington National Cathedral, which had become, if not exactly a *spiritual* home for me, then at least a stone sanctuary of ideas and inspiration, guarded—as the best repositories of dreams and visions are—by a collection of fierce gargoyles.

A towering presence on a high hill in the north Georgetown section of Washington, DC, the cathedral was close to the neighborhood where my father had grown up. I loved it for the soaring scale of its architecture that reminded me of churches in England where I'd spent much of my childhood. Inside, I loved it for its dark and secretive labyrinth of not-open-to-the public nooks and crannies, my favorite of which was filled with flowers for assembling the enormous arrangements used in and around the cathedral.

I also loved it for the interesting characters who came there, none of whom I would have met were it not for this new line of work I'd fallen into, like Alice tumbling down the rabbit hole.

We'd recently done a multi-camera shoot at the Cathedral on the topic of taking away anger, featuring Supreme Court Justice Sandra Day O'Connor and George Stephanopoulos, among others, and moderated by television journalist and lawyer Tim Russert, the longest-serving moderator of NBC's *Meet the Press.*

Stephanopoulos showed up on set as scheduled, despite being sick and feverish. I was impressed he hadn't blown us off. What a professional. An empty hole on the panel would have been impossible to fill at the last minute. Refreshments were not permitted on the semi-circular setup we had in place for our panelists, but Martin said I could bring Stephanopoulos a cup of hot tea, which I did, placing it on the floor beside his chair and periodically refilling it from the kitchen in the flower-arranging rooms behind the nave. He could not have been more appreciative of these small gestures.

Note to self: Regardless of how you're feeling, show up and do your best to be pleasant about it.

Another was the opportunity to sit in on an interview Martin did with Archbishop Desmond Tutu, whose newly established Forgiveness Project was a much needed and mind-opening construct for me those days, wrestling as I was with my residual anger and frustrations in the wake of my divorce.

"Without forgiveness, there is no future," the archbishop said. "Forgiveness says you are given another chance to make a new beginning."

In those post-divorce days when letting go of grievances from the past had been a struggle, his words left me wondering if I could challenge myself to really forgive so that I might move on, less burdened. It was something I would eventually do, but at the time forgiveness was still very much a work in progress.

Even author Madeleine L'Engle had "wrinkled" her way to the Cathedral, sharing her unique meditations on spirituality, science fiction, and, of course, the importance of stars.

Our shoots at the cathedral gave us a pleasant working relationship with its director of communications, Bob Becker, who helped us facilitate most of them.

And when Dave Brubeck came to the Cathedral on his 75th birthday to perform—not jazz—but a Mass he wrote called *To Hope!*

A Celebration, Bob gave me a seat in the section of pews designated as the press gallery for the event. Brubeck's jazz was the soundtrack of many Sunday mornings at home with my parents. And there he was, performing not twenty feet away from me.

As the music soared to the highest reaches of the cathedral's interior stone walls, I watched the musicians play, awash in shards of dancing colorful light streaming through the stained-glass windows. The combination of music, color, and light left me almost breathless with appreciation for the impossible beauty of the moment. If this is what hope looked and sounded like, I wanted in.

When the Mass was over, I left the cathedral swept along in a stream of other jubilant concertgoers, carrying the lights and music inside me. For the first time since I had begun navigating the fraught landscape of the newly divorced, I finally allowed myself to begin feeling hopeful as I drove back home along the Potomac River to my little house and the cheery tulips in the side yard waving hello.

MUSE COMPLEX

AFTER THE SPLIT, Steve and I were now each on our own in terms of child support and dealing with the costs of maintaining modest but separate residences. While it was more peaceful, it was even more difficult to make ends meet.

It would have been easier if either of us had parents nearby who could help. But I didn't have the kind of mother who embraced being a grandmother, at least not in person. In theory she was, but it was always on her own terms. She was the kind of grandmother who, not long after Zoë was born, decided to move more than a thousand miles away and open an art gallery in Florida with my sister, Karen. She visited a couple of times each year while Steve and I were still married and twice paid for us to stay at a timeshare in Sarasota—as long as it wasn't in her house and as long as we got ourselves there. Which we did, making the long, monotonous, 28-hour round-trip drive from Alexandria because we couldn't afford to fly, distracting the kids by having them count the more than one hundred South of the Border signs in each direction.

My father lived and worked in California and was more interested in children once they reached the age where he could discuss ideas with them. Steve's parents had both tragically died in their twenties when Steve was just a child himself.

By this time, Zoë and Leif were both in elementary school so at least childcare was no longer an issue. Fortunately, there were times when I could work from home, times when I could bring them to work with me, and times when they were with Steve. But it was still a juggling act.

I was lucky to have a job with a boss who permitted me to work flexible hours and sometimes from home. I was at the workshop during school hours, but if someone was sick, Steve and I did our best to maneuver around that. Somehow, all of us managed to muddle through until Leif and Zoë were old enough to be on their own.

In the midst of it all, I realized I was beginning to have a bit of a crush on Martin. It was hard not to, given the amount of time we spent together and how enamored I was with the craft of documentary filmmaking.

But did I like *him*, I asked myself, or was it the *job* I liked?

Separating a man from the work he did, or the art he created, was a recurring dilemma for me. I'd made up a little heart test for situations like this: Would I still be attracted to a particular guy if what he did for a living was pump gas? The answer was usually, of course, probably not. It was their dreams and visions that I was swept up in, their *story*. It was watching someone in the process of *creating* something that appealed to me. They were inextricably bound together, which tended to make things complicated.

Because they were artists of some sort, the men who captivated my attention rarely had a lot of money, so I could at least reassure myself I wasn't a gold digger. Unfortunately, I was never smart enough to fall for guys with money, and definitely *never* for guys in suits. I was a dreamer, not a digger.

I was pondering this one day while mowing the grass in front of my little house—a habit I have from my father, who said he always had his best problem-solving thoughts while mowing the lawn or doing jigsaw puzzles. I have a degree in psychology and found the idea of human inspiration intriguing. What *was* it about the muses?

In the following days and months, I spent the time I had to myself researching and reading about muses, both those in the shadows as well as those well known. One of my favorites was Laura Riding, the eerily brilliant poet who lived with her lover and writing companion, Robert Graves. They also lived with Graves' wife and Riding's partner in a rather strange *ménage à quatre*. This unusual domestic situation gradually fostered intense rivalries among the four until Laura, in a melodramatic attempt at suicide, threw herself from a fourth-floor window. Within seconds, Graves sprang after her from a window on the third. Amazingly, they both survived. Despite nearly destroying one another, it was during their fourteen years of writing together that they both produced their most notable work. Each was a muse to the other. Creative and empathetic, their companionship resulted in writings that likely would not have happened but for their influence upon one another.

I wanted that kind of relationship. Mind you, I did *not* envision either Martin or myself jumping from windows to impress the other. What appealed to me was the idea of two creative individuals, not only bringing out the best in one another, but in the process taking their storytelling art to an even higher level, a level that would likely have not been possible were it not for the influence of the other.

I turned my ideas, research, and writing into a book proposal entitled *The Muse Paradigm: Passionate Encounters in the Creative Process*—a behind-the-scenes examination of the muse, the human sources of inspiration both male and female, in the lives of artists.

These would not be studio wenches with vain hopes of parasitic glamour. Those I chose to profile were intelligent provocateurs—quite often equal in talent, if not in recognition. The intention of my book was to weave together a colorful tapestry of some of creativity's most defining moments in the lives of painters, sculptors, writers, musicians, poets, thinkers, scientists, explorers, and theologians. The book would highlight the personal relationships that have aroused and excited profound creative impulses with anecdotes illuminating how and why these relationships came to be, what sustained or broke them, and the ways in which society and culture have been altered as a result of these creative partnerings.

While I was fascinated by the concept of the muse, I did not have a muse complex myself. I had an *artist* complex, I was fascinated by and loved being around artists. But not because I wanted to be their inspiration. No, *I* wanted to be the artist.

But lacking confidence in myself, I thought if I wasn't the *artist*, I could at least be very *close* to the artist. Or write about them. And perhaps that would be enough to scratch that itch.

It never was, though. In time, I would learn to be both my own artist and muse, but that was still a few years away. With documentary filmmaking, I had at least found a foothold of my own in the storytelling world.

Thomas Jefferson and Nick Nolte Take Me to Disney World

IN THE MID-1990s, there were several films about Thomas Jefferson in the works. One was Martin's documentary *A View from the Mountain*—an examination of the issues of race and slavery based upon Jefferson's perspective of the new world from his travels and his home in Charlottesville, Virginia, during the years 1770 to 1826. The title of the documentary came from the name Jefferson gave his plantation: *Monticello*—Italian for "little mountain."

The second film in production was a PBS documentary by Ken Burns. Still in its early stages, it was to be a portrait of Jefferson as a renaissance man: writer, inventor, and architect, and titled simply *Jefferson.*

And then one day at the documentary workshop, not long after we had finished Martin's film on Jefferson, I received a call about a third one. On the phone was a contact of mine at the Library of Congress, an archivist who'd been very helpful when I was trying to find some obscure visuals for the film

"You'll *never* guess who was in here yesterday," he said, barely able to contain himself.

"Who?" I asked.

"Nick Nolte!" he said.

"The actor?" I asked, wondering why he was calling to tell me this. "*People Magazine*'s 'Sexiest Man Alive'?"

"That's the one!" he chirped happily.

"What on earth was he doing at the Library of Congress?" I asked.

"You won't believe this," the archivist said gleefully. I could practically feel him hopping up and down on the other end of the line in his eagerness to tell me.

"He's playing the role of . . ." and here he paused for dramatic effect, "*Thomas Jefferson*, in a new film by Merchant Ivory!"

I was speechless. Each word in that statement came as a small shock. Having helped me with research for our own film on Jefferson, the archivist knew there was a good chance I'd be surprised to hear this.

At the time, Merchant Ivory Productions was well known and respected for their beautiful and iconic films, often based upon novels, and filmed in India or England. Their 1983 film *Heat and Dust*, starring Julie Christie—the British actress born on a tea plantation run by her father in northeast India—was an art house hit in Europe. Two years later, *A Room with a View* brought them mainstream visibility. By the early 90s, they were big enough that Disney's Buena Vista signed a distribution deal with them.

And now they were working on a feature film about Jefferson's years as the U.S. Ambassador to France during the 1780s with Nick Nolte playing the lead role.

[*Monticello* (little mountain) + *Buena Vista* (good view) + A Room with a View: The way the names and titles all lined up thematically—like a payline on a slot machine—appealed to me.]

A semi-fictional account, the working title for the Merchant Ivory film was *Jefferson in Paris*. The screenplay, written by Ruth Prawer Jhabvala, dealt with Jefferson, not long after his wife died, and his alleged relationships with British artist Maria Cosway and Sally Hemmings, the enslaved woman who accompanied Jefferson's teenage daughter, Patsy (played by newcomer Gwyneth Paltrow) to Paris.

According to my source, Nick Nolte had apparently been researching his new role at the Library of Congress. Rumor had it he'd bought a copy of every book ever written about Thomas Jefferson—and read them all. The archivist and I shared a few laughs (and doubts) about this and I made a mental note to see the film when it came out.

A few months later, I got another surprising call. This time, it was Buena Vista Pictures on the line, Disney's marketing arm.

Although it hadn't aired yet on PBS, someone at Buena Vista had apparently gotten wind of Martin's documentary and wondered if they could get an advance copy. I sensed a bargaining opportunity.

"Sure," I said, after checking with Martin, "we can send you one. In return, what can you do for *me*?"

(I never haggle with artists but have no problem doing so with corporate suits.)

The Buena Vista representative thought for a moment, then offered me two passes to a private screening of *Jefferson in Paris* in New York City. I accepted them as a starter offer, but held out for more.

"Do you have any kids?" he asked, offering me a copy of a new animated film called *Toy Story* that Buena Vista was also distributing.

"Yes, and they've already seen it," I said.

"Make me an offer," he said, running out of ideas and, perhaps, patience.

"How about tickets to Disney World?" I asked, never dreaming I'd get them.

There was a pause. And then he said, "OK, but just the passes—I can't do the airfare."

"Deal!" I said happily, looking forward to telling Leif, who was just seven at the time.

A few weeks later, the film passes arrived. Martin and I took the train up to New York City for the screening, relaxing in a pair of plush lounge chairs in a darkened theater at the Todd-AO Studios with members of the press, to watch *Jefferson in Paris*.

Merchant Ivory's take on Thomas Jefferson, quite different from Martin's historical, fact-based documentary, was ultimately a box office flop, a strange aberration in their otherwise illustrious 44-film portfolio.

"After a literate and entertaining roll (*A Room with a View, Howards End, The Remains of the Day*)," wrote Peter Travers in *Rolling Stone* magazine, "the team of producer Ismail Merchant, director James Ivory, and writer Ruth Prawer Jhabvala drops the ball with this droopy, snail-paced, prigs-in-wigs movie. It doesn't help that Nick Nolte is such a lox as Thomas Jefferson. . . . [He] seems to think that playing an introspective man means impersonating a wax dummy."

Ouch.

Martin's *View from the Mountain* aired on PBS in 1995, the same year *Jefferson in Paris* was in the movie theaters. *Jefferson* by Ken Burns aired on PBS two years later. Happily, our press reviews were a lot kinder than those for *Jefferson in Paris* as well as the Burns special:

"Burns' failure to get to the heart of the Jeffersonian enigma is all the more noteworthy in light of *Thomas Jefferson: A View from the Mountain,* the landmark exploration of Jefferson and slavery," wrote film critic Ken Ringle in the *Washington Post*. "Made with a fraction of the resources Burns appears to draw on at will these days, (Martin's) modest but penetrating effort managed to deal both more intelligently and more entertainingly with the central question of Jefferson's life—and do so in much less time."

While working on the Jefferson film didn't get me to Paris, that experience would in time get me to a special mountain—in Italy.

Bill Clinton's Handshake

FROM THOMAS JEFFERSON our attention soon turned to a namesake of his, William Jefferson Clinton. In the fall of 1997, Martin tossed a piece of paper on my desk.

"Here," he said, "I think you'll like this one."

I glanced down at the scrap with his scrawled handwriting. "What's this about?"

"I'd like to interview President Clinton about his friendship with Cardinal Bernardin. Think you can get that for me?" he asked, a challenge in his grin.

Having finished his documentary on Jefferson, Martin was now making a documentary on the late Cardinal Bernardin, his battle with cancer, and his response to a false accusation of sexual abuse.

I wasn't part of the production team working on this film and Martin knew it was a long shot that I'd even get the interview. But he also knew how much I loved a challenge. It took a number of phone calls and a formal written request but, against the odds, I got a private interview approved and we were given a date in January 1998.

Just days before our interview with the president, the Monica Lewinsky scandal broke. Clinton was accused of having pizza—and more—with an intern. As luck and timing would have it, our interview was scheduled to take place between this breaking news and Clinton's scheduled State of the Union address. Awkward to say the least.

Unlike Jimmy Carter, who'd drawn me close to his side in a warm, Southern hug when we posed for photographs together, Bill Clinton took my extended hand and scanned me up and down as he shook it. Under any circumstances—but especially these—that felt a bit weird. I'd kept an open mind coming into the interview, but after that visual appraisal, I couldn't help feeling he was quite likely guilty as charged in the Monica Lewinsky affair.

Rushed into place by the handlers, we set up the interview. President Clinton was sharp and informed, quick with his answers. At one point, however, he mispronounced Bernardin's name. Surprised, I glanced over at Martin's face. Seeing Martin hesitate, I could guess his thoughts. Which would be worse: Correcting the president of the United States or letting it slide and keep the mistaken pronunciation in the film? Martin took the chance at the end of the president's statement and told him. To our great relief, Clinton wasn't at all irritated.

"Let's do it again!" he said immediately in his Arkansas drawl. "Let's get it right!"

I did at least admire that about him.

Afterwards, in appreciation for the interview, Martin gave the president an archival newspaper from his own collection which covered Thomas Jefferson's State of the Union address, thinking he'd like it for the multiple connections. I knew it meant a lot for him to part with this. It was a sincere gesture and a very cool one.

Historian Elizabeth Marvick, writing in *History Today* at the end of 1994, noted interesting similarities between the two presidents, William Jefferson Clinton and Thomas Jefferson.

"President Clinton's pre-inaugural celebrations began in 1993—the year in which Thomas Jefferson's 250th birthday was also widely celebrated. To dramatize the links between himself and the third president of the United States, Clinton journeyed to Washington from Monticello, Jefferson's hilltop house in Virginia, (deliberately following) the path to the White House taken in 1801 by the founder of his party at the start of his presidency.

"Before and since this symbolic pilgrimage, Clinton has followed in Jefferson's footsteps in other ways. A striking similarity between the two presidencies is how the media treated them. The press of Jefferson's time, as of Clinton's, was ever ready to publish reports that the president was hypocritical, irreligious, and amoral. . . ."

Made in partnership with another filmmaker, *Bernardin* aired on PBS in 1998 and was critiqued by the press.

"Viewers will appreciate Bernardin's calm, facing first a false accusation, then cancer," wrote David Finnigan in *Variety Magazine*. "But the program often feels less about him than those he left behind, a wake rather than a discerning portrait of a complex religious leader. Bernardin was a savvy church politician—smiling in public, (then) cracking knuckles, when necessary, in private."

Finnegan criticized the filmmakers for being "unnecessarily soft on this gutsy man" and not "painting Joseph Bernardin for what he was—a flawed, human embodiment of living and dying with deep Roman Catholic Christianity. His memory deserves, and can endure, tougher fans."

Apart from obtaining the White House interview, my role in this film was to get it aired by PBS stations, one by one, city by city, state by state, throughout the entire country as the documentary did not have what's called "common carriage"—airing in the same time slot throughout the U.S. There were 349 PBS stations to court.

Although *Bernardin* was not one of Martin's strongest documentaries, and although I was not part of the production crew, this film was a valuable warm-up act for me. It provided the opportunity to learn (on the job) how to market documentaries, especially on sensitive or difficult subjects, to a disparate group of PBS program executives in a variety of markets—something I would eventually earn a living doing on behalf of independent filmmakers.

It also gave me positive exposure to Bill Baker, the general manager of WNET, the primary PBS station in New York City and one of the most important and influential people in the world of PBS at that time—a man who would soon become a personal mentor to me.

Brenda, my liaison at the White House, told me they only accepted one out of every two hundred requests for an interview with the president. In the game of probability and statistics, we'd beaten the odds. To me, it boiled down to understanding the relationship between what you were asking for and who you were asking it of.

Knowing I'd done that and could perhaps do it again in different situations, under different circumstances—that experience was priceless.

CHEMOTHERAPY, ALLIGATORS, AND SHRUNKEN KIDS

WHEN MY DANISH grandmother was born in 1898, her father named her Karen Margrethe. Soon, however, everyone was calling her Grete. Frustrated, and determined to have a daughter called Karen, my great-grandfather named his next baby Karen as well. (Fortunately, it was a girl.)

As a result of the popularity of this name in my Danish family, I have an aunt named Karen, a great-aunt named Karen, two cousins, and several second cousins. But by far the most important Karen in my life was my big sister.

Despite the ten years difference in our ages, we both married the same year. After our weddings, Steve and I stayed in the Washington, DC area. Karen and her husband, Lou Thomas, a former government computer consultant, eloped to Belize. Steve and I began a family; Karen and Lou began a palm tree business.

Having fallen in love with the country, Lou decided to buy 400 acres along the Belize River in Teakettle Village just outside of the capital city,

Belmopan. He set up a palm tree farm and eventually sold seeds from more than one hundred varieties to buyers all over the world.

Surprisingly, my sister went along with Lou's tropical dream for several years. She would have been more at home in an art studio in Brooklyn or Chelsea, but she was a good sport about it. Using her degree from Pratt Institute, she designed and helped build a house with large, light-filled rooms, ceiling fans, and a long veranda overlooking the river below and the jungle beyond.

She never forgot to send me a birthday card each year. My favorite had a cartoon of a grinning, skinny-legged guy standing next to a smiling woman with soft red hair and the words, "We looked all over to find a card that would represent the real us" on the cover. And on the inside, "But we couldn't find any 'From the Jungle Stud and his Amazon Temptress.'"

This is the best card I ever found! she wrote on the inside.

I can still imagine her laughing to the point of tears when she saw it. I keep it tucked into a framed photograph I have of the two of them, surrounded by a jungle of tall green palm trees. Lou's gray and white beard is closely cropped. He's wearing an unbuttoned blue shirt that matches his Paul Newman blue eyes, which are fixed upon whoever took the photograph. He's smiling. My sister, wearing colorful madras jungle pants and a T-shirt, her strawberry-blonde hair cut short for the heat, turns to look up at him. Together they are a portrait of love and exuberant happiness.

Although he worked hard, the palm tree seed business didn't provide much of an income. Lou was content, however, often looking around with that happy grin of his and remarking, "Just another day in paradise!"

But Karen eventually tired of jungle life in a third-world country. She packed up and moved back to Florida where she thrived as an artist. Even living apart, Karen and Lou stayed close and saw one another regularly.

She bought and renovated a small house just off the Tamiami

Trail near the Ringling Museum in Sarasota, painting it in a soft purple shade. She affixed a small montage of her unique tiles to the outside, where she could see them from the gardens she designed and cultivated.

Karen's colorful tile tables were sold in art galleries up and down Long Boat Key. In addition, she was commissioned to create custom art tiles to be used in kitchens, fountains, and pools. She was written up in the local paper.

She was happy there for several years. Despite her success, however, she was harboring a dark secret. She'd found a lump in her breast. Thinking she could handle everything, she'd had a biopsy done. When she found out she had stage 4 breast cancer, she could no longer keep the news to herself.

"I asked them what size the tumor was, thinking they'd say maybe a marble or, at worst, a ping pong ball," she told me. "But it turns out it was about the size of an orange."

I listened in stunned silence.

"That can't be good," I whispered finally, having no idea what to say.

"No," she said quietly.

She and Mom had plans to visit Denmark together that year so Mom could introduce Karen to all the other Karens we are related to—which is to say, most of the females in our extended Danish family.

Having already had a trip with me to visit aunts, uncles and cousins in Denmark back in the 80s, my mother wanted nothing more than to do the same thing with my sister who hadn't been back to Denmark since her first visit one summer as a teenager. Mom knew she would especially love the Danish design scene, as well as the simplicity and the quality of life there.

But it wasn't to be.

My sister needed to begin treatments immediately, which would leave her too fragile to travel. My mother was devastated.

I suggested she take Zoë in Karen's place and introduce *her* to all the Danish family.

"I'll come, too." I said. "It will be our 'three-generation trip' back to Denmark."

This is my ingrained, knee-jerk response to bad news—looking for something positive to balance out a negative situation, trying to see things through story and imagery. This time, thankfully, it worked.

My mother was thrilled with the idea. It distracted her just enough to give her a temporary respite from worrying about Karen. Ten-year-old Zoë was also very pleased with the idea of this adventure and started packing as soon as I told her, taking care to bring a selection of her favorite hats. And Karen welcomed the temporary respite from the spotlight of our helpless fears and concerns.

Mom, Zoë, and I spent a delightful ten days that summer, eating and drinking our way around Denmark, visiting family and introducing Zoë, weaving in the next generation's threads of connection to the home country of my grandparents.

After the trip to Denmark, I wanted to do something for Leif to balance things out. When I asked him where he'd like to go, he suggested—for reasons still unclear to me—Baltimore. Less than an hour away from our house, this hardly seemed to even out the equality factor. I thought for a while before remembering the passes in my desk drawer at work.

"How about a trip to Disney World instead?" I asked. His face lit up instantly.

Leif and I took Amtrak's 855-mile auto train from Virginia to Sanford, Florida, with my now almost 12-year-old Volvo safely strapped inside. Leif was just eight at the time. He loved eating in the train's glass-enclosed upper lounge under the bright sky, watching how the trees changed from deciduous to tropical palms as we headed south, rolling through different states along the way.

Upon arrival, we retrieved our car and drove one hundred miles southwest across the state to stay with Karen where she was now living in order to be closer to the Tampa hospital where she was getting chemotherapy.

When she opened the door, her head covered with a colorful bandana, it took a fierce amount of self-control for me not to burst into tears. All her lovely strawberry blonde hair was gone. I gave her a gentle hug, worried I might break her in some way.

After me, Karen hugged Leif, teased him about something, and then gave us a brief tour of her apartment complex. Leif could help her by walking her large dog, Cloudy Day, she said, as she showed us their favorite walking paths throughout the abundantly landscaped grounds.

"Watch out for alligators," she cautioned Leif, as we walked around the lake. Leif turned to me in surprise. Was his aunt teasing him?

Seeing his thoughts, Karen assured him she was not. They were common in Florida. Someone in their complex had been chased by one not that long ago, she'd heard. She distracted him with a promise to give him some art lessons.

Alligators, Disney World, and art lessons. Leif's face lit up. This had all the makings of an excellent holiday. He was too young to understand what was happening in the adult atmosphere.

From Karen's little flat, Leif and I drove an hour and a half each day to Disney World, had a fabulous time, and then drove back again at night exhausted. But it was worth it. I wanted as much time with my sister as her illness would permit.

Appropriately, the days were filled with film-themed adventures: *Honey, I Shrunk the Kids*, *Star Wars*, *Indiana Jones*, and *Toy Story* characters, punctuated by Leif's hoots of delight and yelps to come see whatever he'd discovered.

Karen was waiting for us when we got back to her flat after our last day at Disney World. She'd had a good day and had materials laid out for the art lesson she designed for Leif—painting small objects that could then be "fired" in a regular oven. Leif was delighted and got to work immediately.

"He's creative," she said gently to me the next morning, as we said our goodbyes. "Encourage that."

The Man in The Mask Returns—With Half a Million Dollars!

I WAS STRUGGLING in the role of single parent, but I found it easier than being married. During the days Zoë and Leif were with me, I filled our hours together with music, art projects, books, micro soccer, and small adventures. I loved having the kids to myself. In her memoir *The Giant on the Skyline*, author Clover Stroud describes these feelings perfectly as "the maternal intimacy of single motherhood."

But married or single, there were still days and nights of stressful parenting. The midnight ER runs clutching a child with the blue lips of asthma, holding onto the little hand of a toddler who'd just been bitten in the head by a dog while emergency room doctors worked on her wounds—those moments were left to me to handle, as Steve thought I was better equipped to deal with them emotionally. He was probably right.

There were so many things people thought I had the strength to handle. And so, somehow I did, keeping the pain and fear to myself in the blackness of my sleepless midnight thoughts. Keeping my worries from my sick sister. From my parents. Being the strong one carries the disconsolate edge of feeling so utterly alone.

On top of everything else, Steve and I were both plagued and frightened by calls and letters from the IRS demanding money we didn't think we owed. I wanted to suggest to each one of those bastards who threatened what precious periods of calm I was able to muster that they should emulate Willie Sutton and "go where the money was," instead of threatening people who were just barely making ends meet.

I consoled myself with the thought that at least I was doing something I loved, even if it didn't pay well. Documentary filmmaking might sound cool as a profession to anyone who doesn't realize documentary filmmakers need to raise every single dollar they pay themselves, pay others, and spend on production. Like a nest filled with clamoring baby birds, it's a never-ending vicious cycle of needs and mouths to be fed. Much like my home life.

Unless you're Ken Burns, it's a profession and craft that rarely offers a steady paycheck or standard perks like paid vacation and health insurance. Much as I would have liked to continue seeing Dr. Paul Peckar during those tough times, I simply couldn't afford to. So, it was a surprise one day at the documentary workshop when he phoned me.

"Kristin!" his distinctive voice once again boomed into my ear. "Have a minute?"

"Of course," I said, unsure of what was coming.

"I think I may have a project for you!" he said enthusiastically. "Can you stop by my office sometime this week?" he asked.

What kind of project could a psychiatrist have for me? I wondered, hoping he'd heard of a job with steady pay and benefits.

When we met up the following week at his office, he got right to the point.

"A friend of mine is involved in a large art commission," he said. "And I think he wants to make a film about it. So I told him about you!"

His words so surprised me that for a few moments, I was uncharacteristically speechless.

"I don't really know what it's about," he continued. "But I think it has something to do with a wall and a church."

As he gazed down at me through his mask, looking for my reaction, the expression in his eyes softened. "And maybe a piece of art," he added, thoughtfully.

Art? That got my attention. I asked for more details. He told me what he knew about it. The piece of art was to be a 37-ton, 780-square-foot frieze, carved from Italian marble. It would be one of the largest art commissions in the entire country at the time. And his friend wanted a documentary made about it.

"You interested?" Paul asked.

Was I interested in making a documentary film about art? My entire body lit up with the buzz of possibilities.

"Yes, absolutely!" I replied.

I thanked him but he brushed my words aside good-naturedly. He just wanted to help me, he said.

Suddenly, I felt a lot less alone in the world. Instead of thinking of myself primarily as a single mom, this new vision of myself as a documentary filmmaker, or at least part of a documentary filmmaking team, was slowly coming into focus.

I couldn't wait to tell Martin and everyone else at the workshop the good news. We'd still have to convince Paul's friend we were the right team for the job, of course, but with Martin's credentials, I didn't think that would be a problem.

And I was right, his credentials would win us the project.

It's not every day that a half-million-dollar, fully funded project falls into your lap as a new documentary filmmaker. There was only one problem.

Nobody else in the workshop wanted to work on it.

THE NUN FROM NEW ORLEANS AND A NEAR-DEATH EXPERIENCE

"I'M *NOT* INTERESTED," Sister Gretchen said firmly, her New Orleans accent softening the negative impact of her words. She smacked one dimpled hand firmly down on the conference room table for emphasis.

"I don't even *like* the Basilica!" she added, laughing.

Her reaction took me by surprise. *Are nuns allowed to say no to work assignments?*

But then, Sister Gretchen had never matched the image I conjured up when I thought of the word "nun." To begin with, who knew nuns made films?

Martin had called the four of us together around the small conference table at the documentary workshop to discuss the new film project Paul Peckar had sent my way, which turned out to be an astounding half-million-dollar commission.

At least I thought that's what we were there for, but it seemed everyone on the team, for some reason, was quickly coming up with reasons *not* to work on it.

It was Sister Gretchen's reaction that surprised me most of all. She was in her mid-forties and belonged to the Marianites of Holy Cross in Louisiana. I had the vague impression she was on loan to the documentary workshop, sort of like a scholar in residence, devoting her time, energy, and knowledge to the crafting of films that aligned with her beliefs and mission in life.

This was a unique experience for me. Not having been raised Catholic or educated by ruler-wielding nuns, I brought no emotional baggage to the situation. I thought it was interesting to work with her, to see and watch an actual nun up close without needing to convert or join a convent.

Sister Gretchen was as passionate about her work as she was about her native Cajun culinary delights—po' boys, gumbo, and blackened fish—and she had the curvy physique to show for it. She didn't wear a habit, which was kind of disappointing to me, but dressed neatly in slacks or jeans with simple shirts or blouses. Her dark eyebrows arched high above the gold rimmed glasses she wore, often reaching up to the somewhat unruly fringe of her bowl-cut brown bob when something took her by surprise.

Sister Gretchen was an interesting bundle of contradictions. She had a warm and welcoming smile and she loved to laugh, but could be quite fierce. She had no trouble expressing her thoughts and opinions, but she was also very empathetic. It was Sister Gretchen who fed the alley cats behind the documentary workshop and took them to the vet—at her own expense—when they needed attention.

One morning on my drive to work through the historic district of Alexandria, the brakes on my twelve-year-old Volvo failed. A woman dressed in heels and a business suit, perhaps on her way to work, stepped off the curb at an approaching stop sign. I put my foot on the brake. To my shock, the pedal went straight to the floor, not diminishing the car's speed in the slightest. In slow motion horror, I watched my car getting closer to the woman crossing the street.

In desperation, I yanked up the emergency brake with all my

strength and turned the wheels towards the curb, jerking the car to a halt just seconds before it reached the stop sign. In an out-of-body moment, I watched as the woman reached the other side of the street, unaware of how narrowly she'd escaped being taken out by three thousand pounds of Swedish might.

I switched off the ignition and sat for a moment, trembling with the what-ifs. Then I gathered my things, got out of the car, and left it on the street. I walked the rest of the way to the documentary workshop, the scene playing on a loop in my head.

When I reached the back door and walked inside, I found Martin and Sister Gretchen sitting at the small table in the kitchen, chatting over coffee. Seeing them, I broke down in tears. They looked up, surprised. Martin asked what was wrong. I explained the close call.

"But you thought to pull the emergency brake and you didn't hit her," he said after hearing me out. "That's a great ending. Why are you crying?"

He seemed genuinely puzzled. It was Sister Gretchen who came flying to my rescue.

"Oh *Mahr-tin*, can't you see?!" she exclaimed in her New Orleans drawl. "It's just *ehvrything!*"

And with those three words, Sister Gretchen nailed my life exactly. On top of the stresses of my pending divorce, my sister's illness, the endless bills to pay—I had just nearly killed someone.

What was most puzzling to me about Sister Gretchen—but also what I loved best about her—was that you could never accurately anticipate what she was going to say. And this was one of those instances.

Another was the time Martin came up with the idea that we should give away some little thing to anyone who bought our DVDs because, he said, "Catholics love little gifts."

Sister Gretchen looked at him in horror.

"Not *me!*" she said emphatically, smacking the conference room table. "*Ah'm* Catholic and *Ah* like BIG gifts!"

She broke into peals of her contagious laughter as she looked around at each one of us to see our reactions. I loved her at moments like this.

And now here was Sister Gretchen expressing her surprising views firmly once again. She did *not* want to work on this film. Even though it was a Catholic film. Even though she was a nun. Even though it was a half-million-dollar project.

There was a silence around the table as we all digested her response.

And then Greg—the soft spoken, gentle Franciscan monk who always enclosed an original poem to each of us in his annual Christmas cards—spoke up.

"I'll be leaving soon to go back to my order," he said quietly. "This close to the end of my time here, it's probably best I don't begin a new project."

Martin looked down at the table and said nothing.

I didn't understand everyone's lack of interest. After all, we were discussing one of the most desired and also rarest things in our world— a fully- and generously-funded documentary project. That the subject of it was a new piece of art commissioned for the largest Catholic church in North America would have been, I thought, tremendously appealing to this crowd.

But then, I'm not Catholic. How I found myself—essentially a Kierkegaardian existentialist—working with a nun, a monk, and a Catholic filmmaker still completely baffled me.

Paul later told me his intention had been to give *me* the project so I could strike out on my own as a filmmaker. I was touched he'd wanted to help me get back on my feet. Tempting as that idea was, I knew I was underqualified. It did, however, seem a natural fit for the kind of work being done at Martin's shop. So, I was genuinely surprised at the palpable lack of enthusiasm around the table that morning.

Martin adjourned our meeting, and we left the room with no plan.

Kissing the Leper

A FEW DAYS later, on a bright sunny afternoon, Martin suggested we drive over to the Basilica and scout potential shoots for the as-yet-to-be-titled documentary about the creation of the large sculptural wall. It was just the two of us since nobody else wanted to work on the film.

As we walked around the grounds surrounding the massive building, I took photographs of the Basilica's distinctive mash-up of Neo-Byzantine and Romanesque Revival architecture.

"I don't understand why no one wants to work on this documentary," I said, looking up at Martin, who at 6'4" stood a foot taller than me.

Even he didn't seem too enthusiastic, despite it being a completely and generously funded project. At the time, he was consumed with his own documentary on the life of Dietrich Bonhoeffer—the German Protestant theologian from Wrocław, Poland, who, despite his religious beliefs, participated in several assassination attempts on Hitler.

Thoughts swirled in my head. *Might this unloved project somehow be an opportunity?*

We stopped our walkabout beside a tree

across the street from the sprawling entrance steps to the Basilica. I turned and looked at Martin, who still wore a doubtful expression on his face as he stared at the massive structure.

"Let *me* do it!" I said impulsively. "I realize I don't know what I'm doing yet, but I'll find a way. And you can help me figure it out, without it distracting you from your other projects!"

Martin said nothing. I scanned my mind for a visceral image to express my compassion for this unwanted film project.

"It's like kissing a leper!" I exclaimed enthusiastically.

Martin recoiled at my words.

"No, really!" I babbled on. "Nobody wants it. For reasons I don't even understand, nobody wants to touch this project. But I'll work on it, find a way to love it and make something of it. *Trust me!*"

Martin didn't say anything for a few more moments. Then he nodded. Not exactly a match for my knows-no-bounds-enthusiasm, but at least it was something slightly closer to yes.

Here's another lesson worth remembering, I thought: *When faced with something that appears to be unappealing, walk around it—just as Martin and I had literally circumnavigated the Basilica—and look for your point of entry. Something, anything that makes it appealing enough to take on, despite the negatives. Even if only in your mind, walk around it and ask yourself—how is this an opportunity?*

In the short time I'd been at the documentary workshop, I'd often been asked how to get a job in the film business. My advice was always the same: 1) ignore the help-wanted ads (the line's already too long); 2) instead, decide where you'd most like to work; and 3) volunteer or be an unpaid intern while doing a side hustle to pay your bills. Once inside, 4) find something no one else wants to do, and 5) do a really good job with it. When a job opens up, you're already on site and you'll be at the head of the line of applicants because they already know you.

This advice was based upon my own experiences. It was how I got the gig at the television station and how I got my first actual experience as a documentary film co-producer and scriptwriter. There was never a posting for this. But here I was with my dream job because I'd already been part of the team, working more or less unpaid as I tried to find funding for the series *News & The American Character.* Having brought a project into the workshop also helped, of course, but that wouldn't have happened had I not already been working there.

"Kissing the leper," as insensitive as the words may seem, would become a powerful visual metaphor and inner mantra for me over the coming years. A challenge to find a way to embrace things that appear to be unappealing but still need to be done—and done with compassion and a positive attitude. Words said for the shock value, to startle the head open and catapult the mind into new ways of thinking. Embracing what might at first seem onerous or negative or unappealing and still finding some way to like it.

(Many years later, I would encounter an actual leper on a dark road in the middle of the night during my travels in Ethiopia. Seeing him, I thought of my mantra and wondered, with some contrition, if I would really embrace this man in rags who was missing part of his leg and arm. I tell that story in my book, *Lions, Peacocks & Lemon Trees.*)

In the days to come, however, that phrase and attitude would serve me well, delivering me to a mystical moment on top of a minaret on the Blue Mosque in Istanbul, tea with a Lord in London, and to a marble carving studio in northern Italy where the artisans wear newspaper hats as if they're a discarded lyric from a Beatles' song.

I would still be struggling financially, but I would be rich with new ideas and filmmaking adventures. Most importantly, I would have my name on a film and the beginnings of a real career.

And all because I had listened to a friend when she suggested I see Dr. Paul Peckar, and because I'd had the thought to "kiss the leper."

EX NIHILO—OUT OF NOTHING

AMONG HIS NUMEROUS works of art, artist and sculptor Frederick Hart is perhaps best known for his *Three Soldiers* bronze, part of the Vietnam Veterans Memorial on the National Mall in Washington, DC, and one of his Creation Sculptures at Washington National Cathedral, *Ex Nihilo*.

Ex Nihilo comes from the Latin for "out of nothing." The sculpture, unveiled in 1982, is an intriguing, writhing mass of figures, representing God creating the cosmos and man out of a swirling vortex of nothingness.

Out of nothing—could there be a better description of the career I was building for myself?

Knowing Dr. Braddock and his wife wanted to commission Hart to create the enormous *bas relief* that would cover the back wall inside the Basilica, I read up on him.

Hart had been a student at the Corcoran School of Art in the 1960s when he stumbled into sculpture. Having lost his sister to cancer—something he and I would soon have in common—Hart turned his grief into art. He believed it was his moral responsibility to create something that would give hope to the darkness.

"Art," he said, "should be a presence in everyday life." This resonated deeply with me.

After Hart dropped out of the Corcoran, he attended art classes at American University, my parents' *alma mater*. In 1967, he got a job as a clerk in the mailroom at Washington National Cathedral, according to his website, "just so he could pester Roger Morigi, the Italian immigrant who was the Cathedral's master carver, to take him on as a sculpting apprentice." In a short time, Morigi became his mentor and father figure.

In addition to Morigi, Hart was also influenced by the raw, earthy contours in the sculpture of Auguste Rodin. Having spent a summer as a nanny in the Paris suburb of Meudon, just steps away from Rodin's former studio, Rodin was also a favorite of mine. I was beyond excited about making a film that would document Hart's creative process.

Alas, it was not to be.

At this point in Hart's career, he had stepped away from marble in favor of working in transparent and semi-transparent acrylics. Busy with other projects, he passed on the commission.

He did, however, invite the Braddocks, Martin, and me out to his home in the Virginia countryside where a number of his stunning new sculptures were displayed. It was an interesting afternoon, but also a frustrating tease knowing the opportunity to work with him had eluded us.

In his place, Hart suggested hiring a shy young sculptor named George Carr and it became Carr's task to conceptualize a *bas relief* based upon *The Universal Call to Holiness*—and ours to film the process, from rough sketch to installation.

Preoccupied with his Bonhoeffer project, Martin took me at my word when I'd asked to work on the film. He instructed me to pull together preliminary research, come up with a shot list and then an initial draft of the edit plan for the documentary. He gave me some general directions for how to go about this, then left me to it.

I had a room with two windows on the second floor at the back of the documentary workshop, overlooking the alley haunt of Sister Gretchen's cats. It was up in this perch that I began laying out on the floor my research notes and the various storylines we wanted to include, arranging and rearranging them, looking for a sequence of how they would flow when braided together. This took a long time.

Periodically, Martin would come in and stare down at the floor, looking at my color-coded notes and papers, make a few comments, then leave me to rethink the process.

He told me about the rumored rivalry between Washington National Cathedral and the Basilica: the Episcopalians versus the Catholics. Both religious structures are located on hilltops in Washington, DC—the Cathedral in the northwest, just down the street from American University, and the Basilica on a one-hundred-acre parcel of real estate in the northeast quadrant of the city.

Theodore Roosevelt was on hand when the National Cathedral's foundation stone was laid in 1907. Modeled after the English Gothic style of the late fourteenth century, the Cathedral (where Hart worked as a stonemason for many years), is famous for its carved gargoyles and stunning stained-glass windows. It is the second largest church in the U.S.

On the other side of town, thirteen years after Washington National Cathedral's cornerstone was laid, the Basilica of the National Shrine of the Immaculate Conception was erected adjacent to Catholic University, which donated the land.

(In the coming years, Martin and I would go for a life-changing helicopter ride over the Basilica; only it wasn't my life that would be changed—but my father's.)

Titles are important. They need to tell what a film is about but at the same time, leave something unanswered, setting up a little mystery and intrigue. The best ones leave potential viewers with a sense of wanting to know more and therefore more inclined to watch the film.

Musing over the Basilica's uniquely American interpretation of the Byzantine style of architecture—popular from the middle of the sixth century under the rule of the Roman Emperor Justinian until the fall of Constantinople (today's Istanbul) in 1453—I gave our documentary the working title *American Byzantine*.

In just two words, we would be acknowledging the Basilica was not an example of classical Byzantine architecture—anyone with two eyes could see it wasn't—but rather a modern American interpretation of it.

It was also a playful take on *American Gothic*, the famous 1930 painting by Grant Wood of a pitchfork-holding man standing next to a dour and prim looking woman in Iowa—and a tongue-in-cheek nod to the rivalry between the Basilica and the National Cathedral.

DUST TO DUST: THE ITALIAN CONNECTION

TO HELP MAKE ends meet during those first years of singledom, I sometimes worked as a hostess at Panino, a beautiful "white tablecloth" Italian restaurant owned by friends, Lou and Lydia Patierno. It was an hour commute each way, but it was worth it.

The Patiernos and I met when our kids were in preschool together. I think they guessed I was struggling financially and made excuses to help out by hiring me as a hostess on the weekends when they were busiest. The $65-$75 I earned each Saturday night paid for that week's groceries. I even worked on New Year's Eve one year. Lydia seemed to feel badly about asking me, but I didn't have a date and needed the cash more than I needed to go to a party. It turned out to be a fun and festive evening at the restaurant in the warm company of good friends and wonderful food.

I will never forget their many kindnesses to me. I started each evening by running a damp cloth over their laminated menus, removing the dust left by their popular homemade breadsticks. Lou would prepare a special meal for me before the customers started coming in and it was always the best meal I'd eat all week.

One Sunday, Lou and Lydia held a private party for their French partner, René, who was returning to France to take care of his aging father, and they included me in the celebration. Lou's brother Robert, an artist and one of the founders of the Pennsylvania College of Art and Design, was also there. His art hung on the walls at the restaurant. I'd been admiring it for a long time and finally decided to buy one of his less expensive paintings—a nude in hushed turquoise tones with a dark skull hovering in the background. I had to sell a small piece of furniture to pay for it, but it moved me each time I looked at it on my living room wall, reminding me as it did of my sister living with the specter of death hovering just over her shoulder.

Working on *American Byzantine* was giving me the opportunity to watch an enormous piece of art go from sketch to sculpture. George Carr and his assistants had been working in a large warehouse in Pennsylvania he'd rented to accommodate the large clay mock-up and I was anxious to see it. Martin and I, along with Stephen on sound and Richard on camera, drove up for a day to get some footage of the process.

As luck would have it, our shoot happened to fall on National Take Your Daughters to Work Day.

"Want to come with us?" I'd asked Zoë the night before, expecting her to jump at the opportunity to skip school for a road trip.

"No, thanks," she said dismissively, not bothering to look up from the book she was reading.

"But it's National Take Your Daughters to Work Day!" I said.
She rolled her eyes.

"Mama, with you *every* day is Take Your Daughter to Work Day!"

I had to laugh. It was true. When you're a single parent, there are so many times when you have to figure out a way to do multiple things simultaneously, which sometimes means working with the kids in tow. And so, we left without her.

Zoë changed her tune about the next shoot, but that was one I couldn't afford to take her on.

We were following the full-scale plaster model—to Italy. Specifically, to a marble-carving studio in Pietrasanta, where it would be translated from clay into stone by a team of traditional Italian marble carvers.

Dust to dust. This film was developing its own vortex and sweeping me up into it. One night, I was wiping the dust of breadsticks from menus and not long after, I would be more than four thousand miles away, wiping marble dust off my sunglasses at an Italian open-air marble carving studio.

HEAD OVER HEELS IN ITALY

Pietrasanta, Italy

Sunday, May 31, 1998

I awoke this morning in a sun-filled room at the Hotel Palagi.

The white interior with its vivid splashes of colorful art and woven rugs cheered me immensely. I got out of bed and threw open the windows and shutters to admire the view. In the distance, down the hillside, I could see the Tyrrhenian Sea, the portion of the Mediterranean that lies between the western coast of Italy and the islands of Corsica, Sardinia, and Sicily as if surrounded in an earthy embrace.

And if I twisted myself out of the window and looked up to the right, I was able to see the mountains. The hillside was covered in a pattern of aged terracotta roof tiles, little old stone houses, gardens and terraces and painted glass windows.

I unpacked in a state of bliss yesterday, putting everything away in drawers and hiding my suitcase and all other evidence of being a traveler, so I can pretend—if only for a few days—that I actually live here.

In the afternoon, when the marble carvers at Studio Cervietti stopped working for lunch yesterday, I wandered around the town, taking photographs of the streets and homes. This is the quiet time, between 2 and 4 p.m. when the shops are all chiuso—*and everyone is at home eating and resting. Or perhaps, this being Italy, making love.*

There were a few signs of life, however. I walked down the narrow little streets, watching kids kick soccer balls back and forth to one another, and hearing the unmistakable voice of singer Pino Danieli coming from under a house's window shutters. Piano, classical, poured out from underneath another as someone practiced—unseen hands gracing the narrow street with music for those who had the moments to stop and listen.

I ended my walkabout sitting in the sun on the steps of the fifteenth-century St. Agostino Church in the Piazza del Duomo, writing in my journal for a few precious moments as I waited for Martin, Richard, and Ed to reappear.

The sun was shining, the sky was blue, and there were fiori d'appertutto—*flowers everywhere. And everywhere, absolutely everywhere, there was art.*

Filming had now begun in earnest on *American Byzantine* and what a perfect location in which to film. Italian for "sainted stone," Pietrasanta is an interesting little town on the upper west coast of Italy with a centuries-old tradition of marble artisanry. Over the generations, it has become a collective of artisan workshops, including Studio Cervietti, where *The Universal Call to Holiness* was being carved and where we were filming.

With its "magical blend of past and present . . . many artists come to Pietrasanta to study, to work, and to settle down," states the town's guidebook.

"Pietrasanta prides itself on not containing art to prestigious museums and galleries but instead has art all around—especially in the open air—for all to enjoy. More than 300 foreign artists live and study here, forming a unique community."

The production team's initial thought in the early stages of the *American Byzantine* project had been to fly marble carvers from Italy to the U.S, and document the progress as they worked on the art in the parking lot of the Basilica.

"Really?!" I said to Martin. "A parking lot?"

That felt completely wrong, and for so many reasons.

"This is *film*. It needs to be visually interesting. Who will turn on the television to watch a piece of art being made *in a parking lot*?"

Stealing Beauty, the film directed by Bernardo Bertolucci and starring Joseph Fiennes, Jeremy Irons, Rachel Weisz, and Liv Tyler, had come out the year before, in 1996—the year after Steve and I split up. I saw it with my mother, who would go to see anything with Jeremy Irons in it.

I was entranced by this film, imagining myself living in Italy as an artist. The soundtrack was moody, evocative and very cool with songs by Mazzy Star, Portishead, the Cocteau Twins, Liz Phair, Stevie Wonder, Billie Holiday, Nina Simone and others. Whoever put it together was a genius. I purchased the CD, memorized all the songs and played it relentlessly the nights I was on my own, making pasta, drinking red wine, pretending I was living in Italy.

This was the backdrop in my head as I warmed to the argument with Martin.

"Viewers would rather see scenes from Italy than a church parking lot in northeast Washington, DC," I said. "Instead of flying the marble carvers here, why don't we go to Italy and film them there?"

Logistically, we would not be able to film them as frequently in

Italy as we would be able to if they were just across town. But did we need to film them frequently?

Besides, we had to go to Italy anyway to film scenes from the marble quarry where the source material for the carving would be blasted from the mountains, as well as some of the historic places, so shoots at the carving studio could easily be done at the same time.

Thankfully, I got my way and now there I was, waking up in Pietrasanta. In Italy. In another world.

The full-scale model had been cast in plaster, then cut into large pieces and shipped to Cervietti, an old-world studio and workshop in the heart of Pietrasanta, specializing in the reproduction of classical and modern marble sculptures with a strong emphasis on sacred art. Their work was breathtaking, even for someone like me, who was not particularly religious.

Martin and I, along with cinematographer Richard Chisolm and sound guy Ed Roy, spent a few days filming at Cervietti, a *plein air* studio where artisans worked in outdoor sheds, open to the elements, liberating images from massive, millennia-old blocks of marble using brass and wooden instruments and techniques that predated the artisans themselves by many generations.

Inside the primary old building, there were dusty rooms filled with hundreds of sculptures and sculpture models of all sizes on the ground and on the rough wooden shelves; a hushed, still, museum-like gathering of busts and bodies, winged angels, saints and Virgin Marys. More than a thousand sightless eyes were upon us as we passed through the impressive collection of works in an atmosphere that was both magical and slightly creepy.

Outside, we walked around this enclave of dust and light and statuary to a soundtrack of chisels clinking against stone and the gentle buzzing of saws, with clanging church bells in the background—our mouths and apertures wide open to the sights, scents, and scenes around us.

I watched Richard wander through the tall, open-air carving areas of the studio, his heavy camera perched carefully on his right shoulder. Ed followed him closely, hoisting a boom mike high into the air as they worked to capture on film the carvers at work. With his brightly patterned green shirt, Richard was easy to spot moving among the pale white slabs of marble. His black pants had two chalky white handprints on their back pockets, as if one of the statues had playfully patted him on the ass.

All of the marble carvers wore a folded paper hat made from the morning's newspaper, hardly conforming to OSHA standards. But then, we were in Italy, and the priorities were different here.

"How will that keep them safe if a chunk of marble falls on their heads?" I asked Massimo, the handsome Italian man who was our interpreter, negotiator, and handler.

He laughed. "They are not at all concerned about that," he said. "They wear those paper hats to keep the marble dust out of their hair!"

The marble dust, which hung in the air at times like tiny snowstorms, also concerned me.

"Won't working here, with all this dust, give the carvers problems with their lungs?" I asked Massimo. "Like the way coal miners get black lung disease, only white lung disease from the marble?"

He laughed again. "Not at all!" he said.

"Come over here," he gestured for me to follow him through the open yards of sculptures, both finished and in progress, over to a large pile of discarded marble shards and fragments.

"Do you know where these will go?" he asked me. I shook my head.

"They will be sold to the Tums factory, to be made into those little candies that will help your stomach," he said. I looked at him in disbelief.

"No, it is absolutely true," he said. "Tums are made from a mineral called calcium carbonate, found in things like chalk, limestone, and marble."

"Eating marble is *good* for you?" I asked him, a little suspicious he might be teasing a gullible *americana*.

"But of course!" he said, as if everyone knew that. "Follow me!" He made a waving gesture with his hand. So Italian.

We walked back to one of the enclosed sheds where a gray-haired man wearing glasses, perhaps in his sixties, was carving a larger-than-life, muscular statue of a bearded, god-like figure. Massimo called out to him in Italian, saying something I didn't understand.

The carver smiled, carefully set down his tools, then took off his newspaper hat and glasses. He walked a few feet away from the statue he was carving and, to my astonishment, put his arms down on the floor, and swung his legs up in the air into a perfect handstand. Watching the expression on my face, Massimo laughed.

"There, you see?" he said. "This man 'as been carving marble for decades. 'e 'as been breathing marble dust 'is whole life and look 'ow strong 'is bones are! 'E is still doing 'andstands at 'is age!"

Impressed, I was almost ready to lick the floors.

One afternoon, we were invited to pick up a hammer and chisel and try marble carving ourselves. Martin went first, under the supervision of a smiling middle-aged man wearing a simple blue T-shirt, blue jeans, and a newspaper hat. After a few swacks of the chisel, he grinned good-naturedly, then handed the hammer and chisel to me and stepped back to take a photograph while I tried my own hand at it.

Looking at that photograph now, seeing my forehead furrowed in concentration, my fingers grasping the chisel in a death grip, I remember how difficult it was to make even the slightest guided impression in the marble. The chisel bounced or deflected off the stone seemingly with a mind of its own, as if mocking me. Lacking the strength, vision, and expertise to guide it, I made a mess of it. Which made me even more appreciative of the skills and artisanry of those in newspaper hats to render such exquisite works of art. Perhaps that was why we'd been invited to try carving marble ourselves.

We spent several days soaking up this old and otherworldly atmosphere, watching the carvers in the process of rendering the model pieces into marble. Eventually, it would take a team of 23 carvers of all ages more than a year to complete the work.

In addition to Studio Cervietti, we spent a day filming in a marble quarry in Carrara, up in the mountains above Sernavezza in the northernmost tip of Tuscany, where the riches created from compressed sediment of ancient lakes, rivers, and seas have been quarried since Roman times.

The marble extracted here has been used all over the world, from Finlandia Hall in Helsinki to the Saadian Tombs in Marrakesh, to London's Marble Arch and the Rotunda at the University of Virginia designed by Thomas Jefferson and modeled after the Pantheon in Rome. Also, Michelangelo's *Pietá* carved in the fifteenth century.

The Universal Call to Holiness would be carved from one massive block of marble weighing 77 tons. We filmed similar blocks being transported on the backs of what looked like rickety little flatbed trucks, down the mountain roads filled with hairpin switchbacks. The Italians drove with the doors of the cab open, ready to spring out of their trucks if their heavy loads of marble caused them to lose control on the way down.

The quarry kept a crushed vehicle at the top of the road—a reminder to everyone of the dangers of letting their load get out of hand and the possibility of brake failure. Unstable as the trucks appeared to be, they were at least an improvement over earlier times when bulls were used.

The process of extracting the marble is also dangerous. They still talk of a cliff face that collapsed in 1911, crushing ten men on their lunch break.

Despite the dangers, however, Italian men are still Italian men. I took a photograph of one deeply suntanned quarry worker setting dynamite to move the blocks of marble. Perhaps in his thirties, he had shoulder length brown hair, a tattoo on his arm, and was dressed in nothing but a pair of old and dusty tighty-whities. Apart from heavy gloves and construction boots, he wore nothing else. He'd even tucked his knickers up under the elastic, apparently to maximize his tan potential.

When the lunch whistle blew, the dozen or so quarry workers stopped work and walked over to a big yellow Caterpillar front-end loader and stepped into its large bucket to be transported up the mountainside to a lunchroom canteen. Curious, we followed behind on foot. Inside the canteen, we saw table after table of suntanned quarriers, laughing, talking and eating simultaneously.

Charmed by the bottles of wine I saw on each table, and wanting to remember the scene, I raised my camera. Instantly an arm came out, blocking me. I heard the words "*No, no!*" as a finger waved furiously at my camera. They didn't want any documentation of the wine at lunch.

The following day, during a break at the studio, I wandered over to the Bozzetti art gallery in town located in an atmospheric sixteenth-century former convent. Everything I saw and experienced in Pietrasanta made me want to live in a world of artists and artisans, and not just for a few days.

For budgeting reasons, we normally worked long hours on location, with no days off. But this time one of our days fell on Sunday and we had no choice. Studio Cervietti was closed. The four of us dispersed, each to explore Pietrasanta in our own ways.

In the morning, Martin and I wandered around, looking at other artisan studios in town, including one that had a long dining room table with intricate inlaid flower motifs crafted in marbles and gemstones of brilliant colors on its surface. I was immediately smitten with it and wanted to bring it home and show it to my sister. I was certain Karen would also love it and marvel at the craftsmanship. Even if it was the only piece of furniture in my entire house, I would be happy.

Fortunately, Martin's common sense prevailed. That, and the price tag.

Afterwards, Martin and I decided to walk the *Via D'Amore*—a small cliffside trail overlooking the sea that unites the five little coastal towns of *Cinque Terre*—in search of lunch. Along the way, he noticed a large succulent. He stopped, pulled out a knife and (to my horror) etched our initials into one of the plant's juicy leaves:

KF ♥ MD

Why aren't the initials the other way around? I wondered, staring at them.

In the evening, we reunited with the guys. In their explorations, Richard and Ed had met a pleasant young American already living my dream life with a bunch of friends on a hilltop just outside Pietrasanta. She had invited all of us to join them that evening at the little stone house they were renting for a candlelit dinner of traditional homemade *risotto* in their gardens among the olive trees.

As I looked around the large table at the collection of new and old friends laughing and talking over food and wine in the evening glow of the setting sun, I realized these days in Italy marked a turning point, shifting the vision of what I wanted in life in quiet yet seismic ways.

Back home, anxious to hang on to the feelings stirred up in my heart during our days on location, I painted my living room in several of the colors I'd seen on buildings in Italy. To give it that aging Italian slightly moldy plaster look, I scrubbed the paint onto the walls by hand using rags I'd made from one of Leif's old T-shirts.

I also signed up for immersion Italian lessons in DC. Our teacher, Paula, was from Milan. A bottle blonde chick in tight suits and high heels, her day job was working for Baretta, the gun company. While we were not actually learning Italian at gunpoint, knowing that acted as a triggering and subliminal incentive to do well in class.

I got out an old Italian record by Lucio Battisti I'd purchased ten years earlier at the Rizzoli bookstore in Washington, DC—a bookstore founded, ironically, by filmmaker Angelo Rizzoli.

Rizzoli's was located on the C&O Canal in Georgetown and in my pre-marriage, pre-documentary workshop days, I often hung out there on my lunch break or after work just to be in its atmosphere.

What follows is a slight diversion from my tale. Then again, perhaps it was foreshadowing. . . .

The day I walked into Rizzoli's and heard the voice of Lucio Battisti, it was love at first listen. I bought the vinyl album, brought it home and played it endlessly, memorizing the lyrics especially to the title track, *Una Donna Per Amico* (A woman as a friend). Although I often bought books, it was the only album I ever bought there.

Sometime that same spring, I met an intriguing guy with dark hair and captivating dark eyes, a brainy soccer player. He was in Georgetown just for the summer, for an internship during the months between his master's degree and PhD at Harvard. Our places of work were only a block apart along the canal. Mutual friends introduced us.

We went dancing, drank Heineken darks together after work, went to Café des Artistes, and hung out with our friends. Once, he picked me up from my office and rode me on the handlebars of his bicycle all the way across Georgetown to have dinner at a subterranean chili joint he loved—me, laughing and pushing my long blonde hair out of my eyes, trying to keep my balance while holding my long flowery skirt in place.

One night, he invited me over for dinner at his little flat on the east side of the city. In the midst of his cooking prep in the kitchen, he paused for a moment, went over to his record player, selected an album and put it on.

"Listen to this," he said. "I love this song so much I've memorized the lyrics."

As the unmistakable notes of *Una Donna Per Amico* filled the air, I may have stopped breathing. It's quite possible we were the only two people in Georgetown who owned that record. There was likely nobody else in town he could have invited over for dinner who could also sing along to every word, every song. The improbability of it all toppled me head over heels in love with him, firm in the belief that this serendipity was a sign from the universe.

It was, but only for that one summer.

The title proved prophetic. One day in early September, he went back north to Cambridge and Harvard. And the Rizzoli bookstore? Not long after, it too, disappeared. One day it was there and the next, the space stood empty. Like a scene from *The Night Circus*, books, boyfriend, and music vanished overnight.

But I didn't hold any of that against Italy.

In fact, having nearly worn out my Lucio Battisti album, I craved more Italian music. And so, following Massimo's suggestions, I'd brought back CDs by Pino Daniele and the Italian rockstar Zucchero, with whom Massimo said he'd grown up in the nearby Italian seaside town of Forte dei Marmi. I also picked up CDs by Andrea Bocelli and the pop music duo Al Bano and Romina Power.

(Sidetrack: I will later discover singer Romina Power is related through her father's grandmother to author Evelyn Waugh, who will crop up unexpectedly a little later in the making of *American Byzantine*, inside a Lord's toilet, of all places.)

I played my Italian CDs endlessly, translating and memorizing the lyrics. Italian music became the soundtrack of our home for many years, especially the song, "*Felicità*" (happiness), which to this day still makes Leif laugh whenever he hears it.

But these songs served me well. I would return to Italy twenty years later to research a memoir I was writing about my grandmother's time in Rome and find myself not only able to get by in Italian but get by with smiles and laughs from the people I met by speaking to them in rhyming Italian lyrics.

In the years to come, I would also eventually take up marble carving myself and discover a way to take some of the heartaches out of my body by turning them into stone.

There is Meaning in Every Journey

INSIDE ANY DOCUMENTARY workshop, filmmakers are often working on multiple films more or less simultaneously, depending upon what funding has come in. This was always the case where I worked. There were only a handful of employees at any given time and each of us was working on different projects in various stages of production. It kept things interesting.

In addition to *American Byzantine,* Martin was deep into a film that was his heart's passion—about the life, teachings, and spiritual mindset of German theologian Dietrich Bonhoeffer during the 1930s and 1940s. It would be his first feature film, one that would be released in movie theaters instead of going straight to PBS.

"If I sit next to a madman as he drives a car into a group of innocent bystanders," Bonhoeffer famously wrote, "I can't, as a Christian, simply wait for the catastrophe, then comfort the wounded and bury the dead. I must try to wrestle the steering wheel out of the hands of the driver."

He was referring to his own participation in attempts to assassinate Hitler. The intellectual and spiritual journey this devout believer took from "thou shalt not kill" to arrive at this statement was at the core of Martin's documentary.

As one of the film's associate producers, I was part of the crew that traveled to Berlin and other parts of Germany for multiple location shoots in the spring of 1998.

Meanwhile on the home front, Karen was scheduled for a stem cell transfer procedure in her battle against breast cancer the day we left the U.S. Needing to be in two places at the same time, I was beyond stressed. But Karen urged me to go, assuring me there was nothing I could do for her that week. Mom would be with her.

"But please come visit me when you get back," she said. She gave me the phone number for her hospital room, just in case. Reluctantly, I packed a suitcase and left with the crew. As usual, it took several glasses of wine to get me on the plane.

I like Germany; it has been intertwined in my life story since before I was born. If it weren't for Karen's illness, I would have looked forward to spending a week there.

My father was the eldest of three close brothers, all of whom married women from different cultures after serving in World War II.

My father married my mother, a fellow student at American University and the daughter of Danish immigrants. The youngest brother, Frank, married Stella, a charming Ethiopian during the years my grandparents were living in East Africa. And Larry, the middle brother, fell in love with a German ballerina named Ruth while working for the U.S. Foreign Service in Berlin.

I am one of the eight resulting multilingual offspring. Between us, we speak six or seven different languages in various degrees of proficiency.

Dietrich Bonhoeffer was executed by the Nazis in April of 1945, just days before Adolf Hitler committed suicide. Berlin fell to the Soviets and was subsequently divided into occupation zones. The Soviets controlled the eastern portion of the city, while the U.S., French, and the UK controlled the west. As an American, Larry was based in the western section.

Ruth was the eldest daughter of German impressionist painter Josef Bell, who died when she was just five. During the war years, Ruth's mother taught ballet to get by financially, and Ruth and her two little sisters learned to dance at an early age. By her early twenties, Ruth was a professional ballerina with the Berlin Ballet Corps. She met Larry on a blind date in 1949.

Completely smitten, Larry sneaked into the Russian-controlled part of the city one night to see Ruth dance. Russian soldiers sitting near him in the audience suspected he was an American and decided to trick him by asking him for a cigarette—in English. When he good-naturedly complied, they outed him, demanding to know what he was doing in their territory. He pointed to the stage and told them he was in love with the ballerina dancing the role of the little blue bird. Amazingly, they let him go.

Ruth loved telling that story. She loved that Larry risked Soviet punishment by coming to see her dance. She was also proud of the ballets she performed in that had sets and costumes designed by the artist Marc Chagall, whom she eventually had the opportunity to meet, thanks to Larry's next job as a foreign correspondent for the *New York Times*.

One memorable dark and cold winter, when I was fourteen, my family spent Christmas in Germany with Ruth, Larry, and my two cousins. That was the year Aunt Ruth accidentally set the Christmas tree on fire by decorating it with traditional burning candles. It was famous in family lore forever after as the year of the Christmas tree with the large, charred hole in it.

With my heart wrapped up in family memories like a cozy patchwork quilt, I was happy to be back in Germany again—at least until I phoned home.

After checking into our little hotel in a southwest corner of Berlin, Martin thoughtfully suggested I call Karen, an expensive thing to do back then. I dialed the hospital number for her room, but she was in too much post-surgery pain and too drugged-up to speak. She mumbled she was happy to hear my voice but couldn't talk. The call lasted less than two minutes. It was reassuring—and crushing.

We had several days of interviews and location shoots lined up, one of which was at the Tegel prison on the north side of Berlin where Bonhoeffer had been held prisoner for a year and a half. The prison cell was so small, we had to take turns walking into it. With my sister ever present in my mind, I thought about how she, too, was a prisoner—not of a political regime, but a prisoner of her own body and the disease running wild throughout it like a malignant banshee. Bonhoeffer was contained by the physical boundaries of a prison; Karen's own body was her toxic prison. Both were facing death sentences.

Also on this shoot was my delightful workmate, Janna. A recent addition to our documentary workshop crew, she'd been brought onboard specifically for her capabilities with research and her fluency in German. She was elfin-like, creative, cheerful, positive, charming, and invaluable to the project.

Throughout the many interviews we captured on film, including several with Bonhoeffer's former students as well as his niece and Bonhoeffer's reclusive and bedridden twin sister—now in her nineties—Janna handled the delicate task of translating back and forth.

We brought two American freelancers with us—cinematographer Dave Goulding and his assistant cameraman, Gary Waxler.

This shoot was Gary's first trip abroad and his sheer delight at every aspect of the trip was infectious. He chattered away about navigating the confusions of the German language, the cars, German driving on the autobahn, the food, German beer, and the attractive German girls. It was the first time, he told me, that he ate lunch for breakfast and drank Jägermeister. Because his family was descended from Russian Jews who had emigrated to the U.S. just before the Russian Revolution, Gary says his parents would never have traveled to Germany. And yet, here he was.

Rounding out our crew, Martin also hired a German sound tech—a pony-tailed guy named Ulf Herman who greeted us each morning with the words, "Good morning, everybody!" in a Germanic Ringo Starr accent. Initially, none of us were sure how to pronounce his name.

"It's *Uhhllfff*," he said with his dry sense of humor. "It sounds like you are throwing up a little."

At the time of our production shoot, the border between East and West Germany had been open for less than ten years. East and West were still getting to know one another again after 28 years of separation and there was some awkwardness at times. But not between Ulf and Gary, whom Ulf nicknamed "Wax." Ulf began teaching Gary some words in German and, on our afternoon off, took him to see the remains of the Berlin Wall.

"There wasn't much left of the wall to see," Gary later told me. "Just a few small pieces. You could walk through it, like Dorothy inside her house looking out at Munchkin Land. It was also sort of like being in an old James Bond movie."

Afterwards, Ulf and Wax went over to a museum in what used to be the Gestapo headquarters. It still had logbooks listing the names of people they'd killed. Ulf said he had known very little about the Holocaust until he was university age. Gary told me Ulf asked him how, as an American, he felt about what happened, having no idea Gary was Jewish. Ulf told Gary his grandfather was against Hitler, but because he worked for the car manufacturer Porsche, he was forced to join the Nazi party.

Thanks to the making of this documentary, the grandsons of a Nazi and an American Jew began a decades-long friendship. The films we worked on were not just healing *me*; they were also healing others. It was moments like these—one person reaching out to another across the years and political divides—that might help heal the world, I thought, if only there could be more of them.

> *There is meaning in every journey that*
> *is unknown to the traveler.*
>
> Dietrich Bonhoeffer

THE MONEY PIT

TWO YEARS AFTER moving into Jules Renaud's quirky Alice in Wonderland house, where each little room led to another in whimsical and counterintuitive ways, where the tulips bloomed mysteriously in the middle of the yard seemingly overnight, my mother decided she was no longer at peace with the idea of me paying rent.

She had chewed on this for a while before springing her new idea on me one afternoon at a little coffee shop in Alexandria's Old Town. Coffee cup in hand, suspended halfway between the saucer and her mouth, an expression came over her face that told me big thoughts were going on in her mind. Conversation halted as she frowned slightly in concentration. Then she pursed her lips and cleared her throat.

I waited in nervous anticipation for what was coming. Other similarly expressioned moments had yielded bombshells like: "I think I'll leave London and move back to the U.S." and "I'm leaving your father" and "I think I'll move to Florida and start an art gallery with your sister."

But this time was different. This time, it was about me.

"I want to help you buy a house," she said, without preamble.

Shocked and uncertain what this meant or what might be expected of me, I waited a moment before replying.

"Thank you, but documentary filmmaking doesn't pay enough for me to *buy* a house," I said, thinking how stressful it would be to try and hold up my end of the deal. "Reasonable as it is, I can barely make my rent each month."

To my surprise, this was not a deal-breaker.

"I'd rather see you in a house right now, building equity, while I'm still alive," she said. "What's the point of waiting until after I die for you to inherit what you need?"

Even though I'd lived with it my whole life, there were still times when I found her Scandinavian directness somewhat disconcerting.

"I'll put up the down payment," she continued briskly, "and you'll be responsible for the mortgage payments. We'll budget it so they will be roughly the same as your monthly rent." She paused for a moment, looking into her coffee cup as if searching for numbers among the dregs.

"We'll be co-owners," she added, just to keep me in line. "My name will also be on the deed. And in addition to paying the mortgage, you'll be responsible for all upkeep and any renovations."

My first thought was: *Where was this offer eight years ago when Steve and I were about to lose the house of our dreams, the first home Zoë and Leif knew?*

I sat with the idea a bit longer—then realized, well, she's offering it now.

As a former realtor, my mother would be a good partner. And it wouldn't be the first place I'd owned, nor the first I'd renovated. Two years out of college, I'd scraped together the money to buy a little garden apartment south of Alexandria, not far from the Potomac River. I sold that for the townhouse Steve and I were living in when we got married. Two years later, I sold that for the little mid-century modern fixer-upper of my dreams— and nightmares.

The mid-century modern house was owned by a retired international airport architect named Harry. From someone I knew through work, I'd heard the neighbors were concerned about him—and the house—and rightly so. Unable or unwilling to pull himself together after the death of his wife, Harry spent most of his days sitting alone in a decades-old, brown faux Eames chair among the shelves of books that lined the walls he'd painted brown. Long transparent beige drapes hung over the floor-to-ceiling windows. Altogether, it was a tableau of suspended animation in shades of depressing brown.

Each day, Harry stared through his nicotine-stained glass wall at the surrounding woods, smoking, brooding, and drinking. Periodically, he got up and walked into the old kitchen, with its once-contemporary white metal cabinets on which he'd optimistically painted black and yellow geometric shapes decades ago. Now a fading ode to a previous era of design, the cabinets were dinged and rusted out in places. He prepared his dinners on a vintage range top coated with tufts of cat hairs glued in place by the grease of many meals.

Harry had neglected himself and the house for years. He didn't appear to shower or bathe. His family and neighbors were both frustrated and concerned. One of them was a lawyer I knew through work. Unhappy with what he could see of Harry's house from his own backyard, he encouraged me to try and buy it. There was only one problem: It wasn't for sale.

"Knock on the door and make him an offer!" the lawyer encouraged me, desperate to see a change. I thought about it. Hollin Hills was a super cool neighborhood architecturally, with '50s era homes thoughtfully and discreetly situated throughout its wooded setting. It had even been written up in *Life* magazine. Having not yet seen the inside of the house and therefore having no idea what I was getting myself into, I mostly thought, *why not?*

Steve and I talked it over, then drove over to see it later that week. Wordlessly, we pulled up at the house, which we could barely see through the overgrown trees and shrubs surrounding it. Well over six feet tall, I thought Steve might appear intimidating to Harry, so I asked him to wait in his truck. I ventured cautiously through a thicket of bamboo and across a small patio of broken bricks and weeds as Steve watched me, ready to spring to my rescue if needed help. I knocked on what turned out to be the kitchen door and held my breath. Nothing happened. I knocked again. A moment later, I heard the sound of footsteps slowly shuffling closer and closer toward me. Then they stopped.

The door jerked open and there stood Harry. He was tall and lean, somewhere in his seventies, with long, gray, unkempt hair reaching down to the frayed collar of his baggy old sweater. One shaking hand gripped the countertop to steady himself, the other held the tail end of a burning cigarette. The reek of stale smoke nearly overwhelmed me.

"Yes?" he said, peering down at me through dirty glasses, like a ghastly and ghostly character from a Dickens novel.

I hesitated briefly before telling him my name. Hoping to establish some semblance of credentials and connection, I also told him the name of the architecture firm where I worked. His eyebrows went up ever so slightly, but still he said nothing. The cloud of smoke emanating from Harry, which covered him like a shroud, and from within the house's darkened interior, made me cough involuntarily.

"My husband and I would like to buy your house," I said, wiping my eyes.

"It's not for sale!" he bellowed gruffly, and perhaps just a bit defensively.

"Yes, I realize that," I said.

I'd heard tales about how he and his stylish wife would dress up just to go motoring around the neighborhood in their classic convertible, waving at the neighbors. Hoping to appeal to those happy memories, I told him we were a newly married young couple with a small child. I told him how much we loved the wooded setting and the architecture of this neighborhood.

"And so, we were hoping you might consider selling your home to us," I trailed off, not sure what else to say.

"It's *not* for sale," he repeated sternly. From the glimpses of the rooms I could see behind him, I thought perhaps it was just as well. It felt as if my own "great expectations" for this house had manifested themselves into a creepy male version of Miss Havisham.

"Okay," I said. "I apologize for disturbing you."

I turned and began making my way back through the bamboo thicket and thorny, unwelcoming barberry bushes, out toward fresh air and Steve.

"Wait!" I heard him say. I paused and turned around.

"What would you give me for it?" he asked. The lawyer had told me Harry's daughter was after him to move somewhere he could be better cared for and perhaps that was on his mind.

"$150,000," I said, having been coached by the lawyer as to a suggested price.

"Well," he said grudgingly. "I'll think about it."

I pulled a business card from my pocket, hoping the architecture practice where I worked might at least reassure him, and handed it to him. He grasped it in his long, thin, yellowish fingers and looked at it for a moment, his cigarette sloughing ashes down upon it. Then, without another word, he turned around and slammed the door behind him.

Several weeks passed before we got a call and an invitation to come back and see the inside.

On the appointed day, Steve and I passed through the rooms quickly, partly because it was only 1100 square feet in total and partly because we could barely breathe. The combination of stale smoke scented by cat piss was so thick we were tempted to reach out to try and brush the air away from our faces. The house had just one bathroom. The fixtures were all original and from the '50s. We stared at them, trying to imagine how much cleaning we would have to do before we felt comfortable bathing and potty-training two-year-old Zoë here.

Glancing into the old tub, I noticed a little dead cricket lying still, its matchstick limbs akimbo.

Eventually, either encouraged or ultimatum-ed by his daughter, we settled on a price a few thousand higher than what I had offered. Three months later, the house was ours.

Someone suggested I pick up Harry and bring him to the attorney's settlement offices, to make sure he would actually be there. With his aura of decrepitude, smoke and alcohol, I wasn't thrilled at the prospect of having Harry riding shotgun in the car beside me, but I wanted this house.

The morning of settlement day, I rolled down all the windows in my car on the drive over to the house of my dreams and nightmares. To my surprise, Harry was ready and waiting for me. He'd tamed his wild hair slightly and donned a dress jacket for the occasion. I told him he could not smoke in the car, and he complied. I don't recall what we talked about during the twenty minutes' drive to the lawyer's office, but I do remember my heart breaking just a little at the thought of how difficult this must be for him, for so many reasons.

Steve met us there from his jobsite.

As we walked to the conference room, I noticed a bottle of champagne on the table. The lawyer led us cheerfully and briskly through the paperwork. When it was all finished and everyone had signed, he pushed back his chair and stood up to offer his congratulations. Harry's long shaky arm shot out to make a grab for the bubbly. After a slight tussle, the lawyer managed to wrest it from him, telling him it was for the new owners, not for him.

Later, Steve and I wandered through the house for the first time as owners, taking turns drinking from the champagne bottle and struggling with a knee-buckling case of buyers' remorse. What the hell had we just done? The flue wasn't even attached to the furnace, Steve noticed—how on earth was Harry even still alive? I saw the little cricket's body still in the tub—three months after I'd first seen it—and took it outside for a respectful garden burial.

A few days later, we began the demolition of the interior, stripping out as much as we could, taking it down to slab and bare walls. Parts of it were like an archeological dig. Steve kept shouting out to me in disbelief and surprise as he took up not one but two layers of indoor-outdoor carpeting in the kitchen, only to find two additional layers of linoleum buried underneath. Channeling the character of the Count from Sesame Street he cried out, "One floor covering! Two floor coverings! Three floor coverings!"

Gradually, a long pile of appliances, rotting carpets, kitchen flooring, old furniture, and odd shelving accumulated along the road. Contractor friends came over, helping us when and where they could, and we paid them with warm pizza and cold beer. We bought fresh new appliances. I found an ad for fifteen feet of beautiful rosewood kitchen cabinets secondhand and a friend installed it all for us. Although we didn't have any money to spare, we did hire a cheerful, three-person cleaning team to literally shovel out the room the cats used, then clean and sterilize it. That was something we couldn't ask anyone to do for free and neither Steve nor I had the stomach for it.

Once again, a film came to my rescue. I think it was Steve's idea to rent *The Money Pit*. Over takeout and a bottle of wine, we watched it every night of that first week of renovation. Exhausted, sore, and filthy from the day's efforts, we took some consolation that our house wasn't as bad as theirs.

"On the bright side," Steve would almost always say, pouring another glass of wine as we watched the circular hallway staircase collapse over and over under Tom Hanks or the bathtub crash through the floor for the fifth time, "our house is all on one level!"

Our favorite feature of the house—and the main reason for buying it—was that each room had an entire wall of glass windows. I put my hand through one of them while scraping it clean and had to stop to pull out the shards and bandage it up. Then Steve had an accident that required having his head stitched up. But the idea that little Zoë would grow up in a house with nature always at her own eye level kept us going. What eventually emerged was a beautiful and simple little gem of a mid-century modern house with gleaming glass walls, surrounded by nature.

We lived there until Leif was born. Then Steve's business came apart at the seams.

Seven years later, a few days after that cup of coffee, Mom and I went house-hunting, something we both loved to do and do together. Eventually we found one she and I and the kids could all agree on—and one that she and I could make work financially.

Zoë and Leif liked how close it was to their friends' houses; I liked how close it was to the Potomac River with its wonderful eight-mile-long bike path; and Mom thought it was a good investment. We bought it and the kids and I moved in.

I painted a colorful jungle scene in Leif's bedroom and Zoë and I wallpapered her room with photographs of her friends. The redesign and restoration of the gardens along with the complete renovation of all three bathrooms would come later, as time and funds permitted.

This was the house I would fill with the colors of Italy and Italian music.

THE ART OF FORESHADOWING

April 24, 1998—Linda McCartney died last week from breast cancer. She was 56. I think Karen gave up any hope to recover when she heard Linda McCartney died. I could hear it in her voice. "With all their financial resources," she said to me, "it wasn't enough. She still died." Paul McCartney described himself as "shipwrecked" over his wife's death. I can't even imagine.

Martin is in Brussels for a shoot. He told me he woke himself up at 4:30 this morning just so he could call to say goodnight to me at 10:30 p.m. He also told me he'd seen the London Times *with Paul and Linda McCartney on the cover and immediately thought of me. He bought a copy of the paper to bring back to me, along with a copy of* Paris Match *and a small crêpe pan. He remembered I'd had an intense craving for crêpes last summer— and now I'll be able to make them myself!*

FORESHADOWING IS A technique used by filmmakers and writers to keep audiences and readers in their seats—either to keep them watching or to keep them reading.

The best foreshadowing sets the stage and prepares the audience for what is to come, even if the audience is unaware of it, dropping subtle hints and clues about future developments and plot twists while being subtle enough to avoid giving away the plot.

Foreshadowing is a tease and, as with the best teases, you aren't necessarily aware of what's happening until some point in the future, when you've had time to reflect and look back.

After her initial chemotherapy, Karen was in remission for nearly six months. During those months, she was happy and hopeful. We were all happy and hopeful.

The little loft condo Karen was living in at the time had a small spiral staircase that led up to her studio. One day, on a whim, she decided to paint the railing gold. Just the idea of doing that delighted her.

She was about halfway done with her task when the phone rang. It was me, calling to check in on her and tell her about the kids and our latest documentary film escapades—anything to entertain and distract her.

She later told me it was while listening to me prattle on that she paused painting for a moment and put her hand under her armpit, to gently massage away the tightness that had built up from the repetitive brushwork. And that was when she felt the swollen lymph nodes and realized the cancer had returned.

But hearing the excitement in my voice about an upcoming film shoot, she kept this frightening news to herself until my next visit a few weeks later when she found the words to tell me in person.

Lou was also visiting Karen at the same time. She'd already told him, and he'd immediately flown up from Belize to be with her. Thank God for Lou. I watched as he teased her by purposely draping his damp towels on her furniture or pretending to turn left while driving after she'd told him to turn right. Each time she yelped at him in exasperation. And each time he laughed, his blue eyes twinkling in delight as he admitted he was doing it "just to see if she was still in there," still the Karen who was so particular about everything, still the artist he knew and loved so much. And all the time, doing his best to mask his own pain from us.

Lou and I went with Karen to see her oncologist at the hospital. Having studied her latest test results, the doctor gently suggested she might think about getting in touch with hospice.

Lou and I took this to mean we still had time to find someone who could cure her. I remember how foolishly and lovingly optimistic we both were, thinking she'd been granted a reprieve.

But Karen, as always, was way ahead of us. Her normally relaxed face was rigid with stress and disappointment as she fought back tears. Hearing the word hospice, she realized she likely had less than six months to live.

In the following days, Lou and I struggled to find alternative scenarios to release Karen from the disease-imposed limitations on her future and restore her natural optimism. Privately, however, all three of us were filled with the dark and breathless despair you dare not give voice to.

It was at the worst of these moments that I remembered a scene from a documentary Martin had produced prior to Karen's illness. It was a tiny, fragile lifeline of an idea, but I grasped onto it like a lifejacket in a turbulent sea.

Martin's film, *Final Blessing,* explored how individuals with incurable illnesses might be able to experience positive moments in their lives, despite living with a death sentence. The final blessing was to be able to seek these moments out and notice them, despite the keen awareness they could be their last.

I'd only been on one shoot for the film, and it was one I found extremely difficult. It was an interview with Mattie Stepanek and his young mother, Jeni, both of whom had dysautonomic mitochondrial myopathy—a rare and fatal disorder that had already taken the lives of Mattie's three older siblings. Six or seven years old is much too young to be facing a death sentence. But Mattie was already writing the poetry he called "Heartsongs." His heroes were Oprah Winfrey and former president Jimmy Carter and, by the time he died at 13, he had met them both. Mattie also published seven books of poetry and essays on peace, several of which made the *New York Times* bestseller list.

Apart from the interview with Mattie and his mom, I had only a slight familiarity with the rest of the film's content and characters until the day I happened to pass through our basement edit suite while Tim was working on the rushes from another interview. It was with Ira Byock, a physician and advocate for palliative care in Missoula, Montana, and author of the book *Dying Well.*

While there, Martin had also captured interviews with a few hospice patients. Focused on whatever task had brought me down to the basement, the interviews played on like background noise until I heard a man say how lucky he was to have gotten cancer. I stopped in my tracks, thinking I had misheard.

"Tim, would you back that up and play it again for me, please?" I asked.

He did, and I listened in disbelief once more to the man on camera say how lucky he was to have cancer. His diagnosis had given him a warning, he said calmly, and with that warning, enough time to get his affairs in order and tell everyone how much he loved them before he died—something that would not have happened had he been the victim of a heart attack, gunshot wound, or car accident.

I was struck by his perspective, not realizing how much I would need it in the very near future.

When I was younger, I used to play a simple head trick on myself when something happened that I didn't like. I would try to think of something even worse, then ask myself, "Which of the two would you prefer to have happened?" And the answer, of course, was the thing that *had* actually happened. Ahh, well then, I'd say to myself, you got your wish! Things aren't nearly as bad as they could have been. For some reason—even though I was the puppet master—this simple trick often worked, permitting me to feel *I* was the one who made the choice, even if I had created and stacked the odds myself.

This man's words were a reminder to be aware of the privilege of choice, even if the choices are self-invented as a framing and coping mechanism. This attitude is what would make the difference between six months of despair and six months of gratitude in the last days of Karen's life. The unthinkable *was* going to happen. With medical know-how and expertise seemingly exhausted, the only weapons and guides available to us were in our minds and hearts.

And with that realization, Operation *Final Blessing* was put into action.

OPERATION FINAL BLESSING

"I FEEL SO helpless," I told Karen in tears as I was leaving. "All I can do is to come back as often as possible and spend time with you."

"That's all I want, honey," she said in matching tears, hugging me gently goodbye. "Just come and see me."

And so launched operation *Final Blessing*—an imperfect storm of creative ideas and care and quiet moments together. Everyone contributed what they could, and Karen was rarely alone. Martin gave me short leaves of absence, sometimes coming down to Florida with me to see her. Steve watched the kids, or they took care of themselves. Incredibly, friends gifted me with their frequent flyer miles. Lou flew up from Belize to spend a week each month with her, renting stacks of movies they could watch together. Mom, as well as Karen's friends living nearby, were almost always on hand.

I carry a kaleidoscope of images from those six months in my heart. One of them is the time I accidentally dropped one of Karen's hand-blown wine glasses on the floor as I was washing it. I held my breath as the noise of its shattering reached the ears of my artist and design-loving minimalist sister. She turned at the sound and, to my great surprise, just smiled and said, take it easy honey, don't worry about it. That almost made me feel worse. That was the I'm-dealing-with-cancer-there-are-bigger-things-to-worry-about sister speaking, *not* my perfectionist sister.

On one of her good days, Karen and I gently explored a large enclosed market of secondhand treasures she had discovered not far away. I still have the two glass candle holders I bought that day.

Helping my sister also meant taking her much beloved dog, Cloudy Day, to get her nails trimmed. Cloudy was a large, beautiful mix of breeds weighing about 80 pounds. The year before, I'd found an umbrella from a museum store with clouds on the inside and gave it to Karen. It delighted her. Cloudy was her only child and she loved her passionately. And because Karen couldn't bear to hear her yelp when her nails were trimmed, she put me through the torment of taking care of that while she waited in the car, reading a book.

Sitting together on her bed one night, Karen propped up against the cushions, we went through a small basket of jewelry she'd collected over the years, all of it either vintage or handmade by artisans. She gave most of it to me, keeping only a few pieces to have "just a little bit longer."

Eventually, Karen had to let go of the idea of living independently and moved into Mom's house. Mom gave her the master bedroom, moving her own furniture out so Karen could bring her three large bookcases and have the comfort of being surrounded by her collection of art books. She dressed every morning, then held court from atop the neatly made bed on the days when making her way into the living room seemed beyond her strength.

On one of those atop the bed days, she'd asked if I'd do her a favor.

"Sure," I replied automatically.

"Would you change my dressing for me?" she said. After her mastectomy, the pads and odor-absorbing charcoal filter needed to be changed regularly.

"Sure," I said again. "Just tell me what to do."

She gave me directions, watching me intently as she did—not, I later realized, because she thought I would do something wrong, but because she knew what I was about to see. She knew it was a big ask.

I climbed up next to her, gently removed her blouse, then unbandaged her chest, trying not to flinch or show any expression as I gently peeled back the reeking bandage from what looked like a blackened bombsite where her left breast had once been. I had to bite back tears at the sight of my sister's once lovely body, which now looked and smelled like the plague. Of course, I didn't know what plague victims' bodies looked like, but surely it must have been a hellish nightmare like this.

Following her quiet directions, I gently cleaned the area, applied a fresh charcoal pad and bandaged her up again.

"Thanks for doing that honey," she said. "I know it was tough."

"I love you!" I said, looking at her. "I'd do anything for you."

The words came more from my heart than my mouth, and they came without thought or warning. This was something we never said to one another—ours wasn't that kind of family. Tears came into her eyes as if she was only just now realizing how much I cared for her. Difficult as it was, that moment was another *final blessing*.

That evening, we all piled into her room to watch one of the movies Lou had rented. Karen, fully dressed and wearing some of her artisan jewelry, reclined on the bed. Mom, Lou, and Martin brought in chairs from elsewhere. But I had the premier seat in the room; I climbed up on the bed and settled myself carefully next to my sister because *I* was her little sister. And I could claim that spot next to her like nobody else could.

I don't recall what film we watched. What I do remember is looking around at everyone's faces gathered in this room, all there because we loved Karen so much. All of these moments, all of these final blessings—we would not have had them, I kept reminding myself through my tears, had she died in a car accident.

In celebration of my brother's 50th birthday, Mom decided to gather everyone for a small dinner at a nice restaurant in Sarasota.

Martin flew down with me. My brother Pip arrived from Washington, DC. Lou flew up from Belize. And Karen dressed up in one of her favorite artisan-made Blue Fish outfits and put on a little makeup and jewelry. She looked stunning and normal, as long as you didn't look too closely. By then, her left arm was painfully swollen, a result of trapped fluids with nowhere else to go post-lymph node removal. Someone unintentionally brushed up against her in the restaurant, and I saw the color drain from her face as she very nearly screamed out in pain.

By then, she was living in hospice. Karen, the most intuitive of us all, was always a step ahead. After a few months living at Mom's, she announced one day she'd like to drive over to the hospice facility to take a look at it. My mother balked. There's no need, she told Karen. You can stay here, I'll take care of you.

But even with her own pain and fears, my sister was prescient of the emotional toll her illness was taking on others, especially Mom. She didn't want to die in Mom's house, she told me. She didn't want to do that to her.

We'll just go for a look, she told Mom. Eventually, my mother agreed, just to humor her. Off they went, my sister taking nothing with her but a book.

There was only one room available at Hospice of Sarasota, but it was spacious and filled with light from the many windows which overlooked the stream and grove of orange trees just outside. There was even a small private terrace. Karen looked around and decided it would do.

To my mother's complete surprise, she announced she was going to stay. Could Mom please go home and bring back some of her things later?

The thought that Karen had looked at the room with the full awareness that this was where, in the weeks to come, she would die, haunted me. I cannot imagine the courage, heart, presence of mind, and selflessness it took for her to make that decision. Despite having all of us close at hand, she was so alone inside her thoughts and her ravaged body. And, short of a medical miracle, there was nothing any of us could do about it.

My mother, realizing she'd been outmaneuvered, complied.

When Karen moved in somewhere, she *moved in.* And living in hospice was no different. Within twenty-four hours, her room was transformed. She had gently instructed the hospice staff how to better arrange the furniture (she was right about that) and had Mom bring over the Japanese white paper lamps from her own apartment to replace the hospice ones, filling the space with a soft glow. She also had Mom bring over a few books, some of her favorite clothes, her art supplies and sketchbook, and a beloved and colorful kilim rug, which she draped over a table (most likely to hide it).

From that moment on, Karen never spent the night alone—my mother made sure of that. A rotation of friends visited. Her best friend Charlotte Kellogg, who lived on the other side of the state in Palm Beach, came frequently. Charlotte's husband, Chris, grew roses. Each visit, they brought a bucket full of them, filling Karen's room with the scented blooms. Mom and Charlotte took turns playing Scrabble with her.

Sometimes there were several of us with her at the same time, which was fine, except that none of us were very good about keeping track of who'd given her a push of morphine and when. During one of those overly helpful times, Karen announced she wanted to go outside for a walk. We bundled her up and brought her out into the winter gardens under the old orange trees. Suddenly she motioned for Chris to stop pushing her wheelchair.

"Look at that!" she said, pointing up at the fruit hanging in one of the trees. "Can you see those letters?!"

We glanced at the tree, then at one another. When no one responded, Karen got a little impatient with us.

"There!" she said, adamantly, pointing to one of the oranges. "That's an 'e.' And that next one," she said, pointing to another orange, "that's an 's.'" She was smiling up at the tree, happily trying to rearrange the Scrabble tiles she thought she saw hanging from its branches.

"What words can we spell out with all of the letters in *this* tree?" she asked, pointing to another.

That's when it occurred to us that in our anxiety and love to make sure Karen was as pain free as possible, more than one of us had pushed the little IV plunger in her arm, accidentally tipping the scales with her dosage. But she seemed happy, and even happier when she looked around and realized she'd said something that made us all laugh.

Another *final blessing*. I was beginning to count them like prayer beads.

And then there was the pillow talk. In one of her many artist lives, Karen had developed a passion for needlepoint. She created amazing contemporary designs, needling them mostly into pillows. She stitched one for each of us, each different and very much *us*. At one point, she and another artist friend had opened a shop in the trendy, aptly named town of New Hope, New Jersey, to sell her work, as well as yarns and kits.

Mom kept her pillow out on the sofa in her living room. In lovely shades of cream, green, and gold, there was a row for each of us in the family—Dad, Mom, Karen, Pip, and me. During her last weeks, Mom later told me, Karen picked up the pillow and, tracing her finger over the squares, said our names, our present relationship status and what she thought the future held for us.

"Mom and Dad—divorced," she said. "Pip—divorced. Kristin, in love with Martin and *probably* going to get married. And Karen and Lou," she said softly, "*divorced but in love forever.*"

When Mom relayed this story to me, I thought it weird that my sister had added the word "probably" to the story of me and Martin. As far as Karen knew, Martin and I *were* getting married.

Drinking Jack Daniels in Hospice

I DON'T RECALL a moment when Martin said the words, "Will you marry me?" There was that moment when he spontaneously carved our initials on a yucca plant in Italy, "KF loves MD," but I don't recall any declarations of love, any getting-down-on-one-knee moment. And there was no ring, just something of a loose understanding. More than anything else, it seemed a very pragmatic and practical idea, a logical next step.

On a flight down to Florida with me, he began planning the details. Our wedding would take place at Washington National Cathedral, he said, because we both loved it and we spent a lot of time there for shoots. And he would ask Greg, our sweet Franciscan monk, to officiate.

We told Zoë and Leif of our plans and they seemed to approve. Over the years, they'd spent a lot of time with Martin and got on well with him. And so began the search for a new-to-us house big enough for the four of us.

Ironically, we found one tucked away in Hollin Hills, the same wooded wonderland of mid-century marvels where *The Money Pit* house was located. I loved the neighborhood and still knew some of the neighbors. It seemed perfect. Symbolically, we put in an offer on Valentine's Day and it was accepted.

The first call I'd made, naturally, was to Karen. Now that she was living in hospice, we spoke every day. I knew she'd like the house. During the call she mostly listened. She wasn't feeling well, she told me, but she wanted to have a vision in her head of where I would be living.

"Send me a video of it," she whispered. I promised to do that.

Martin and I had flown down to see her the week before. We stayed at Mom's house and went back and forth to see Karen a few times a day for short visits so we didn't wear her out.

One evening, as we pulled into the parking lot, I broke down in tears.

"I can't take this," I sobbed to Martin. "I never know what we'll face each time we go back. *Will she even still be alive?*"

Martin turned off the ignition and looked at me. Then he put his arms around me and held me. He told me he'd be with me, we'd be together, it would be all right, and it would make my sister happy.

"Besides," he said, trying to cheer me up. "We have the bottle of Jack Daniels she asked us to bring her. We can't *not* go in."

Patients in hospice can have alcohol—the staff doesn't mind. You're dying anyway, they rationalize, so where's the harm? Their entire mission is to have you feeling comfortable, happy, and as pain- and worry-free as possible during your remaining days. The staff at my sister's hospice in Sarasota was made up of the most lovely, supportive, and empathetic people I could ever have wished for her. For all of us.

I gradually pulled myself together and mopped up my face. Martin got out and came around to my side of the car. He offered his hand and helped me out. As we walked through the front doors together, I could hear what sounded like a party going on somewhere inside.

Well, that's a bit disrespectful, my sad self thought. Martin stopped, a listening expression on his face, as he tried to figure out the source of the revelry.

"Is that coming from *your sister's room*?" he asked.

Astonished, I looked around and realized the party noises were indeed coming out of Karen's room. We crossed the lobby and stepped inside to find her room aglow from the light of her soft Japanese lamps as well as from the spirits of those gathered around her. *My sister was having a party!*

It turned out she'd asked *everyone* to bring her a bottle of Jack Daniels—me, Martin, my mother, and two of her artist friends. Once again, she was dressed in her favorite Blue Fish outfit and holding court from atop her neatly made bed. She was delighted with each new bottle and each bouquet of flowers she was presented with. There were jokes, stories, and laughter. My sister was in the finest of high spirits, thanks to the combination of family, friendships, JD, and morphine. The party lasted until nearly 10 p.m.

Two days later, it was a quieter scene. My mother never wanted Karen to be alone at night and usually stayed with her. On our last night in Sarasota, I asked her if we could spend the night with Karen instead. "Of course," she said.

Martin settled his long frame onto the sofa while I put together an arrangement of cushions on the floor. All night, I listened for the sound of her breathing, keeping watch over her for what seemed like hours, before gradually dozing off to the sound of her gentle intermittent breaths.

In the soft shades of early morning, a change in Karen's breathing pattern seeped into my consciousness, awakening me. Startled, I raised my head quickly to look at her, worried she had left us while I was sleeping and not paying attention.

But she hadn't.

She was lying still, but awake, and she was watching me. How long she had been watching me, her little sister, curled up like a puppy, asleep on the floor at the foot of her bed, I wondered.

Wordlessly, we gazed at one another. A long, lingering moment passed. And then she raised her right arm slightly, her fingers held in the three-letter sign language arrangement Martin had taught her.

I love you, she signed.

Without speaking, I held my own fingers up.

I love you, I signed back to her.

Crossing her index and middle fingers over one another, frowning slightly with concentration, Karen signed back silently, *I really love you.*

In tears, I mirrored her gesture with my own hand. *I really love you!*

She looked at me silently for another moment, then she rearranged her fingers again, this time flying them gently through the air to say, *I will always love you.*

That is the last image I have of her. Karen died five days after Valentine's Day.

Phone Calls and Paintbrushes

THE PHONE AT the documentary workspace rang periodically, as it usually did, that Friday morning. Ever since Karen had slipped into a coma, I hadn't been able to focus on work. I tried to make myself useful by painting the walls a color that cheered me up—Scandinavian white. But as I was painting, all I could think about was my sister, lying in hospice, nearly one thousand miles away from me.

When the phone rang at ten minutes past ten, however, it sounded different. There was something in that particular ring.

I froze, paintbrush in hand, listening.

Please, I whispered to myself —*can I have just one more minute?*

Not only was she my big sister, Karen was also my counselor, my mentor, my friend, and my best critic. She was my other self—the older, wiser, more confident, more artistic me that I could only dream of being. We were ten years apart but crafted from the same genetic pool and bound together through the shared cultural experiences of a common—and uncommon—upbringing. It was a mutually satisfying relationship. I looked up to her and she looked out for me.

All my life, Karen had been my teacher. She was always there before me, guiding me, giving advice, suggestions, ideas—all cleverly hidden in the guise of telling me what to do. From boyfriends, clothes, makeup, hairstyles, to when I would lose my virginity, my choice of husband, and, of course, anything to do with how I set up my home, she always had an opinion. In fact, I couldn't remember anything she *didn't* have an opinion about.

Ours was a joyous rivalry with constant taunts to each other and the competition in differing fields of creative endeavors. Despite our age difference and the peripatetic ways of our family lifestyle, we always found chunks of time to spend together.

In 1964, our family had moved from a fifty-acre tree farm in rural New Jersey to the heart of London. London in the '60s was magical—Mary Quant and miniskirts, Carnaby Street, the mods and rockers, the Beatles and the Rolling Stones—and my 18-year-old sister took full advantage of it.

When I was eight and Karen was eighteen, she and I were walking along a street in Chelsea when a car full of young guys drove by. They leaned out of the window, whistling their appreciation. My sister laughed.

Honeybunch, she whispered to me. *They're looking at you!*

For a hopeful moment, I was excited. *Me?!*

And then, as the car passed by, I realized that of course it was my sister they were admiring. I think that's when I first realized how beautiful she was with her creamy pale skin, strawberry blonde hair, and green eyes.

Karen left London later that year to attend Pratt Institute in Brooklyn and pursue her interest in design. Before leaving, perhaps as consolation to her sad little sister, she came up with the idea that we would exchange letters using fake names while she was living in New York. We chose Peter Cook and Dudley Moore, our favorite comedians at the time and stars of the show, *Not Only But Also*. I was thrilled when the first airletter arrived from New York addressed to "Ms. Dudley Fellows." "Pete" was a better correspondent than I, writing to me often about art school, fashion, New York City—and of course, boys.

In the late '60s, Karen invited me to spend a week with her in New York. She took me to Greenwich Village to see the artists and to Central Park. We shopped at her neighborhood grocery stores and she took me out to small inexpensive restaurants. Being a very pragmatic older sister, she also taught me to clean her "loo"—her idea of rent for the visit.

Years later, in between my high school years, we lived together at our mother's small A-frame beach house on Long Beach Island for a summer. Karen took her responsibilities (me) very seriously and monitored any possibility of a social life (i.e., meeting boys on the beach) quite fiercely. She taught me how to make macaroni and cheese out of a box and we indulged in what would become a decades-long ritual: hand-me-down fashion shows, both of us collapsing in laughter at how easily everything that looked so stylish on her, looked so awful on her skinny little sister.

After I graduated from college, Karen visited me during the years I worked in the Georgetown neighborhood of Washington, DC. We watched the latest French foreign films and decided to dress like Catherine Deneuve in *The Last Metro*. In a vintage clothing store on Wisconsin Avenue, she tried on a black cocktail dress from the '40s that seemed tailor-made for her curves.

I really missed my time, she said wistfully, turning this way and that, admiring her reflection in the mirror. *I look great in these clothes!*

Despite the constraints of an unpredictable artist's income, Karen was capable of spontaneous and overwhelming generosity. After my marriage to Steve ended and I was living in the house with the tulips, she came to visit me and the kids for a few days. She and I spent an afternoon at the Torpedo Factory in Alexandria's Old Town—a collection of artists' studios in a former munitions factory—and both of us fell in love with the same painting by artist Connie Slack. We sat in two chairs in front of it for some time, gazing at the canvas.

"You really like it?" Karen asked me. I nodded.

Two hours later, it was hanging in my living room, a riot of colorful flowers lighting up my little house, bringing joy and energy to the space.

"*I* will own it," she said firmly before she left. "But as I don't really have the space for it at my place, why don't you take care of it for me?"

And of course, she never reclaimed it.

Art was her everything, and she was always eager to share it. In her final months, in addition to teaching Leif to paint and fire clay, she spent time with Zoë painting shells they found on the beach with watercolors.

During my last night by her side, I kept watch over her as she struggled for breath. I was torn in half, both wishing her peace but also wanting desperately to cling to what was left of her. There was still so much to do. We had talked about visiting the art museums in New York City together and the many art scenes in Italy. There were so many places I wanted to experience with her.

Six months earlier, it was Karen who had a paintbrush in her hand when she realized the cancer had returned. Now at the documentary workshop, it was me holding a paintbrush and bracing myself for bad news. Six months between paint brush strokes—as if those two paintbrushes were a pair of parenthetical arms wrapped around that precious space of time and moments together, our bittersweet months of final blessings.

Martin answered the phone. I heard him greet my mother by name, then fall silent, followed by a few murmured words. Then I heard him lay the receiver gently on his desk.

Everything was still, suspended for a moment. Softly, he called my name.

RUNNING ON EMPTY

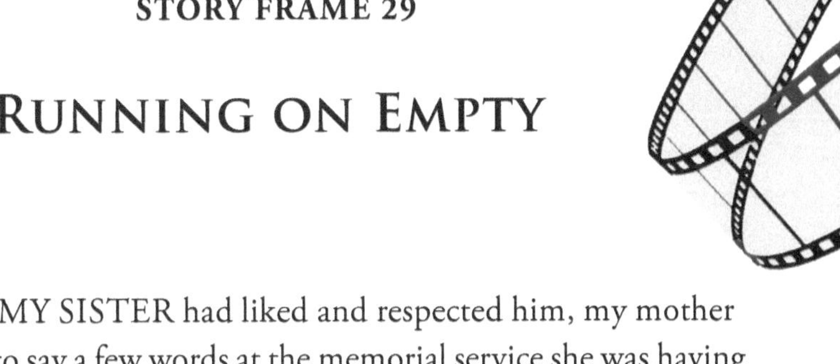

KNOWING MY SISTER had liked and respected him, my mother asked Martin to say a few words at the memorial service she was having for Karen the following month, which he graciously agreed to do.

In addition to writing his own eulogy, Martin encouraged me to speak as well. I hesitated at first, but he persisted. It was easy and cathartic for me to write about Karen. But saying the words out loud, knowing I'd never see her again and that my treasury of stories was now of a finite quantity—I wasn't sure I could manage that without breaking down.

Martin coached me, suggesting I add in a little humor where possible, knowing the gathering of mourners would appreciate the opportunity to smile or laugh. He showed me how to type my words out double-spaced, in all caps with pauses and other directions written in to make it easier to read them aloud to an audience.

And so I wrote about the London years, our *Last Metro* vintage clothing shopping spree in Georgetown, the purchasing of the large canvas of flowers at the Torpedo Factory, and other favorite anecdotes that I felt showcased her spirit and personality. He had me read what I'd written out loud to him over and over, coaching me on my pacing until both of us felt I was as ready as I would ever be to do the unthinkable, the unimaginable—to speak at my sister's memorial service.

We flew back down to Sarasota. My mother had made arrangements for a service at a small Lutheran church near where she lived. Walking in, I noticed there were cheerful little plastic flowers along the sidewalk. An avid gardener, Karen would have *hated* fake flowers, I thought. I hated them on her behalf. Then I reminded myself, this service and its location in a church wasn't really about Karen; it was for those she left behind, especially our mother. Details like that simply didn't matter.

I remember very little of the actual service. Martin thoughtfully made a recording of me speaking and gave me the tapes, but I've never been able to listen to them.

One of the most meaningful tributes to Karen came after the memorial service, back at the documentary workshop. And it came from Bertch, our freelance gaffer, the head electrician on most of our shoots, and the guy in charge of the layout and design of the lighting. Bertch was a very sweet guy, tall, a bit shy and a bit awkward, often blinking at the world and those around him from behind his spectacles. He was quick to laugh at a joke and fiercely loyal to those he cared about.

Bertch was interested in how things worked and how they were put together, useful attributes for a head electrician. He freely admitted to having ADHD, attention deficit disorder. One time he disassembled his Volvo to fix something, but he never got around to doing it. Month after month, the Volvo lay in parts around his living room like weird metal steampunk furniture. Rather than put it all back together, he eventually decided it would be easier just to buy a second, second-hand car.

In addition to working on our documentary shoots, one of Bertch's main gigs was weddings. A *Washington Post* "Lifestyle" article once described him as spending his weekends "trying to make electronic sense of other people's happy occasions." That was Bertch in a nutshell: on the sidelines, in the shadows, sweating the details, always wanting the best for others.

We looked out for one another in small, and not so small ways. Ten years older than me, he sometimes played the role of a big brother. Once, a nearby restaurant owner was rude to me during a meal all of us from the documentary workshop were enjoying together. Martin ignored this uncomfortable situation, the words that silenced everyone at our table. It was Bertch who, as we left the restaurant, wordlessly put his arm around me and held me close as we walked the few blocks back to work.

Another time, we had a shoot in the city on a miserable weather day, an interview with a Catholic bishop at his residence. Bertch seemed unsettled when he arrived. Coming in through the front door, he thoughtlessly, and uncharacteristically, threw his wet slicker down on some very nice wooden furniture. Concerned with possible marks, I retrieved his wet things, hung them somewhere else and mopped up the chairs so he wouldn't get in trouble. Then I offered to do a drinks run for the crew. I bought containers of juice for everyone except Bertch. Having read that caffeine can calm down some ADHD traits, I brought him two cokes. It worked a charm. He was fine halfway through the first bottle.

Not long after Karen died, I came into work and found a card on my desk along with a pre-paid entry form for the 10th anniversary Susan G Komen 5K Race for the Cure in Washington, DC. It was from Bertch.

Even though he knew I wasn't a runner, this was a touching gift from someone who didn't know how to console me. Although he never said or wrote this, I think what he wanted to say in his sweet, slightly awkward way, was—*If we support the Race for the Cure, maybe you won't get breast cancer and die like your sister.*

I had eight weeks to prepare. That weekend, I bought a pair of running shoes.

On the fifth of June, participants gathered early in the morning for a sunrise breakfast on the grounds of the Washington Monument, featuring a ten-star salute to survivors with Al and Tipper Gore. Afterwards, the survivors, some sporting pink bandanas over their bald heads, and their families ran through the streets of Washington, DC together. Seeing them made me sad. In a crowd of about 50,000—I was running alone.

I ran for my sister. And I ran with appreciation for Bertch.

He also gave me a copy of a book titled *Hilary and Jackie: The True Story of Two Sisters Who Shared a Passion, a Madness and a Man.* Written by Hilary du Pré, it was the story of her sister, Jacqueline, and her life as an international cellist, her marriage to conductor Daniel Barenboim, and early diagnosis with multiple sclerosis. It was also the somewhat shocking story that Jacqueline shared her husband with her sister. Apart from being a book about sisters, it had nothing to do with me and Karen. But that was how Bertch's mind worked, and I loved him for it.

In the years to come, more documentaries—*Not as I Pictured, Inheritance,* and *Full Circle*—would come to my rescue, providing me with visions for how I could navigate the wake of Karen's death in a positive way.

Whereas *Final Blessing* helped me deal with a pending loss, these films would give me opportunities to go beyond that loss to help others, and in a more impactful way than running through a city in the early morning hours. Working with these films, I would be able to reach potentially tens of thousands of viewers—if not more—with scientific information and true stories.

But as I crossed the finish line in DC that day, somewhere in the middle of the pack, these films were still way off in the future. They hadn't even been made yet. The filmmakers had not yet had the life experiences that would inspire them to create a documentary film on the topic. One filmmaker's wife had yet to discover she had breast cancer. Another filmmaker had yet to read an article, which had yet to be written, that would make him think of the grandmother he lost to breast cancer, understand how her doctors had failed her, and then decide to do something about it. And one filmmaker did not yet know he himself had cancer.

These filmmakers had not yet raised the funding needed, nor picked up their cameras, nor assembled a team to help them make these films. At that moment, none of them knew who I was, nor did I know them.

But we were already destined to be connected. In future years, our paths would cross on a topic painfully close to all our hearts as the four of us—each in our own way—found a measure of healing by helping others mitigate their own suffering.

In the meantime, another unexpected plot twist rocked my world within weeks of my sister's memorial, and it needed my immediate attention.

A Plot Twist in Four Little Words

A PLOT TWIST is a literary technique that introduces a radical change or unexpected occurrence in the anticipated outcome of the plot, changing the direction of the plot from where we thought it was going. Plot twists are designed and intended to be disrupters.

And just as they can happen in films, books, and video games, plot twists can also happen in real life.

Martin sold his house. With Mom's permission, I borrowed my half of the down payment from the equity in the home she and I owned together near the river to purchase the house Martin and I had fallen in love with in *The Money Pit* neighborhood, where Martin, the kids and I would soon be living.

Martin moved in first. Or rather, his belongings did. Busy with one of his film projects, he asked if I could oversee the men moving his furniture and possessions into the new house. I love doing this and was happy to take care of the move for him.

A few days after his things were in place, Martin asked me to come over for a cup of coffee in the kitchen of our new home. We had what was now a years-long habit of talking about projects and work over morning coffee.

I showed up at the agreed upon time, parked my car under the trees and walked inside. It was a sunny and lovely May morning, a few days after my birthday and about a month after Karen's memorial. It seemed like there was an almost tangible scent of fresh new beginnings in the air, but it was probably just the lilacs in bloom that stirred up these feelings of optimism inside me.

Walking into the house, I glanced around at the new arrangements and felt pleased with how everything looked. I found Martin sitting on a stool at the kitchen island, facing the wall of windows. I sat across from him, with my back to the view of the garden, looking at the kitchen cabinets instead. It wasn't my preference—normally I would always take the opportunity to look out the windows, but for some reason this didn't feel like a sitting side by side moment.

How often, I wondered, *do I find myself ceding the better seat, the better view, the credit, the limelight—to others? I do it automatically, generously, almost reflexively, and I do it more often than I ever get it back. Why is this?*

There were two mugs of coffee in front of him. I noticed an awkward expression on his face as I reached for one. I smiled and greeted him. I'm sure there were the routine pleasantries. Or perhaps there weren't. Maybe he said a few words to me about *American Byzantine*. Or perhaps he didn't. But what he did say next is forever seared into my memory.

"I've changed my mind," Martin said quietly, not making eye contact.

He didn't say what he'd changed his mind about, but somehow, I knew. The documentary filmmaker with whom I had worked for more than six years, *with whom I had just bought a house*, the man I thought I was going to marry and live with, now suddenly didn't want any of the things *he* had been advocating for.

In just four words, I lost house, husband—and job.

There were no tears, no angry words, no accusations, and no pro-testations. In fact, I don't recall saying anything at all.

After the loudest, longest moments of silence, during which we both studied the cooling remnants in our coffee mugs as if that was where the answers might lay hidden, I reached into my pocket, pulled out my key to *our* new home and put it on the counter. Then I stood, walked through the house and out the front door. I got into my car and drove away.

I never asked him why. Part of me didn't want or need to know.

The relationship's ephemera—the photographs, cards and notes from him I've held onto over the years—show that once upon a time he was crazy about me.

Last night you looked radiant. I was so proud to be with you. Thanks for a beautiful evening! . . . I see you're sad today, is there <u>anything</u> I can do? Please! . . . My fondest wish is to hold you close, so close all your burdens vanish into air . . . I carry your smile with me all week . . . Today moments will pass as if they were hours. My thoughts will only be with you . . . Be my love forever, is that clear? Today and always. . . .

I remember feeling the same way, too, once upon a time, and still have some awkward poetry and songwriting to show for it, none of which I ever showed him.

> *I love a you, you may not know*
> *The one the camera caught off guard*
> *The one too tired to try so hard*
> *to impress the already fallen.*
>
> *I love a you, you may not know*
> *The imperfections you hate to show*
> *The thinning hair, to me so fair,*
> *I love all of what you are.*
>
> *I love a you, you may not know*

Exhausted at last, I watch you sleep,
Delighting in your peace.
I love all the moments you don't know I'm watching—
the flashes of you that belong only to me.
I love a you, you may not know.

Somehow those giddy, romantic feelings dissipated over the course of making a film together. It's possible it just came down to the simple mathematics of storytelling. It was his documentary workshop and naturally, he wanted things his way.

But for me, it was a lopsided equation that ultimately didn't work. I had ideas of my own and I wanted to see at least some of them somehow woven into our work. Stephen, our sound tech who by now had become a good friend, once remarked that my frustrations stemmed from Martin being a journalist, whereas Stephen saw me as more of an artist. Martin was newspaper, magazine style reporting, and interviews; I was sculptures, stories, and canvases.

To be quite honest, part of me was strangely relieved. Which led me to think there must have been something inside my head or my heart that wasn't in favor of the idea of marrying Martin, something I had either ignored or suppressed.

I had my own house, which the kids and I were still happily living in. We hadn't yet packed even a single box. The good news was the three of us didn't have to uproot ourselves and move. I'd never really cared whether Martin and I were married or simply carried on the way we'd been. Marriage had always seemed more important to him. I just wanted to keep making interesting films together.

What *did* upset me, what shocked me beyond the reach of tears, was the imminent loss of my job at the documentary workshop. Despite the hundreds of thousands of dollars I'd raised for him, in addition to the valuable work I'd done in terms of production, research, press, and what felt like a million other things, Martin didn't want me there anymore.

A few weeks later, well into the wee hours of yet another dark and sleepless night, I had a Scarlett O'Hara moment. I got out of bed, went downstairs. Feeling my way around my desk, I found a pen and a handful of small white index cards. I turned on a light, sat down and carefully numbered them, one for each of the next five years, beginning with the year 2000 and the start of the new millennium. And then, in the stillness of the night, with my slumbering children lost in their dreams upstairs, I sketched out what I wanted to accomplish each year. These index cards became my vision board. Determined never again to have so many rugs whipped out from underneath my feet, the first item on the first card read: "Be my own boss."

I added: steady work, a raise in salary, and the IRS situation dealt with. On cards 2 through 5, I wrote:

- take a sculpture class
- learn to cook
- learn Italian
- write more letters and read more books
- get hired by interesting people to do interesting shoots in interesting places— or work for myself
- write several books, which will be glowingly reviewed by people whose opinions I respect!
- start college savings plans for the kids
- be debt free—own my car and my house

There were many others. I wrote until the cards were completely covered. The penultimate item on the fifth card was, "Be able to work anywhere I want in the whole damn country!" That, to me, was freedom.

Martin once told me I was the most resilient person he'd ever known. Of all the compliments he had given me, that one was my favorite, the one I held onto. I knew I was resilient, but no one had ever said that to me before. I also knew that *resilience is a choice.*

One by one, I would cross off each goal from the cards as I achieved it. It would take me five years, but I would eventually be able to cross off even that next-to-last item on card number five when I packed up my car, my kids, and our dogs, leaving all the toxic memories of the DC area behind me, and drove west to a new home in the Blue Ridge Mountains. I wouldn't go there for a job, or love, or money. I would move there simply because it was beautiful and that was where I wanted to live. It felt good there.

That left just one goal still to be crossed out on the cards. It was a big one—one that would take me two decades to accomplish. But I would ultimately scratch that one off, too.

In the meantime, there was still a film to finish with the man who no longer wanted to marry me.

NOW WHAT?!

HOW COULD HE do that to you?! you may be thinking. I was wondering the same thing—especially considering the timing. Martin ended our future together just a few weeks after he'd spoken at Karen's memorial service and within days of the first birthday in my life without my sister. Yet, despite feeling melancholy over this, I couldn't help but notice that having dodged a second marriage, along with all its encumbrances, I also felt a bit relieved. I felt *free*. And that felt good.

It took a while, but once the initial shock of Martin's announcement wore off, I realized he was probably right to pull the plug on the relationship and kick me from the nest I thought we were building together. It's possible he sensed in me something that chafed at being under someone else's wing, something I may not yet have understood about myself at the time—an innate desire to strike out and be completely on my own, working on my own ideas.

American Byzantine, however, was not yet finished. I'd written the first draft of the script and knew the characters, research, locations, subjects, and funders better than anyone else. It was me who brought the film—and its significant funding— into the documentary workshop. The awkward reality was that we still had to work together to complete the project. Navigating relationships—in all their complexities—is often part of making documentaries.

Over the next seven months, Martin and I continued to stumble along awkwardly, both trying to be amicable and trying to avoid one another. Eventually, we would have to deal with rewrites, the editing process, and the creation of the film's soundtrack.

And before we could begin that, we still had location shoots in Ravenna, Italy, and Istanbul, Turkey. We were also headed to London where I'd booked what I hoped would be a fabulous interview with one of the world's preeminent Byzantinists, John Julius Norwich—a member of the British House of Lords and, in the words of *The Guardian*, "a man of many enthusiasms."

Even though I would be traveling with Martin, I should have been looking forward to all of this. But the truth was, I was nervous. What was holding me back was not Martin, it was that I was scared to fly—and with *very* good reason.

MY FEAR OF FLYING GROUNDS A 747

I WAS THE sister, daughter, and granddaughter of flying professionals. My brother had flown F-somethings—4s or 16s, I could never remember which—in the Marines. My father was a former vice president of Eastern Airlines. He'd also been the director of operations for British European Airways during the years we lived in London. My grandfather, a former advisor to Emperor Haile Selassie, had been chairman of the board for Ethiopian Airlines in the 1950s. And then there was me, scared to fly.

This was the source of a lot of teasing within my family.

I felt I had good reason for my reticence to fly, however, having had a handful of bad flying experiences, the worst of which happened when I grounded a 747 in Switzerland—all by myself.

When I was twenty-eight, I flew to France to meet up with my Danish boyfriend and a group of forty jovial Danes for a week of skiing in the Alps. Getting there involved taking three Pan Am flights, *all* of which had problems, including an aborted takeoff in the snow at JFK.

Sadly, my Danish boyfriend and I got along

even worse than my efforts to traverse the French Alps on skis. Everything was fine during the day: The sun was shining, the scenery was beautiful, the skiing was great, and the stops for hot chocolate on the way down the slopes were always a welcome treat. But in the evenings, drinking beers at a bar called "33," we bickered over relationship expectations. Older than me by several years and already a father, my boyfriend wanted to hang out with other families whereas I, still in my twenties, wanted to party in the evenings with the singles.

At the end of the week, I packed up and flew from France to Switzerland where I boarded a 747 in Zurich for the flight back to New York City. Waiting for takeoff, I looked out the window and noticed a large hole—larger than my arms could encircle—in the wing of the plane. Through it, I could see the tarmac below.

As the plane began to taxi to its takeoff position, I decided to ring the flight attendant button. When she arrived, I explained I was a nervous flyer, that I had just broken up with my boyfriend, and even though I may have had a few pre-flight Heinekens, I was concerned about the large hole in the wing.

"Is that okay?" I asked, pointing through the window. The flight attendant bent over to take a look. The polite expression on her face vanished.

"*Fuck!*" she said, confirming my fears. "No, that's *not* okay!"

I sat still in my little haze of beer, listening in as she spoke with the flight deck on an intercom behind my seat. Meanwhile, the plane continued taxiing to its takeoff position. Once there, it turned to face the runway. The engines revved. I held my breath wondering what on earth would happen if we took off with a large hole in the wing.

A few moments later, the engines cut back. As the plane turned to taxi back toward the airport, the captain's voice came on over the loudspeaker with an apology and the news (to everyone but me) that a problem with the plane needed to be checked out. Once we arrived back at the gate, we were asked to disembark and wait in the terminal.

I passed the time shopping, reading and having another Heineken, just to calm my nerves.

A few hours later, Pan Am announced the plane was unable to fly. We were grounded overnight in Zurich until they could book us on another flight the following day. We were asked to return to the plane, retrieve our carry-on belongings, and pick up a voucher for the airport hotel.

I just grounded a 747! I thought with a weird mix of fear, surprise, and—to be honest—a touch of smug satisfaction.

As we left the plane with our carry-ons, the flight attendants stood in a line by the exit doors. One of them pointed at me and remarked, "There's the troublemaker! Thanks to her, I won't have my date in New York tonight."

I was shocked at her hostility. In my beery haze and now boyfriend-less state, tears filled my eyes. I made my way off the plane where I found a group of five people, perhaps in their sixties, lined up in the lounge outside the exit tunnel. It turned out they were waiting for me.

"There she is!" one of them exclaimed, pointing at me.

What now?! I thought, blinking through a fresh wave of tears.

"Don't tell me *you're* mad at me, too," I sobbed, regretting that extra beer.

"Mad at you?!" one of them said. "Why on earth would we be *mad* at you? We think you just saved our lives!"

I stared at them in surprise. Melodramatic as they were, these words felt so healing compared to how I'd just been treated by the Pan Am flight attendants. Having witnessed that, the five friends had decided to take action.

"This is the woman who saved our lives!" they began shouting to the other passengers in the terminal, much to my embarrassment. I just wanted to slink away somewhere and pull myself together. But they had a plan.

"You're not going to stay at the crappy airport hotel Pan Am booked us in," one of them said. "We're taking you downtown. You'll stay with us at The Stork Hotel!"

"I can't afford that," I protested. I'd already overspent my budget for the ski trip.

"Don't you worry, we're so grateful you spoke up, we'll pay for your room," another said. "And we're also going to take you out somewhere nice for dinner!"

They were good to their word.

A few hours later, as I looked around at my five new friends in the lovely restaurant they'd chosen, I couldn't believe any of what had just happened. The airlines held onto our suitcases, so we were all still wearing the same clothes which, in my case, was a ski sweater and black pants. Not appropriate for a restaurant of this caliber but when my hosts explained our situation to the staff, we were welcomed in anyway.

As we exchanged stories and got to know one another a little over the food and wine, we discovered the son of one of the couples lived in the same small town in Pennsylvania where my mother worked. Even more improbably, he lived in the *same* small historic building, in an apartment above my mother's real estate offices.

What were the chances?

We pondered the weird serendipity of my mom and their son passing by one another, perhaps daily, more than four thousand miles away from where we were eating, laughing, and chatting. That discovery lent a strange but sweet meant-to-be-ness to the circumstances of the disabled plane that had brought us all together.

The following morning, we shared a taxi back out to the airport to board a different 747—one we hoped didn't have any holes in it. I found my seat and checked the wings, just to be sure. As other passengers passed by, some of them called out and asked me how the plane looked today. That would have made my father and brother roar with laughter to hear people asking *me* this question—me, who knew absolutely nothing about planes.

When I eventually got home, three flights later, I told my brother,

Pip, what had happened. He guessed the plane may have hit a bird either on its takeoff or landing in Zurich. When airplanes are taking off, he explained, the flaps on the wings help produce more lift. They also allow for a steep and more controllable angle for a plane during landing. But when the plane is on the ground, the flaps, which are not extended, would cover up any damage to the wings. It turned out there was no above-wing inspection protocol for planes at the time, only an on-the-ground inspection.

At my mother's urging, I wrote a letter to Pan Am, detailing the incident, to which I eventually received a toothless response, handwritten in pencil on a sheet of corporate stationery. Not long after came the news that Pan Am was in a precarious financial situation. They filed for bankruptcy six years later.

"What could go wrong, did," Stanley Gerwitz, Pan Am's VP for External Affairs, was quoted as saying at the time. "It was the most astonishing example of Murphy's law *in extremis.*"

When I thought of the flight attendant who missed her date in New York City, I will admit to feeling just a touch of *schadenfreude.*

But now, in order to finish the filming for *American Byzantine,* there were a lot of flights ahead. Fortunately, another film came to my rescue.

FRENCH KISSING
MY WAY TO ITALY

FOR A GLITTERING moment in time, Ravenna, Italy, was the capital city of the Western Roman Empire—and its architecture shows it.

"Selected for its isolation," wrote historian Robert Wernick, "the city became the center for miraculous works celebrating divinity . . . a beachhead of antique civilization in the rising seas of barbarism. It was crowded with sumptuous palaces and churches."

Lazy and cowardly as Roman Emperor Honorius was, he at least had the presence of mind to stay one step ahead of the barbarian hordes roaming throughout his domains. He accomplished this by relocating the capital of the Western Roman Empire in the year 402 from Milan to Ravenna.

Strategically located a few hours south of Venice on the Adriatic coast, with the vast marshes of the Po River acting effectively as a large moat, Ravenna was relatively safe from direct assault.

To explain the sources of inspiration behind the architecture of the Basilica in Washington, DC, and the title *American Byzantine,* Martin and I set off to film some of those sumptuous churches.

We had visited Ravenna briefly two years

earlier to scout the locations, decide where and what we would film, and in general get our bearings for how these stories could be woven into the tapestry of our documentary. Along with the marble carvers of Pietrasanta, this was one of my favorite parts of our film.

Karen was still alive back then. As a tile artist, she would have loved seeing the mosaics and tiles of Italy but, too sick to travel, she told me I was to be her eyes. She loaned me her Canon AE1 single lens reflex to photograph it all for her, a camera I still have.

During our first visit, I'd taken photographs and sent her colorful postcards with little stories of what we were seeing and doing, along with notes of encouragement for any progress she was making in her battle against the cancerous barbarians inside her body.

And now, two years later, Martin and I were returning to Ravenna for the actual film shoot.

A close friend, knowing I hated to fly, had gifted me a thermos of mimosas for the cab ride out to Dulles Airport. Much as I appreciated his thoughtfulness, it may not have been a good idea.

I stepped onto the curb in front of the departures terminal where I saw Martin. Thanks to the drinks, I had my exit strategy ready.

"I don't want to go, let me stay," I told him. "I'm worried about my kids, they need me and what if the plane crashes? Really, it will be okay. I've organized everything, you'll be fine."

The words tumbled out between tipsy tears, a babble of nonsense as I fumbled through my backpack to give him the all-important production binder with the carefully choreographed details and time-lines—names, dates, locations, players, permits, emails, and mobile phone numbers.

The tricky dance of permissions and wire transfers began, of course, with the Catholic church, in the person of Monsignor Guido Marchetti at the Diocese di Ravenna. His very name sounded to me like something from a dark Italian opera and added a touch of intrigue to the shoot. A payment of more than one million lire was needed to film at San Vitale for the day, which sounded appalling until I calculated the conversion and realized it was only about $500.

Ravenna's lovely tourism director, a woman named Grazia, arranged access to San Vitale and the other buildings, negotiated the town permits on our behalf, and helped book a hotel.

We'd assembled a dream team, with rhyming names like Italian poetry. Silvio, Luca Nonni, and Cristiano Nanni would provide the camera gear and all the lighting equipment. Marina Ferretti, our government-provided interpreter, would coordinate with the staff at San Vitale and help with the feeding and care of the crew.

Martin was all too aware of my fear of flying. For the "house of many colors" shoot, we had taken separate flights to San Antonio. A few days before I left, I discovered a chunky envelope in my desk drawer at the documentary workshop. Inside was a rosary and a small note in Martin's handwriting.

> *I thought I would give you a little something to reduce the shakes when you fly Saturday. When I was seven, a nun gave me these rosary beads and told me they would always mean God was protecting me. Carry them safely to San Antonio. Nothing but good will happen. See you there. M.*

Even though I considered myself an existentialist non-believer, the rosary comforted me. I carried it in my pocket and touched it frequently during the flights there and back.

But I'd long since returned the rosary to Martin and had no such totem with me now. Martin ignored my protestations and began piling our suitcases and gear—ten pieces in all—onto a curbside cart. Then he told me to get it together.

"You're coming," he said, slinging the last one up on the pile. "This is *your* shoot. You've done all the work to organize it. Come on, let's go."

He grabbed my arm firmly and steered me into the airport. We checked the suitcases and gear bags.

"Okay," he said, after we'd cleared security. "Now let's find the bar."

A few hours and two beers later, I took the middle seat next to him on the plane. Channeling Meg Ryan in the 1995 film *French Kiss*, I tried to distract myself from takeoff by chatting with the guy sitting on the other side of me. I don't recall what we talked about, but he was not Kevin Kline and it wasn't about sex. I think it may have been about geology and Italy. On the other side, Martin read a book in stony silence, ignoring me.

Much to my surprise, I found myself enjoying the flight. It occurred to me that my anxieties may not have been about flying *per se,* but perhaps had something to do with the process of *getting ready* to fly? Perhaps about leaving Zoë and Leif? What if something happened to them while I was more than four thousand miles away?

And of course, something *did* happen.

We landed safely and made the drive to Ravenna without incident. Once there, we checked into our rooms at the Hotel Bisanzio (Italian for Byzantium), conveniently located just three blocks from San Vitale, the location for our primary shoot.

Knowing I was stressing over potential home fires, Martin suggested I call the kids if it would give me some peace of mind and get me to pull focus on the shoot.

I dialed the number of the house where Steve lived with his new wife. Leif, who had just turned nine, answered.

"Hi Mom!" he said, then paused. He tried to muffle the phone with his small hand, but I still heard him say the words, "Should we tell her?" I presumed he was talking to Zoë.

What's going on, I wondered. *I've been gone less than twelve hours!*

"No, *don't!*" I heard Zoë hiss fiercely to her little brother. I could imagine her pinching his arm to add a little emphasis to her words. "*Not until she gets back!*"

"I heard that," I said, doing my best to sound calm. "So now you have to tell me!"

Wild imaginings ran through my head while I waited, listening to the small whispers from so far away.

"Here, *give* it to me!" I heard Zoë say in a tone of exasperation to her little brother. And then, speaking into the phone she said, "Hi Mom. Dad's getting divorced."

Steve had been remarried less than two years, but it hadn't gone well. *And this is when he decides to tell the kids their lives are going to have another major change, when I'm four thousand miles away from them?* I always felt responsible for managing their happiness, for damage control. Why couldn't I shed that for just one week, like a heavy backpack, and leave it hanging on a tree or in a storage locker somewhere back home?

"Okay, no worries, you two, you'll be fine!" I heard myself saying brightly into the phone, not believing a word of what I was saying. "I'll be back home in a few days and then you can tell me all about it."

After a few I love yous, I put the phone down, changed from my travel clothes, and washed up. Work was calling. Sleep deprived and trying to quell my anxieties, I put on my game face and went down to the lobby to meet Martin, find some coffee, and discuss the production days ahead.

In order to reach into the upper recesses of some of those ancient churches, as well as provide a more dramatic effect, Martin had decided to rent a Jimmy Jib—a versatile camera and crane combination with a counterweight on the opposite end of the crane to balance the weight of the camera. Filmmakers and cinematographers like its ease of movement for pan, tilt, and zoom angles. Its reach of up to thirty feet allowed for dramatic, sweeping visuals, which are exciting to watch and perfect for the architectural heights and crevices inherent in this particular shoot. Using this camera would enable us to access the mosaics in the upper reaches of these churches in a way that wasn't available to visitors, bringing the ancient figures in the mosaics down to earth and eye to eye.

Between getting the permissions, wire transfers, and insurances needed, in addition to finding local crew and gear and then coordinating everyone's disparate availability, planning for this shoot had taken months of preparation. The paperwork alone—emails and copies of letters—was more than an inch thick. But it was essential to the story we were telling.

The Byzantines, of course, didn't have films, documentaries, photographs, or graphic novels as mediums with which to tell stories. What they *did* have, in addition to paintings, were mosaics. They told the Church's stories using thousands of tiny squares of colorful glass, stones, and ceramics known in Italian as *tesserae*. Together, these bits of glass catch and bounce and reflect the light in a colorful dance designed to dazzle those who gaze upon them and make them believers.

First on our shot list was San Vitale, which, despite its plain exterior, contains a jewel box treasure trove of frescos and mosaics that still sparkle as enticingly now as they did more than fourteen centuries ago.

We set up to film an interview with mosaics expert Wanda Frattini Gaddoni, author of *Ravenna: Art and History*. This was the one on-camera interview Martin said I could do, perhaps because I was more comfortable talking about art.

"In the early 400s, after Ravenna was declared the capital of the Roman Empire, all of the best artists were invited to come decorate the city's public buildings with visual stories in fresco, marble and glass," Wanda Gaddoni said gently when camera was rolling.

"And these works of art acted like a *biblio pauperum*—a visual bible of stories—as most people at the time were illiterate. Instead of reading, they could see and feel the stories on the walls all around them, kind of like an illustrated book."

Kind of like a graphic novel, I thought, *intrigued. Or, a storyboard.*

"According to the Byzantines, our world is considered to be an *illusion,*" she explained. "The real, the only world, is represented behind the golden background (of many mosaics) which is acting almost like a barrier, a curtain, between our world, which is an illusion, and the real world, which lies behind it—but our eyes can't see it."

At the end of our interview, Wanda motioned me closer.

"Hold out your hand," she instructed, smiling. I did as I was told. Into my upturned palm, she placed half a dozen old stone *tesserae*. I still have them in my studio—a handful of tiny, precious memories from that film shoot.

The concept of the golden barrier caught my imagination. And so, during a break, I wandered around until I found some dark and narrow stone steps to the side of the apse—an area off limits to the public—hoping our film permit would grant me access. There was no one around to ask, so I climbed up to a narrow stone balcony overlooking the apse to get a closer look. Emerging from the dark stairwell, I came face to face with the large ancient mosaics and was startled at the physical sensation in my body looking these figures eye to eye. I think it was the closest I've ever come to a religious experience—and all the more powerful for being a surprise. Art transcends language.

The rest of the shoots in other buildings went well. To celebrate the end of three successful and interesting days on location, on our last evening in Ravenna, Martin and I ate dinner at a charming little restaurant called *Spasso Bistrot*. Afterwards, we walked around and window shopped, enjoying being among Italian families out for the evening *passeggiata*, pretending we were part of them and not just passing through briefly.

We were in Ravenna for a tantalizingly short time. But what I saw and experienced left me wanting more. In my usual effort to bring a little of my travels back home with me, I bought the most appropriate and inappropriate treasures of all—glass. I was unable to resist buying a mirror attached to an old and heavy piece of wood and hand decorated by an artist in a beautiful pattern of blue and gold *tesserae*. I also bought a fragile handblown glass carafe with two impossibly slender and fragile glasses in pastel gold, blue, and rose tones. All of which, of course, had to be carefully packaged for travel, then hand-carried four thousand miles home due to their fragility. After some teasing, Martin offered to carry the heavy mirror for me.

Boarding our transatlantic flight clutching my precious packages, I saw with dismay that our seats were in the very last row—the last to disembark from and often the bounciest during turbulence.

To my surprise, it turned out to be a delightful flight. As we made our way across the ocean, our flight attendants became increasingly chatty and attentive, gifting us an entire bottle of Italian white wine. Just before landing, they handed us another bottle to take home with us—so they didn't have to inventory it, they said, winking.

It was during this flight that I realized that getting on a plane to fly *back* home was not nearly as stressful as getting on one to fly *away* from home. That was a helpful insight for me, cutting, as it did, my worry time in half. And no, I don't think it was the free bottles of wine.

Filming in Ravenna was another turning point in my career. It gave me the confidence that with clear instruction as to what was needed, I could negotiate and organize an international shoot for a small crew—and do so despite a language barrier.

What's more, I *enjoyed* navigating the customs and quirks of another culture. This would serve me well in the future.

Next, we were heading to Istanbul—and a very nearly catastrophic film shoot.

A Character Without a Script in the Wrong Movie: Lights Out in Istanbul

A FEW WEEKS later, we were back in the air again. This time we were flying to Istanbul to capture more footage for *American Byzantine*. Specifically, we were going to film the interior of Hagia Sophia Grand Mosque. Its name alone hints at its multifaceted life as a religious structure.

Built at the direction of Emperor Justinian between AD 532 and 537 as the Christian cathedral of Constantinople for the Byzantine Empire, this impressive structure has alternated over the centuries between being the fifth largest church in the world and a Muslim mosque, depending upon who the rulers have been at the time. Hagia Sophia, Greek for "Church of Holy Wisdom," is one of the best surviving examples of Byzantine architecture and a key influence in the architecture of the Basilica in Washington, DC.

Martin and I had been to Istanbul a few months earlier to scout the location—a quick couple of days to assess what was needed to film the interior and exterior of this extraordinary building. To figure out what would be, in Martin's vernacular, "the money shots"—the dramatic visuals that would stand out in the film and tell the story of the building's architecture.

On our flight there, I got into conversation with a lovely Turkish woman sitting across the aisle from me. Her name was Bingul—Turkish for "a thousand roses," she told me.

By the time we arrived at Atatürk Airport, A Thousand Roses and her husband had invited us to their home for dinner, a harbinger of other warm encounters yet to come in Istanbul. It's a lovely thing to be invited inside someone's home when traveling—especially someone whose parents had given her such a poetic name—and I very much wanted to do this. But Martin politely declined, for reasons he didn't elaborate upon.

During our first visit to Istanbul, we'd visited the Kapalıçarşı, the large indoor covered market—a maze of 61 "streets" with more than 4000 shops under domed ceilings painted in bright Turkish patterns. Once upon a time, it was the super mall of the Mediterranean, unrivaled in terms of abundance, variety, and the quality of its offerings.

Inside the walls, it was lively, buzzing, and confusing, with vendors offering price negotiations over cups of aromatic tea, especially for those interested in Turkish carpets. Tempted as I was by them, I chose instead a simple, colorful, hand-painted bowl that was more in my price range.

Moments after I left the shop, the bowl fell through the flimsy bag it had been wrapped in and shattered on the stone floor. As I stared at the pieces, heartbroken and wondering what to do, a man from another stall immediately rushed over. He picked up the pieces and brought them back to the vendor from whom I purchased the bowl and indignantly demanded a replacement for me—which I got, thanks to his help. Whether it was theater for the tourists, or a real knight in Turkish leather, I don't know. Either way, I appreciated it.

I wasn't the only person shopping that afternoon. On our way back to our hotel, I watched from our car windows as a man walked down the street with a refrigerator mounted upon his back.

After we'd finished our initial scout of Hagia Sofia, Martin and I lingered in the nearby Basilica Cistern, a subterranean collection of pools fifty-two scary stone steps below street level. Built during Justinian's reign to provide storage for water from the mountains for the city's inhabitants, the cisterns are an architectural wonderland filled with hundreds of marble columns, each thirty feet high, holding up the vaults and arches of its roof. One of the columns was carved with the head of Medusa turned upside down—to negate the power of her gaze, so it was thought.

Atmospherically lit, the pools glowed in soft turquoise lights with ruby and gold lighting overhead. Ethereal flute music played by a small group of musicians enhanced the otherworldly atmosphere. I would love to have shot some footage there, but there was no logical way to fit it into our story. James Bond had been way ahead of us anyway; the cistern was used as a location for the film *From Russia with Love*.

Istanbul was a magical and entrancing place to spend time. It's good we took in what we did during those days, for when we came back for the actual shoot, it was all work and things went quite wrong.

To begin with, somewhere between Paris and Istanbul, Air France lost our luggage. That's an inconvenience for any traveler, but for a film crew, it's a costly and serious problem. The gear is expensive, and the crew gets paid a day rate on location, whether or not they are able to work. Air France promised to have it to us the following day, the day before we were to start filming.

Fortunately, we had a distraction. Having heard about Hülya Biren, an experienced Turkish "fixer," from our cinematographer, Dennis Boni, we'd arranged in advance to hire her to help facilitate arrangements and technical issues on location. A fixer is someone with local knowledge and contacts who understands the film business and is skilled at solving problems, especially in foreign countries where you and the crew don't speak the language, and don't know local crews and supply houses where gear can be sourced. They can be critically important on international shoots. And, depending upon who your fixer is, they can also be a lot of fun and provide a deeper cultural understanding.

We were staying at the Armada Old City, located almost in the shadow of Hagia Sophia. Feriha Ishtar, our wonderful contact at the Turkish Embassy in Washington, DC, had made the arrangements for our *pro bono* accommodations there. When checking in, I noticed on the hotel stationary their slogan was "Where Istanbul Lovers Meet." It's too bad Martin and I were no longer in love, for the hotel had an astonishing rooftop restaurant that offered a breathtaking, magical view of both the Blue Mosque and Hagia Sophia.

I reached out to Hülya soon after we got to our hotel and explained what happened to our gear and luggage. She immediately offered an empathetic and novel solution: *Why don't you come to a party instead?*

It turned out she was hosting a celebration that evening in honor of her father, Işik Biren, retired vice admiral of the Turkish Navy. It was his birthday and there would be interesting people for us to meet, she promised. I told her we'd been traveling for the past eighteen hours and none of us had a change of clothing.

"It is not a problem," she said, laughing pleasantly. "We understand and we don't mind. Please come anyway!"

That evening, the four of us—me, Martin, Dennis, and his assistant cameraman—showed up at a very chic, expensive nightclub with its all-white decor wearing our grungy, transatlantic, already-seen-three-countries travel clothes for Hülya's father's birthday party. The champagne was flowing, the music was sexy, and the general vibe was contemporary and quite dazzling. Apart from us, everyone was dressed in what looked like the height of European fashion.

From time to time, Hülya appeared at my side, quietly pointing out a famous pop singer, television personality, or dignitary. Having no idea who any of them were, I felt like a character without a script in the wrong movie, with no one on hand to fix my wardrobe or makeup. Not that I'd ever *had* that experience; I just wished I had on nicer clothes as well as proper makeup and clean hair, because this was a very cool and unusual party. Despite our appearance, no one made us feel unwelcome or inappropriate. I was able to take care of *that* all by myself.

Hülya also introduced me to one of her close friends, Emine, the daughter of Turkey's Minister of Culture. Emine explained to me that Turkish culture is not just one homogeneous entity—that Turks are a mixture of, in her words, "many different blood, earth, religions, and traditions." Her words only added to the intrigue and appeal of Istanbul.

I could have partied all night. But having a shoot (we hoped) the next day, we reluctantly tore ourselves away Cinderella-style, long before the party was over, and made our way back to our hotel.

When we first scouted Hagia Sophia, Martin thought that due to its immensity, it would be most effective to film it using a Steadicam, a heavy stabilized camera the operator straps on with a special body vest. Designed with a unique bearing system that rotates freely and smoothly, permitting sideways and up and down shots seamlessly, the Steadicam's basic function is to isolate the movements of the camera from the person operating it, which it does very effectively. It's so heavy that while not in use, it hangs on its own special rack.

Martin told me I'd seen Steadicam footage and likely not even realized it. He mentioned a film that had come out the previous year, *Shakespeare in Love*, starring Gwyneth Paltrow with Joseph Fiennes as a young Will Shakespeare and a dastardly Colin Firth as Lord Wessex.

Martin loved the way the film's dance scene had been shot and thought we could get a similar effect inside the cavernous Hagia Sophia. Before coming to Istanbul, we'd watched the film again, this time together, so I could visualize what he was talking about. Martin pointed out how the camera moved around the young couple, enclosing them in a 360-degree continuous shot, like an embrace. To me, one of Martin's most appealing characteristics was his interest in teaching me what he knew about the art of documentary filmmaking.

Martin hired Dennis Boni, veteran of hundreds of film projects and a specialist in Steadicam cinematography for the shoot. Dennis was fun to be with on location. In no time, he'd learned how to say the numbers to his room in Turkish, as well as necessary words like beer, peanuts, and toilet—and was teaching them to us as well.

The following morning, our gear cases and luggage were in the hotel lobby, much to our relief. We stashed our things in our rooms, then headed over to Hagia Sophia so everyone could see and discuss angles and setups. We were scheduled to shoot the following day.

Monday morning, we arrived early. It was the only day Hagia Sophia was closed to the public and we had to film everything that day if we didn't want any tourists in our footage. If we didn't, we'd have to wait another week to get another opportunity. And, of course, we'd have to go through the tedious permissions process and paperwork all over again.

While Martin organized the setting up of crew, lighting, and gear, the Turkish interpreter assigned to us gave me a quick tour of the upper areas and the significant Byzantine mosaics still visible among the large Muslim symbols that had since been added to the walls. When I commented that some of the mosaics were incomplete, he remarked with an air of resigned sadness, "Yes, many of the little tiles have jumped off the walls"—as if discussing hundreds of tiny suicides.

I shot some location stills and was back downstairs as filming began. All went well for the first few hours. The crew was shooting a key mosaic when suddenly, the huge lights on the scaffolding went out, plunging us into blackness.

While the crew stumbled around in the dark, double-checking the lighting equipment and electrical sources, our interpreter materialized from the gloom to inform us there was a power failure in our grid of the city affecting nearly a quarter of Istanbul.

I made a panicky call to Hülya who quickly set things in motion, including a scrambled frenzy to find a generator somewhere close by that was large enough to power the tall portable stage lights needed to light the cavernous interior adequately. Martin and I paced impatiently, worrying about costs, overtime, and getting the rest of the footage we needed.

A generator arrived an hour and a half later and filming resumed. Dennis asked me to pull focus for him while he was shooting B-roll as his camera assistant was busy with other tasks. I was rarely asked to handle gear—and with good reason. Nervously, I put my fingers on the rim of the camera lens and turned it gently as Dennis counted down slowly, patiently coaching me. We did this three times before his assistant returned and took over, and Dennis was able to dismiss me with a good-natured laugh.

Even though I failed to do it smoothly enough for Dennis to use, this teaching moment stayed with me. As someone who is all too often going in too many directions, thoughts, and ideas at once, I've used the term "pull focus" as an internal mantra or self-correction ever since, trying to notice when I'm scattered and need to gently focus the lens of my mind on the task at hand.

Due to schedules, availability, and practical logistics, Martin, Dennis, and I needed to anticipate what architectural details to get—both inside and outside—*before* interviewing Lord Norwich, our main expert on Byzantium. We had to figure out what footage we might need as underlying B-roll to help visualize Norwich's words in the final cut.

To pull this off, you need a pretty good idea of your script and edit plan. But sometimes you just have to hold your breath until you get to the edit suite and see how it all weaves together, and if the resulting film tapestry makes sense—or not.

Before organizing the Istanbul shoot, I'd bought a copy of Norwich's book, *A Short History of Byzantium,* and had perused it carefully to get an idea.

The following day was spent getting "establishing shots"—footage that would visually explain Hagia Sophia's location and setting.

Istanbul is uniquely situated at the intersection of two continents and is divided by the Bosphorus Strait. Hagia Sophia and the Blue Mosque are both located in European Istanbul. Wanting a distance shot of them both from across the water, we trekked over the bridge and up a long hill on the Asian side of Istanbul to capture the view. There was a park with playground equipment. We set up our tripod and camera, and it wasn't long before we attracted a small group of friendly young boys in soccer jerseys interested in the gear and in having their photographs taken posing with it and the film crew.

While camera was rolling, the call to prayer started. Slightly staggered from minarets all over the city, the wailing sounds amplified as they crossed the water. We paused filming to take it all in, this religion that comes at you from the air.

I'd been sleeping with the shutters of my hotel room windows thrown open so I would be awakened by the morning's first call to prayer instead of an alarm. Even though I was neither kneeling down nor stopping to pray, I listened in stillness each time I heard it, unable to express exactly how or why it moved me.

Ravenna wore its religion on its walls, a delight for the eyes. But here in Istanbul, it was carried through the air; you breathed the sound of it in with each breath. I loved the sensual experience of both locations. These moments filled hidden crevices inside of me I'd not realized were empty.

With help from Hülya's friend Emine—along with a small contribution toward its upkeep and maintenance—we'd received permission to film from the top of a minaret on the Blue Mosque. In all respects, this was indeed a "money shot."

Martin, Dennis, and I clambered up narrow, circular stone steps, twisting around and around until we emerged into daylight at the top of one of the minarets. There was hardly any space to maneuver, but it offered a fantastic view of the rose-colored walls of the many-windowed dome of Hagia Sophia as seen across the beautiful public gardens laid out between the two religious structures.

There was only enough space for two of us at a time and we had to be quick about it, as we were only permitted to be up there providing we got back down before the next call to prayer went out. We had perhaps twenty minutes to get the shots.

As cinematographer, Dennis had to be there. And so, Martin and I took turns squeezing in and out of the tiny space. Martin went first to discuss shots with Dennis. After he left, Dennis motioned for me to come out.

"Let's take photos of each other up here!" he said with a smile.

What a great idea. I took one of him and then he took one of me I call my "Christiane Amanpour photo" after one of my idols. I'm dressed in black with a multi-pocketed, khaki Banana Republic vest, looking (I hoped) professional and journalistic while reporting from some exotic location. It was fun in the moment.

Later that evening, our last in Istanbul, the two guys dispersed to check out the city on their own. Martin and I decided to have dinner at the hotel.

Before our meal, hotel proprietor Kasim Zoto invited us to watch dancers perform the Turkish tango—something I wasn't even aware existed. It was an exotic delight to watch.

Afterwards, we sat down at a table under the stars on the hotel's roof terrace. Our dinner of Turkish delights included *Peynirli Muska Boregi,* spinach and cheese filled pastry triangles, accompanied by a bottle of Kavaklidere Çankaya white wine crafted from Emir, Narince, and Sultana grapes selected from Anatolian vineyards. With its views of Hagia Sophia and the Blue Mosque, both dramatically lit up against the night sky on the hill above us, it was one of the most surreal and magical restaurant experiences I've ever had.

Kasim appeared periodically to check on us. Seeing I was a little underdressed for the cool night air, he reached into a large copper kettle near our table and brought out two warm and soft ivory-colored blankets, draping one over my shoulders and one across my lap. He was a handsome man and I almost purred under his attention.

Such a waste, I thought as I watched him walk away, to not be in the company of someone with whom I was in love. Ahh well, at least I was here. This moment, this location, this view—everything had been such a surprise.

Had it not been for that impulsive twenty dollar donation and that brief entanglement with Sophia Loren's bedsheets, I thought for the thousandth time—*the stranger's shoes, taking a friend's advice to speak with someone who'd been blown up by a package bomb, which in turn led to this whole film adventure—any of those turns not taken, those instincts gone unheeded, and I wouldn't be here gazing at the stars from a rooftop in Istanbul.*

It was all so unlikely. What on earth, I wondered, might happen next?

LONDON: CLOUDY WITH A CHANCE OF EXPLETIVES

AFTER WRAPPING THE Istanbul shoot, Martin and I flew to London, a city of many good memories for me.

Having spent a third of my childhood there, it was a homecoming of sorts. Even my enunciation skewed slightly British when I was in London, an accent I'd acquired as a defense against classroom bullying in one of the several British schools I'd attended.

Back then, it was the London of the Swinging '60s—the Beatles, the Kinks, and the Rolling Stones. It was during those years that Mary Quant took the fashion world by storm with her invention of the miniskirt. "Dedicated Followers of Fashion" prowled Carnaby Street looking for hip clothes. Julie Christie dominated the movie screens. And Mick Jagger even paid a surprise visit to our flat overlooking the Thames, hoping to purchase it so he could be close to the home of his then-girlfriend, Marianne Faithfull.

Jagger's visit was a foreshadowing of what Cheyne Walk was soon to become. After Marianne Faithfull bought 48 Cheyne Walk from friends of my parents, Ron Wood bought a house down the street (number 103), and eventually Keith

Richards also moved to Cheyne Walk a few years later. Even for a little kid, it was an incredibly exciting time to live there.

Our home on Cheyne Walk was more associated with writers than musicians. We lived in a block of lovely and gracious flats overlooking the Thames River called Carlyle Mansions. Built in the 1880s, it was named after the writer Thomas Carlyle, who'd lived around the corner on Cheyne Row. The block of flats was nicknamed the "Writers' Block" for the many writers who'd lived there, including Henry James, T. S. Eliot, Somerset Maugham, and Ian Fleming. Fleming is said to have written his first Bond book there, *Casino Royale.*

And now here I was back in London. It sounded and smelled like childhood. Were I to have been blindfolded, I would still have known where I was by the pings of the bells on the buses, the sound of them pulling away from bus stops, the taxis, and the smell of exhaust fumes.

In an effort to be budget conscious, I'd booked us tiny rooms in a tiny hotel just off Sloane Street. Accurately described as a "doll's house," it was only a few blocks from both Harrods and the high school I went to in Lennox Gardens. It was so small, the hotel's lift opened onto the sidewalk. Upon arrival, Martin and I stepped in and took it up a flight to check in at the little hotel lobby. We had the afternoon free and did some Christmas shopping at Harrods and along the Brompton Road, my head filled with the gentle buzz of happy memories.

Our interview with Lord Norwich the following day was to take place at his home, which was not far from St. John's Wood, where I'd gone to the American School in London for sixth grade.

As luck would have it, the evening before our scheduled interview, Lord Norwich was speaking at the Royal Albert Hall on behalf of the "Venice in Peril" organization, of which he was chairman. And so, Martin and I went to listen to him.

During the evening, Norwich spoke about the history of Venice and made a compelling case for helping the city's flood mitigation efforts. In his lifelong passion to understand and help the city, he'd visited Venice more than two hundred times.

"The Italians are totally *crushed* by the weight of their artistic heritage," Norwich explained. "Every town and every village in Italy has got *so much* to be preserved—the list is *endless,* and they *can't* do it all themselves. And, after all, it's *we* who go there for our holidays and enjoy them."

Even though we would be asking him questions about Byzantium and not Venice, watching his presentation gave us a pretty good idea of what to expect when we interviewed him.

When the lecture ended, it was still too early to call it a night and go back to our hotel, so Martin and I decided to put in for a pint at a pub along the way. As Martin opened its front door, we were greeted by the warmth and noise of a lively crowd of individuals, beery voices vying with one another to be heard over the general hubbub.

Martin persistently worked his way to the bar, his height helping him make progress through the layers of chatting professionals recently liberated from their workplaces. He returned with a pint in each hand and offered one to me. We toasted and I took an appreciative sip; it was cool and crisp, a lovely footnote to the day.

There were no available seats, so Martin and I stood side by side, not saying anything. I drank my beer, watching the happy crowd around us and yearning to be a part of it all. I wanted to enjoy this night as a grown woman in the city of my childhood. I wanted to mingle and chat with its interesting mix of patrons as if I was a local and this was my regular stop on the way home from work.

How could we start a conversation, I thought, pondering the possibilities. Especially, how to do it with Martin—a towering introvert—standing awkwardly and somewhat ill at ease by my side. After some moments, inspiration hit. No longer terribly concerned with what Martin thought of me since he changed his mind about everything six months ago, I tilted my head up to share my thought with him.

"I have an idea," I whispered loudly. "I want to get into conversations with people here."

"But we don't know anyone," Martin said.

"Maybe we can start by introducing ourselves and tell them we're conducting a little research for a project," I said.

"What project?" Martin asked, ever the straight guy in the room.

"Just for grins, let's ask them what expressions and euphemisms they have here in the UK for making love or having sex," I said enthusiastically. "Let's ask people how many languages they know how to say that in!"

I have no idea where this idea came from. Martin was, understandably, a bit skeptical. Or perhaps appalled—it was difficult to judge from his face. Either way, he did not look enthusiastic.

"Tell them we're documentary filmmakers," I laughed, ignoring his expression. "Say we're doing some research. As we're Americans, I'm sure we can get away with it. You don't have to worry," I added. "It's not as if we'll ever see any of them again."

"Here, give me your notebook and pen," I said when he made no move. "Let's go have some fun!"

Looking extremely uncomfortable, he handed both over to me and I nudged my way into the crowd.

"Pardon me," I said to a couple of guys discussing football. "We're American journalists and we're researching a story on how to say, 'Will you have sex with me' in different languages. Can you help us out?"

Conversation stopped. Then they looked at one another and grinned, as if they could hardly believe what they were hearing. One of them laughed and responded immediately with some British slang.

He called his mates over and explained what we were doing.

"*Vamos a follar*," one said. "Spanish!"

I wrote down his words.

"*Niqons*," another said. "That's French for 'let's fuck.'"

Others chimed in, calling out to friends for additional phrases. Soon I was in the middle of a dozen or so men and women in their twenties. They crowded around me, offering phrases enthusiastically as I tried to scribble them all down on the pad. Everyone was laughing, everyone wanting in on the fun. More joined in until it seemed the entire place was shouting out terms and expressions in a cacophony of languages.

Eventually Martin decided to join in. I handed him back his pad, keeping a piece of paper for myself, and watched as he tentatively approached a couple to make his first ask. Within moments, he was at the center of a large group, laughing, easy to spot above the crowd. Writing furiously fast, he was engaging with people, his face lit up. He was enjoying himself.

Pub patrons—trying to outdo one another in their knowledge—tossed words and expressions at him in many languages. More invitations for conjugal relations came flying through the air.

"*Lass uns ficken*! German!" shouted someone.

"*Déanaimis* fuck! Irish!" shouted another.

Both of us were now scribbling as fast as possible.

"*Scopiamo*!" said someone.

"What's that?" I asked.

"Italian!"

"*Davay yebat*. Russian!"

I was right. This *was* an international crowd. Or at least, a well-traveled crowd.

"*Seikōshiyō*. Japanese!"

"*Prod'me do prdele*—Czech!"

"*Dē cudā'l kariē*" someone said.

"And that language is?" I asked, having no idea how to spell it.

"Punjabi!" came the response.

Eventually, we exhausted the impressive knowledge of the pub patrons. While the game had played itself out, it seemed to have also sparked a lot of tangential conversations and who knows, perhaps even new friendships.

"There," I said to Martin with a smile as we eventually eased our way out of the pub, several drafts later. "That's *one* way to start a conversation with complete strangers!"

We walked slowly back through Knightsbridge, quietly window-shopping along the way to our doll's house just off Sloane Street. At the hotel, we got into the little lift on the sidewalk, then parted ways to get a good night's sleep in preparation for the next day's interview at the home of John Julius Norwich.

Much as I would have liked to have kept the list as a souvenir—it had been *my* idea, after all—Martin put it in his pocket and I never saw it again.

A Man of Many Enthusiasms and What I Discovered in His Loo

"OH *NO!*" I exclaimed. The words had popped out of my mouth before I realized it.

I was reading one of the London morning newspapers over a cup of coffee before Martin and I headed over to Lord Norwich's home for our interview.

"Bad news?" Martin asked, looking up from his own newspaper and coffee.

"Yes," I said. "Parliament, under Tony Blair's government, has just passed the House of Lords Act!" I hastily scanned the article looking for one particular name. And then I found it.

"About half of them got the sack, including Lord Norwich! And on the very morning we are scheduled to interview him—how's *that* for crap timing?"

Martin looked startled. Normally, this kind of news would barely have registered with either of us. But as we were in London to film an interview with Norwich himself, I was worried. After nearly five years of working on this documentary, he was our last and most important interview.

Norwich was considered the preeminent Byzantinist at the time. A scholar, journalist, and broadcaster, in the late 1980s, he'd set out to write a history of the Byzantine empire from its creation by Constantine the Great in the fourth century to its fall to the Turks eleven hundred years later. The three volumes of *Byzantium* appeared between 1988 and 1995. I had a copy of *A Short History of Byzantium*—a more reasonable 421 pages.

There was no better expert on the topic for us. Getting an interview with him was a huge leg-up for the documentary. Martin told me we could fly to London after our shoot in Istanbul and interview him—*if* I could book it.

Not knowing how exactly to accomplish this, I began with Parliament, specifically the House of Lords, looking for guidance. I found a phone number in a directory at my local library and placed the call to London.

"Good afternoon, Houses of Parliament," a disembodied voice answered, surprising me.

You can just call them up and they'll answer?!

I explained I was a documentary filmmaker calling from America, trying to get in touch with Lord Norwich in order to interview him.

"Hold one moment, please," came the polite response.

Moments later, the voice returned.

"Here's his home number," he said graciously in perfect BBC accented tones.

Wait, *the home number for a member of Parliament?!* Surely, I had heard wrong. But no.

I rang the number. I was surprised when another polite voice answered, female this time, and even more surprised when she put Lord Norwich himself on the phone. He heard me out, then cheerfully offered to sit for an interview. We agreed on a date and time in November. And then, even more astonishing to me, Lord Norwich gave me his home address. It turned out he lived in the little Venice part of London. How appropriate, I thought.

I hung up, feeling a bit starstruck and shared the good news with Martin.

"Can you believe that?!" I'd said, still a bit in shock. "The House of Lords gave me his *home* telephone number and he gave me his *home* address!"

I couldn't fathom that happening in Washington, DC, if I called to get a number for someone in the Senate or House of Representatives.

Two months later, here we were in London and Lord Norwich had gotten the sack the same day we were set to interview him.

"As I have his home phone number, do you think we should call him?" I asked Martin. "Perhaps it would be thoughtful to reschedule."

Martin pondered for a moment before responding, "Nope. We're here now and the camera is already booked. Let's just show up and hope for the best."

I was very intrigued to meet this man, so I hoped like crazy it would somehow work out. Lord Norwich seemed, from everything I'd read, the very personification of British peerage. On his father's side, he was descended from King William IV and his mistress, Dorothea Jordan.

Norwich's father was the late Duff Cooper, a conservative politician and diplomat, and World War II Minister of Information. His mother was Lady Diana Manners, a celebrated beauty and society figure, said to have chosen her wealthiest 17 friends as her only child's godparents—Lord Beaverbrook and the Aga Khan among them.

Lady Diana was also a close friend of novelist, biographer, and journalist Evelyn Waugh, who was so smitten with her he modeled his character "Mrs. Stitch" after her.

Writing in *The Guardian*, Jeffrey Manley would later describe Norwich as "a man of many enthusiasms—for books, music, architecture, paintings—and his great talent was to be able to convey those passions to the public at large, through books, radio broadcasts, and in nearly three dozen television documentaries from the BBC."

That was almost an understatement.

In addition to being a writer for thirty-five years, Norwich had also served as editor for *Great Architecture of the World*, *The Italian World*, and *The Oxford Illustrated Encyclopaedia of Art*. He often contributed to *Cornucopia*, a magazine devoted to the history and culture of Turkey. His television documentaries included *The Fall of Constantinople*, *The Antiquities of Turkey*, and *The Gates of Asia*.

Intriguingly, Norwich was also the father of Allegra Huston, a result of his affair with film director John Huston's wife, the ballet dancer Enrica Soma.

Intelligent and well-educated with degrees in French and Russian from Oxford, Norwich had inherited the title Viscount Norwich upon his father's death in 1954, a title he'd apparently now just lost.

At the appointed time, we rang the front doorbell of Lord Norwich's beautiful home, a large detached Victorian house on Warwick Avenue in the "Little Venice" part of the Maida Vale section of London.

The nickname "Little Venice" is said to have come either from the poet Robert Browning, who lived there in the second part of the nineteenth century, not far from Norwich's house. Or, perhaps Lord Byron, who may have been the first person—fifty years earlier—to compare the area to Venice. Regardless of the origin of the nickname, it was a very appropriate place for Norwich to call home.

The housekeeper opened the front door, but Norwich himself was right behind her, perhaps six feet tall and robustly British looking.

"Come in, come in!" he said, his arm gesturing in a sweeping circle to welcome us into his home.

He ushered us through the spacious entry hall into a large library lined with bookshelves weighted down by hundreds of leatherbound books with gold embossing on them.

"Lord Norwich," I said. "We're so very pleased to meet you. Thank you for permitting us an interview."

"Not at all," he replied. "Delighted! Only I *must* tell you straight off that I'm not 'Lord Norwich'. Technically, my title is—or rather, *was,* until today—*The Right Honourable, the Viscount Norwich, CVO.*

"However, I think that's a *dreadful* mouthful, don't you?" he said laughing. "Please, just call me John Julius."

He went on to say he didn't really mind at all getting the sack, that it was actually something of a relief as he could now just write and not be bothered with "all that other stuff."

His Oxford education came through in his manner of speaking—upper class, well-articulated English. His grayish-white hair was combed back neatly. He was wearing a blue button-down shirt underneath a tweed jacket. The blue brought out the blue in his eyes, I noted with appreciation.

(Sidenote: It makes it so much easier when the subject of your interview knows and understands what looks good on camera, and what doesn't. You want viewers to concentrate on what interviewees are saying, *not* what they are wearing or wondering who on earth did their makeup or hair, and didn't they have a mirror somewhere they could check themselves in, etc.)

Norwich, of course, was a pro. He was 70 years old at the time and had done this a hundred times before, perhaps even more. He answered all our questions directly. His enunciation was wonderful, very British, very confident, and he gestured effectively with his hands to illustrate his points. One could hear the italics when he spoke.

Having done the research, read the books, and made the initial contact with Norwich, I would have loved to do the interview. Martin, however, decided to do it himself.

Although I was disappointed, having Martin do it left me with lots of free time inside my head, space I filled with musings about how nice it would be to go out to a lovely dinner somewhere special and listen to John Julius talk about Italy or the Byzantine Empire all night long. I'd never met such an interesting man. Nor have I since.

At the end of the interview, as Martin and the cameraman packed up the gear, I waited for a pause in the conversation, then asked John Julius if I might use the loo.

"Yes, yes, of course, my dear!" he said immediately. "First door on the right in the front hallway."

There was no problem locating it off the spacious square front hall. Inside, the walls were adorned with framed photos and letters from famous and interesting people. I paused to read some of them while washing and drying my hands. One especially caught my eye. The salutation was to Lady Diana, John Julius's mother, and signed by author Evelyn Waugh.

I returned to the sitting room as the last gear bag was being zipped up, the last case closed.

"I have a question for you, John Julius," I said with a smile. "Are *you* the 'little shit'?"

The room fell silent. All eyes turned to me. Martin stood still—shock, horror, and disbelief on his face, but I no longer cared. His reaction didn't matter and besides, what more could he do? He'd already fired me from his life months ago.

I smiled at him serenely, then I looked back at Norwich. He didn't look shocked at all. In fact, there was just a hint of bemused puzzlement on his face. Then, to my immense relief, he threw back his head with a great roar of laughter.

"You read Evelyn Waugh's letter to my mother!" he exclaimed. "Yes, yes, that was *me*, 'the little shit' he was referring to!" He appeared delighted I'd noticed that particular letter.

I brought out my copy of *A Short History of Byzantium* and asked if he'd sign it, which he did.

Martin and Kristin,
With thanks for a particularly sympathetic
and enjoyable interview!

JOHN JULIUS
LONDON *12.11.99*

As we prepared to leave, I put my hand out to shake his, but John Julius hugged me to him in a warm embrace.

"Wonderful, my dear, thank you for this interview. I look forward to seeing your film!"

This handsome, intelligent, and lovely man of many enthusiasms lived another nineteen years, but unfortunately, I never had the opportunity to see him again. How very lucky I was to have met him at all. For the hundredth—or perhaps the thousandth— time, I thanked that little impulse I'd had to give my local PBS station twenty dollars. It was my best investment ever.

Tiny Bubbles and Time-Lapses

A TIME-LAPSE IS a film technique in which a cameraperson takes a sequence of frames at certain intervals to track how an image changes over time. When time is collapsed and the frames are shown at a normal speed, the action is sped up and you can see movement and change. It's just like the actual filming process, but with all the boring frames in between the interesting ones compressed or removed. Think of an image you may have seen of a flower blooming from a bud over the course of just ten seconds.

That fall, the marble carvers in Italy laid down their chisels and took off their newspaper hats after putting the finishing touches on *The Universal Call to Holiness.* Thought to be one of the largest relief sculptures in the world, it needed to be cut up into sixteen pieces, some of which weighed as much as 9,000 pounds, in order to be shipped to the U.S. Once it arrived in Washington, DC, via trucks, it took a large crane to lift the pieces into the Basilica.

That was just the beginning of the logistical complications. Transporting the large blocks of stone required the invention of a special 300-foot-long rail system that allowed the pieces to be pushed manually across the Basilica's marble floor.

Inside, an enormous scaffolding had been erected to facilitate the process of attaching the *bas relief* to the back wall of the Basilica. Using a system of cables, handles, and chains to guide the indoor crane, the engineers in charge oversaw the manual securing of each unwieldy block of marble into place. It took nearly two weeks for this installation to be completed.

Because of the length of time involved, Martin decided to film it using time-lapse—a clever idea to get us over the humps of that tedious process and whip our potential viewers through those two weeks of laborious engineering details in less than a minute.

While waiting for this to happen, we also captured some aerial footage of the Basilica. A local helicopter company helped us facilitate the special permissions needed to fly and film over Washington, DC. Once again, cinematographer Richard Chisolm came along to film it. Luckily, the weather gods were with us and the sun shone on our only day to shoot.

Although I didn't know it at the time, that helicopter ride would come back five years later and impact my life in a way I could never have imagined.

Richard filmed the art installation and also my interview with one of the installers who had come from Italy to help oversee the process—a handsome guy I'd nicknamed "Italian eye candy" (but just in my thoughts).

Throughout the five years it had taken us to get to this point with the documentary, Martin and I were asked to present our progress on *American Byzantine* at the annual meeting of the Basilica's Board of Directors.

The first time this happened, Martin and I arrived in suitable business attire and waited in the anteroom for our turn to be called in to speak before the assembled members and Catholic dignitaries in the conference room.

We'd each prepared comments, covering different aspects of the film's production. When the door opened, we rose to go in. Martin went first but as I attempted to step through the door, the Director of Communications extended his arm, blocking my entry. Puzzled, I looked at him.

"Just Martin," he said. "*Not* you."

Martin turned around to see what the problem was.

"But she's the co-producer of the film," he protested.

"That may be," the Director of Communications replied. He gestured to the assembled bishops, priests, and other male Catholic figures sitting at the tables inside. "But they're not used to listening to women."

I gasped in shock. His words stung as if he'd physically slapped me across the face. *Not used to listening to women?!* How on earth could this still be happening on the cusp of the twenty-first century?

Nothing either of us said could dissuade him, however, and I was left to cool my temper and burning cheeks in the sitting area.

Hearing what had happened, Dr. Braddock intervened on my behalf the following year and I was permitted to speak.

Following these meetings, we were usually invited to attend a formal dinner afterwards at Washington, DC's Omni Shoreham Hotel—a very comfortable and sumptuous setting.

Not having been raised Catholic, I observed these gatherings like a journalist instead of one of the faithful. I noticed in surprise how much alcohol the assembled bishops and cardinals consumed. I made a comment to the director of communications about it.

"Yes!" he laughed in agreement. "And no beer or wine for them—they like the *hard* stuff!"

At one of these dinners, an announcement was made that there would be a special toast in celebration of the 90th birthday of one of the Cardinals. Flutes of champagne appeared on trays passed by waiters, as if by magic. Once served, we were asked to raise our glasses in a birthday toast.

We were told the birthday Cardinal would like to mark the occasion with a song he wanted to sing for us, even though he was in a wheelchair and quite doddery. Expecting "Happy Birthday" or perhaps "Ave Maria," I (and, I suspect, everyone in the entire ballroom) was astonished when he launched into a quavering version of "Tiny Bubbles." A Cardinal, singing a song about champagne? There seemed to be no end to the surprises.

The last dinner I attended, I was seated next to the Archbishop of Baltimore, William Henry Keeler. Archbishop Keeler had studied in Rome and was a leading figure in the restoration of the Basilica. He was a kindly and gentle man, and during the course of our conversation, I found myself telling him about my sister. Archbishop Keeler listened quietly as I spoke. When I came to the end of my words, he gazed at me intently and asked if it would be okay if he gave me a blessing. I told him I was not Catholic, but he assured me that didn't matter.

"Well, yes—then, of course," I said quite honestly. "I'd *love* to have a blessing."

He asked me to bow towards him. Then he placed his warm, comforting hands on either side of the top of my head and very quietly intoned some words, none of which I can recall, unfortunately.

What I do remember is feeling—for those precious moments— strangely at peace.

IT'S A WRAP

*"Getting over a painful experience is
much like crossing monkey bars.
You have to let go at some point in order to move forward."*

C.S. LEWIS

"IT'S A WRAP" is a phrase often used in filmmaking to tell actors and production crew that the filming of a particular scene or film has finished. "Wrap" may (or may not) have its roots as an acronym for "wind, reel, and print." Some are relieved to hear these words; others are not.

I don't recall Martin ever using this phrase on any of our shoots, but the essence of it hung in the air as we approached Christmas 1999—and my last paycheck.

In my case, it wasn't a clear wrap. Instead, the last of my days at the documentary workshop ended with more of a slow fade, another film term.

In January 2000, Martin and I parted ways, each to pursue our own paths. He moved onto the next film project, and I tumbled headlong back into the dark abyss of no work and no steady income. He switched me from salary to hourly, but with not quite enough hours to get by on. With no savings to fall back on—because it was all I could do just to pay the bills—I began the desperate search for another job.

Fortunately, over the past seven years, I'd amassed a solid network of friends and connections in film and television, mainly through the Washington, DC, chapter of Women in Film & Video—a non-profit organization founded two decades earlier by four pioneering filmmaking women.

WIFV is the premier collection of people in media in the DC metro region—a vibrant, creative community of professionals with national and global connections. The previous year, I'd been asked to serve on its board.

I also knew people at Discovery Channel, National Geographic, BBC, and, of course, PBS. I had connections to production crews at government departments and in the private sector, film festival organizers, writers, editors, sound techs, cinematographers, and gaffers. I had a lot of independent filmmaker friends. I even had connections in New York, Los Angeles, and other parts of the country.

Despite all of this, it didn't take long to realize nobody *hires* a documentary filmmaker. Documentary filmmakers have their hands full managing their own projects and trying to get paid. They are already doing the work themselves. I knew this from my own experience, yet I was still surprised and disappointed at the closed doors and lack of opportunities. I worried obsessively—how on earth would I take care of myself and the kids?

During the first months of 2000, Martin and I met periodically at Misha's Coffeehouse in Old Town in Alexandria for progress updates on *American Byzantine* over mugs of strong black coffee. I often used Misha's as the space where I met friends and colleagues for job leads, interviews, and freelance work.

It was also often the setting for my writing sessions even though, between the coffee machines, music, and chatting patrons, there was never a shortage of noise. Misha's had its own unique "room tone." I liked those ambient sounds and found them soothing. And whether they were playing Ray Charles, jazz or punk, the music almost always matched my mood. If not, I adapted to it. The odd art on the blue and yellow and green walls was always interesting, and I found the nonsensical mix of chairs and tables strangely comforting. Misha's offered just the right amount of distraction. I could relax and think and write in its atmosphere.

Bonhoeffer, the last film I worked on at the documentary workshop, was finally finished. It had a limited run in movie theaters before its PBS release.

I took Zoë and Leif to see it at the Avalon Theater on Connecticut Avenue in the northwest part of DC. Stephen, our sound guy, came with us. Over the years, he'd become a good friend, and we stayed in close touch. I always thought he had something of a Roy Orbison vibe about him, and I mean that in a good way. Stephen's sight is better, and his hair was no longer dark, but I think their voices are similar (even though I've never heard Stephen sing.) Periodically, I invited him over to the house to have dinner with me and the kids. He was the one who taught Leif how to assemble a working computer from parts.

Zoë and Leif both dozed off within the first half hour of *Bonhoeffer*. I let them sleep until the end when I woke them up so they could watch the credit scroll and see my name on the big screen, if only for a nanosecond. I wanted them to know who I was in my other, non-mom life. Having accompanied me on numerous production shoots, they likely already had a pretty good idea, but I wasn't taking any chances.

Over our last coffee together at Misha's, Martin told me he'd given the shoes he'd been wearing the first night we met—the shoes that had started everything—to a homeless person he'd encountered during a shoot in Los Angeles. I was surprised he'd done this and surprised he made a point of telling me; he knew their significance to me.

Then again, perhaps it was a fitting way to end things. As my sister used to say when encouraging me to get rid of something—*Honey, it's time for someone else to have a turn.*

I tried to settle my bruised ego and ruffled feathers with the thought that perhaps the shoes would bring a little magic and a new path to someone else who desperately needed it, just as they once did for me.

More than anything else he'd said to me, giving away those shoes telegraphed Martin's message loud and clear: Our time together was over. It was time for me to let go and reach for the next monkey bar, even if I couldn't yet see it and it felt like my hand was just grasping at air.

My mother knew Karen had given Martin a beautiful tile table she'd designed and crafted, most likely as an advance wedding gift to both of us. It was one of the best pieces she'd ever made. The cost of it in the gallery on Long Boat Key in Sarasota where she sold her designs would have put it well beyond my range. It bothered Mom that Martin had kept it and not given it back to me after breaking off our relationship.

"You should get that back!" she told me, angrily. "If he's not marrying you, he shouldn't keep it. Karen would *not* have wanted that!"

I didn't know how to respond. Yes, of course I wanted her table back, and felt he should have given it to me after he broke things off. But I couldn't bring myself to go back into what had been, for such a brief time, "our house."

My mother was quiet for a few moments. What she said next surprised me.

"Would you mind if *I* went over there and got it?" she asked.

I looked at her in astonishment.

"No . . ." I said, wondering how that might turn out. My mother was far braver in this moment than I was. But then, she didn't have the emotional baggage I was carting around inside my head and heart.

She didn't say anything more. But a few days later, she drove triumphantly up my driveway with the table in the back seat of her car. Seeing it again, I almost broke down in tears. Together, we brought it in and from that moment on, Karen's beautiful table has had pride of place in my house—wherever I've lived.

"I always thought of Martin as your second husband," Mom said, over a celebratory glass of wine that evening.

I swirled the wine in my glass, as a montage of the responsibilities I'd been given and the many skills I'd acquired over the past seven years ran through my mind: art history researcher, associate producer, co-scriptwriter, location scout, driver for talent, interviewee make-up person, production assistant, international location scout, international location manager, grant writer, permits and international visa coordinator, transportation coordinator, U.S. president interview-getter, past U.S. president meeting-getter, national broadcast airdates coordinator, fundraiser, and publicist. I'd even managed to wrangle a Distinguished Alumni Award for Martin from his *alma mater,* Boston College, because I knew someone on the board from a previous job.

"That's funny, I always thought of him as my second *degree,*" I replied. "My film degree."

And, unlike the shoes—*that* was something he couldn't give away to anyone else.

PART II

METAMORPHOSIS

---

a transformation, such as that of magic or by sorcery

*"You can't always stop bad things from happening to you.
But remember, you can't stop the good things
from happening to you, either
—often when you're least expecting them."*

CAROL ORSBORN, PHD, *THE ART OF RESILIENCE*

ANXIETY GOBLINS

Journal notes, March 2000—The anxiety goblins attacked again during the night. I awoke this morning feeling restless and unsettled. . . .

AS MY PAYCHECKS from the documentary workshop trickled to an end, it seemed as if a massive door had slammed shut on the most interesting career I could ever have imagined for myself. Like a dark fairy tale, a huge and immovable rock had rolled across my only path into the magical world of telling stories and making films.

In addition to working on documentaries, for the past few years I'd also been researching and writing a nonfiction book of my own, *The Muse Factor*—a psychological, non-fiction study of muses and their relationships with artists. Who would those artists be and what would their music, art, sculpture, and writing be like were it not for someone who happened to cross their paths at just the right time, altering the trajectory of their creativity?

I loved this book project. So did my agent in Washington, DC. An author who'd been interviewed in one of Martin's documentaries facilitated the introduction. The agent invited me in to speak with her after reading my book proposal and told me it was just the kind of "smart, sexy, and intelligent" book she was looking to represent. I floated out of that first meeting high on a cloud of possibilities.

I was assigned an in-house editor and together we worked on crafting a proposal they would shop to potential publishers. For a while, my book was at the top of their whiteboard. What a thrill it was to see my name up there.

A year passed as I worked diligently on whatever changes they asked me to make, reshaping my proposal over and over to meet their suggestions.

The agent sent a copy of the revised proposal to an editor she knew in New York City. It came back several weeks later with a lot of comments in red ink. I was dismayed and wished the editor had instead seen a copy of my original proposal. It wasn't long after that my agent told me she couldn't spend any more time on me and my book—we were finished. Another heart-wrenching rejection on top of the loss of my job. Disheartened, I put my writing aside to focus on finding paying work.

> *March 17, 2000 . . . I've decided to make the bike path along the river my partner in the creation of my book. It's been a wonderful source of inspiring new thoughts and potential solutions. So many ideas have occurred to me as I've walked along it over the past two years—not only for this book, but beyond this project as well.*

Each day, I walked for miles with our dogs Zydeco and Bandit along the bike path that meandered through the trees along the Potomac River from Mount Vernon to Old Town, Alexandria. These walks renewed me. That, and the kids. When I was with them, I was okay.

> *March 11, 2000 . . . Zoë's basketball game was the highlight yesterday, it's so exciting to see her play. Afterwards, the three of us spent the rest of the day together, sharing the little things, a story from school, a lyric from a song, or a quote from a film*

we just watched. Just low-key and together, both of them doing their own thing at these ages—Leif with his video games, Zoë with her movies—and Zydeco bouncing around and barking, making us laugh. Leif acting goofy to entertain us and Zoë pretending not to be amused. Leif spontaneously grabbing the video camera to record the moment. The phone ringing, friends calling . . . And always the food, everyone's cooking now, even Leif. Something's always being prepared, something's always being consumed. These lovely days together. . .

But the hardships kept coming. With no steady income, the bills started to back up like toxic sludge in a clogged drain. The IRS continued to hound me over a disputed return from my married years. My father's health began to falter. His brother, my beloved uncle and mentor Lawrence Fellows, whose multi-country career as a foreign correspondent for *The New York Times* inspired me to want to tell stories from other lands, died unexpectedly from a heart attack. Having just lost my sister to cancer, I worried the same fate would befall me. Despite having Zoë and Leif with me at least half of each week, I'd never felt so utterly alone. At least they were fine, I kept reminding myself. And that thought kept me going.

After Karen's diagnosis, I knew I should be doing self-exams in the shower. But I didn't. If there was a lump, I didn't want to know. I simply couldn't handle any more stress or potential catastrophes, not even if my feel-no-evil cowardice harmed me further down the road. I did manage a yearly check-up with my doctor, holding my breath in anticipation of bad news each time. But that was all. Each time I got the all clear, I thanked my breasts and wondered if my sister was still looking out for me.

A few days after the one-year anniversary of Karen's death, Dr. and Mrs. Braddock, the sponsors of *American Byzantine*, invited me to join them in their box seats at the Kennedy Center to see a production of Shakespeare's *Otello* starring Placido Domingo—who was, according to Philip Kennicott writing for the *Washington Post*, one of the greatest Otellos of the century.

I enjoyed the production, even though the plot riled my feminist blood. The costumes were great, especially Iago's—black leather pants with a pattern of holes in vertical stripes and a black leather tunic, which I thought looked surprisingly hot on him.

Following the curtain call, Mrs. Braddock ushered me backstage to spend a few moments post-performance with Placido Domingo. She meant well, but there was nothing remarkable in our meeting. While Placido Domingo was shaking my hand, he looked right past me at the line of others waiting. A group of brassy women snapped his photo without first asking permission. A group of Japanese businessmen closed in upon him with their own cameras, as if he was a tourist attraction. I felt demeaned and groupie-fied to be among these fans. Mrs. Braddock encouraged me to ask for his autograph, but I shook my head. It would only remind me of the man who didn't even make eye contact with me when being introduced. I understood that it wasn't the man, it was the circumstances—but still, what meaning would it have?

The encounter that made the far bigger impression on me that night had already happened—and it was not with any of the performers. During the intermission, a kindly woman in the neighboring box leaned over and began talking to me. She introduced herself as Becky Dukes.

In the course of our conversation, the topic of cancer somehow came up and I confessed my almost paralyzing fear of dying before my kids were out of the nest. She looked startled and then very sweetly gave me a few words of encouragement. A survivor herself, she told me not to worry. I had a long way to go yet, she said, and I would do so in good health.

Oddly enough, I believed her—mostly because I wanted to. But also because there was something so grounded, affirming, and wise about her. After the performance, she asked for my card, saying she'd be in touch.

I never heard from her again, but it didn't matter. Those words from a stranger—words I would not have heard had I not been working on a documentary film—comforted me and quieted the dissonance in my head, at least for the time being.

Her words were a prelude to what happened next. Unbeknownst to me at the time, I was about to step into flow. . . .

FLOW AND FLOWING

Morning journal, April 2000—Some days are just more tentative than others. I don't really feel my feet are securely beneath me all the time.

Feeling lonely and at loose ends yesterday, I momentarily considered calling Martin to see if I could come over to the house, crawl into bed with him and just be held. The thought lasted only a moment or two before I realized how hungry I was. So, I went downstairs and made dinner instead.

Morning journal, May 8, 2000—I had a vivid dream about Martin last night. We were working on location—me, along with everyone else from the documentary workshop. When Martin tried to put his arms around me, I asked him not to touch me. I awoke, feeling strange. . . .

Morning journal, May 19, 2000—The "Ghost of Employment Past" dropped off my last paycheck yesterday. It was not a comfortable visit. How different from the days when he would come over to my house to discuss the art assignments for the Thomas Jefferson documentary over coffee. I kept wishing my telephone would ring, any excuse to escape his presence.

FLOW: THE PSYCHOLOGY of Optimal Experience, a book by Hungarian American psychologist, Mihaly Csikszentmihalyi was published in 1990, but it didn't pop up on my radar until ten years later.

In his book, Csikszentmihalyi describes a state of consciousness he called "flow," during which people experience deep enjoyment and creativity, a state in which positive experiences are unleashed and sustained. To achieve it, he says, we just need to order the information that enters our consciousness.

Easier said than done, I thought.

Having often experienced that lovely state of flow when everything seemed open and positive and creative throughout the years of working at the documentary workshop, I understood what he was talking about. But how could I get back into that state now that I was no longer in that atmosphere?

I read about *Flow* on a Friday afternoon in an article I found on the internet.

The following day was Saturday, our once-a-week shopping spree day, when the kids and I piled into our old Volvo and set off to see what useful and necessary treasures we could find at yard sales.

That morning, we drove down along the river to Mount Vernon to check out a community yard sale in a friend's neighborhood of contemporary wood and glass homes, surrounded by gardens and green spaces. With houses like these, I thought, they should have good stuff.

And they did.

We spent nearly an hour browsing, during which time I found a pair of brand-new shoes for Leif as well as art supplies for both kids. On the front lawn of the last house, I noticed a couple of books on a blanket. I hesitated a moment. We were all hungry and wanted to get back home. But then I decided to walk over and take a look. And there—one of just four books for sale—was a paperback copy of *Flow,* waiting for me to notice it. For a dollar, it was mine. I started reading it that night.

Two weeks after I found that copy of *Flow*, I was asked to be a judge for the CINE Golden Eagles Television Awards. I spent a morning at American University, my parents' *alma mater*, watching two films on economic development and four on sports. Yep, that's me, an expert in both fields. Fortunately, lunch was included, which offset the cost of the gas to drive there and back.

Three weeks after finding *Flow*, with my finances getting precariously meager, I got a call offering me a two-day location scout ($600) in Washington, DC, for an upcoming PBS pledge special. That was followed by a callback for an audition to be considered as the host of a pilot television travel show, which was followed by a request to send in my resume for consideration as a producer for a pilot series on female spies.

I also responded to a query from a production company looking for a typical teenager's room for a production shoot, offering Zoë's room which, though small, was cute and bursting with personality. We'd painted the walls bright colors and using a poster from her favorite television show, *FRIENDS*, as our jumping-off point, covered the walls with a montage of photographs of Zoë and her friends. I told her I'd split the location fee with her, if there was one. She was pleased at the thought of the potential income.

Four weeks after finding the copy of *Flow*, I got a callback about a job interview with the BBC. I was surprised to hear from them after the initial telephone interview with a headhunter who thought I didn't have enough "British TV experience." I didn't have any at all, of course.

I did not get any of these gigs.

But just five weeks after finding *Flow*, however, I did get a surprise phone call from Dr. Braddock, the man whose foundation had funded *American Byzantine*. It was a call that would change my life, but not in the way I might have anticipated.

Two Phone Calls
and a Face

Look at every exit as an entrance somewhere else.

Tom Stoppard, playwright and screenwriter

AMERICAN BYZANTINE WAS finished, and I was both thrilled—and unhappy—with the results.

I was happy to see my name in the credits as co-writer and co-producer. But to be honest, it felt like watching two different films play out side by side, Martin's version of the film interlaced with my own. Artistically and narratively, I felt it wasn't cohesive. It looked like something made by two people who were not in sync—because that was exactly what it was. It started out strongly, but somewhere in the telling of the story it began to dissipate. Just like our relationship.

Regardless, the film still needed to make the leap to broadcast and Dr. Braddock was calling that morning to check on my progress getting it on the air on PBS stations around the country. After listening to my update and having heard about the recent split from Martin's documentary workshop, he kindly asked how I was doing.

Uncharacteristically, I thought about my response for a moment before answering. And then—equally uncharacteristically—I told him how scared I was. Horrified, I listened as a breathless rush of despairing thoughts came tumbling out of my mouth, gasping for air.

"Once this project is finished, I have *no* work lined up. *Nothing.*" I heard myself say in a confessional half-whisper. "I can't find another film, and I've been unable, despite a lot of effort, to find any job in my profession. I'm a single parent. I have no savings. I don't know how I am going to pay the bills, hang onto my house, and feed my kids."

There was a pause at the other end of the line. And then, he chuckled softly.

Had I said something funny?

This wasn't the response I'd been hoping for.

"Kristin," he said gently. "May I give you some advice?"

I had just confessed I was completely broke to the funder of my film. Could I have sounded any more desperate, unprofessional, and pathetic? Hardly. Was I interested in advice from him?

"Yes," I said, hoping to hear him say he would give me a grant to fund another film.

There was another pause. And then this lovely, gentle, intelligent older man said five words I never expected to hear from a self-made, multi-millionaire scientist and engineer.

"Let go and let God," he said.

Pardon me?

I couldn't believe my ears. These words didn't have the ring of steady paycheck potential to me. I wanted to scream into the phone: *That's it?! How's that going to pay the bills? I just confessed my desperation, my fear of defaulting on my mother's mortgage, and not being able to feed my kids. You're a successful, professional, entrepreneurial, millionaire businessman—and that's all you've got for me!?*

Worried my thoughts were so loud he might hear them, I forced myself to thank him politely, then hung up as soon as I could.

By now I was no stranger to tough times and uncertainty, but that night was possibly the worst one yet. Alone in my dark bedroom, the kids sleeping peacefully in theirs, blissfully unaware of the financial precipice we were precariously perched upon, I tried to rationalize my devastating disappointment in what had pretty much been my last hope. Alone, frightened, and bereft of resources and ideas, Dr. Braddock's five words of advice floated around in my head like ephemeral wisps of clouds—thin, vaporous, useless. Not to mention, somewhat ironic.

Although I'd spent the past seven years working for a Catholic filmmaker who explored religion-based stories in documentary format, the closest world view to mine is basic existentialism as laid out in the writings of Danish theologian Søren Kierkegaard. Life isn't inherently coherent, meaningful, or particularly conducive to happiness, he wrote. It's up to *us*, as individuals, to work to create order, meaning, and happiness—if that's what we want. The personal responsibility perspective of this appeals to me. I also took it as a sign from the universe that I happened to be born on Kierkegaard's birthday—May 5th.

At that moment, however, I wasn't thinking about Kierkegaard. Unable to sleep, alone with my fears, struggling to admit to myself that I was out of ideas, options, and possibilities, and that I might need to swallow my pride and apply for public assistance, I decided to follow Dr. Braddock's advice that night. What the hell? I thought and floated my thoughts grudgingly up towards the dark sky of my bedroom ceiling.

Hello. I have reached the point of no options. It has been suggested I let go and get out of Your way. So, here You are. Take it all! Do what You will with it. I'm going to take the night off.

And with that, I gave myself permission to part with my anxieties until the sun came up and drifted off to sleep.

The following morning, my cell phone buzzed just after I'd dropped the kids off at school.

"*Kristin!*"

The voice of a different Dr. B. boomed into my ear by way of greeting. It was Dr. William F. Baker, the general manager of the largest PBS station in the country, WNET in New York City. Although he'd been our executive producer for both *Final Blessing* and *American Byzantine*, it was unusual for him to call me.

"I've got a project for you!" he continued, without waiting for a response. "It's called *The Face: Jesus in Art.* Are you interested?"

The film was already finished, Dr. Baker explained, and it was stunning. A multi-million-dollar epic, it was a beautiful celebration of two thousand years of paintings and mosaics of Jesus that included Giotto's frescoes; works by Michelangelo, Leonardo, Rembrandt, and Grunewald; as well as fourteenth-century Ethiopian images, Latin American, and Asian art; and more contemporary examples by Marc Chagall, Andy Warhol, and African American folk artist William H. Johnson. Directed by Craig MacGowan, the film was shot by Dean Cundey (*Who Framed Roger Rabbit, Back to the Future, Hook, Jurassic Park*) and featured a state-of-the-art morphing technique of the paintings by Christopher Cundey, his son. The film was narrated by Mel Gibson, Edward Herrmann, Ricardo Montalban, and Patricia Neal.

Would I be interested, he asked, in marketing his film to PBS stations around the country? And doing the film's national press, as well as organizing—on his behalf—the film's world premiere at New York City's iconic Radio City Music Hall?

I was speechless. It would be at least half a year's work. And—an art film on *Jesus?* The irony of it all was astonishing.

My metamorphosis from being in documentary film production to becoming a documentary film consultant had begun.

A Wrangler is Born

I ACCEPTED THE project, of course, even though I was scared to pieces to represent not only a multi-million-dollar film, but also the personal dream project of the general manager of the most important PBS station in the country. A film with a lot of celebrities—including Jesus!

Jesus . . .

When Dr. Baker asked me to come up to New York City for a meeting to discuss everything he wanted me to do for the film, I decided to take the opportunity to bring ten-year-old Leif along with me and make a mini holiday out of it. He'd never been to New York City, or any city of that size, before, and I was curious to see his reactions to it.

In order to do this as cheaply as possible, we took the train instead of flying and stayed with my cousin Gail and her boyfriend at their apartment in midtown. On the train, I gave Leif some money for lunch and suggested he go check out the food car. He was delighted to go explore by himself. He returned fifteen minutes later with a soda, a huge piece of pizza, and an equally huge grin.

Walking around New York City, Leif thought

it was very cool that I could just put my hand out and a big yellow taxi would pull over and take us wherever we wanted to go.

"What a magical city!" he said. Or something to that effect.

"You know I have to *pay* those yellow cars, right?" I said, at the risk of bursting his happiness bubble, but it didn't seem to dim his enthusiasm.

During our few days there, we visited a great burger restaurant and an interactive science and technology museum I thought he'd enjoy.

He was very into magic at the time. Gail took us out to lunch at a small restaurant she liked and laughed and applauded when Leif did his magic tricks at the table. That night, she asked him to do his tricks all over again for her boyfriend at his apartment, which Leif was only too happy to do.

In between the fun things, however, I did have to spend several hours at the WNET studios for an organizational meeting about the project. Having nowhere else to put him, I brought Leif with me. I was a little worried about showing up for this important meeting with a kid in tow, but the staff there was very nice and set him up in a small room with a tall stack of VHS tapes to entertain himself. I thought he'd enjoy being the master of his own private screening room, but the tapes were all "boring PBS stuff," he told me later. Oh well, at least he had the taxis and train rides.

Over the next four and a half months, I worked like crazy from home to create a launch event at Radio City Music Hall with long-distance help from their staff.

My first task was to fill the seats of what was the largest indoor theater in the world for the world premiere of Dr. Baker's film.

There are 5,960 seats—*a lot* to fill. To accomplish that, I somehow needed to convince thousands of people to pay between $12 and $40 for a ticket to see a shortened version of the full 90-minute film they'd be able to see for free on PBS just ten days later.

Instead of trying to find and convince nearly six thousand people to buy a ticket, I came up with the idea to bring them in by the busload. I put together a campaign to entice Catholic churches all over the state of New York to make it an event and literally bus their congregants to the city for the evening. Thankfully, it worked. And between that and local publicity, we were able to get a body in about 75 percent of the seats in Radio City Music Hall.

My second task was to get 348 PBS stations all over the country to put *The Face: Jesus in Art* on the air during Easter Week. In this case, I was offering them a multi-million-dollar, star-studded film, produced by the number one PBS station in the U.S., about Jesus for Easter Week. There was no dogma, just an art extravaganza of images most viewers had likely never seen, rendered with intriguing, state-of-the-art storytelling. Regardless of one's personal belief, this was a beautiful and beautifully crafted film to dazzle viewers at Easter.

The airdates had to be confirmed station by station, market by market, by me. After mailing out hundreds of copies of screening VHS tapes, I did most of the follow-up work by telephone because you could do that back then. Things are different now, but in those days, it took hundreds of calls and conversations to encourage PBS station program directors to watch the film, then schedule it in a favorable broadcast slot.

My third task was to do the national press and the national religion press—a monumental responsibility knowing I was representing an expensive (in terms of public television productions) film for the biggest PBS station in the country, one with a lot of hopes and expectations around it. I also helped shape the graphics package, reaching out to Miguel Tejerina, a lovely editor and graphics artist from Argentina with whom I'd worked at the documentary workshop. Miguel created his own "face" of Jesus composed of hundreds of tiny images digitized together. It was stunning and Bill Baker loved it. It was used for all the film's press materials.

Any one of these tasks would have been a full-time gig over a four-and-a-half-month period. But I had been hired to do them all simultaneously and mostly on my own. It was a clown-at-the-circus act, keeping plates spinning atop broom handles. To get press reviews for *The Face*, I had to first get it on the air. But there was only so much lead time, so the press effort for each market had to start the moment I had a confirmed airdate. Multiply this by two hundred or so markets across the country and, well, you get the idea.

Somehow, I pulled it off. I didn't give myself time to think or get nervous. I just wanted to do a good job. And not just a good job, I wanted to excel.

In the end, *The Face: Jesus in Art* did spectacularly well with airdates on nearly every PBS station across 98 percent of the U.S. Nationally and regionally, the press responded enthusiastically to the film. I had taken a chance by strategically pitting *The Face* against a Discovery Channel documentary that was releasing at the same time, *What Did Jesus Look Like?* Strangely, the final image of what Jesus may have looked like was included in their press materials. Talk about a spoiler alert! Why bother watching the entire film when they've given you the answer right up front? I made sure to include that observation in my pitches to the press, and it worked.

Ultimately, I was able to present Bill with an impressive binder of press clips nearly two inches thick that included cover and feature stories, including one in the *Washington Post*.

And then came the premiere at Radio City Music Hall.

This time it was Zoë's turn for a New York City adventure. My mother came with us. My wonderful German Aunt Ruth, the former ballerina, came down from Westport for the premiere.

WNET paid for a suite for us at the New Yorker Hotel, also known as the "Grand Old Lady" for its iconic architecture. It was built with its own private power plant and included an underground tunnel to Penn Station. Nikola Tesla lived in the hotel until his death in early 1943. Throughout the 1930s and 1940s, NBC broadcast live from the Terrace Room, where big band acts like Benny Goodman, Woody Herman, and Tommy and Jimmy Dorsey performed. In 1948, The New Yorker installed television sets in 100 of its guest rooms, one of the first hotels in the U.S. to do so, then marketing it as the hotel with "the greatest number of television sets under one roof." It seemed only appropriate that we stayed there.

In 1959, Senator John F. Kennedy organized an airlift initiative that provided scholarships and expenses for Kenyan students in the U.S., including stays at The New Yorker. One of those students was a young man named Barack Obama, Sr., and it was on this trip that he married Ann Dunham, the mother of President Barack Obama.

While I was checking us all in, the desk clerk told Zoë that Jennifer Lopez had recently stayed there, which thrilled her. She took photographs of our rooms and the lobby of the hotel with the little instamatic camera I'd given her for the trip to show her friends when she got back home.

And then came the big night.

The film's name was lit up in bright lights on the iconic building's wrap-around marquee, and the Music Hall, while not quite at capacity, was at least gratifyingly filled with people eager to see *The Face: Jesus in Art.*

With the theater's Art Deco architectural style, its beautiful, stepped arches designed to mimic the sunrise, and its more than 5,000 house lights, it was a stunning setting for a premiere. The night was a huge success, and I could finally breathe a sigh of relief.

I treasured times like these when I could bring Zoë and Leif along with me. Zoë and I stayed in New York City after the premiere, just the two of us, so she, too, would have her own special adventures there, as Leif had.

She was into basketball and music at the time and so we went to Madame Tussauds to see Michael Jordan and Central Park to see the John Lennon *Imagine* mosaic. Having seen *Sleepless in Seattle,* she wanted nothing more than to visit the top of the Empire State Building in person and see the exact place where Tom Hanks finally met up with Meg Ryan. I mentioned this to Bill, who immediately loaned me a pass permitting us to queue jump the tourists and take the elevator straight to the top. Zoë thought this was brilliant—not having to wait in line made her feel like a celebrity herself. She wanted to know if we had a "Bill Pass" for anything else.

I had to return the pass before leaving the city. Wandering through the halls of WNET on my way in and then out again, I got to pondering why Bill Baker, with a staff of well over 600, had asked *me* to do this project for him? He could have chosen anyone from his teams. Perhaps they were all too busy to take this on. From his role as our Executive Producer for *American Byzantine*, he knew I loved art and loved it enough to fight for it. I think he also saw that working with films on the topic of religion didn't scare me—rather, they fascinated me from the perspective of an outsider.

To be honest, though, it's still a mystery to me. Stressful as they were, my experiences working on *The Face* ended up being like getting a quick master's degree in broadcast marketing.

Getting films on the air is not something that happens automatically. The primary PBS stations around the country are required to air PBS's national program schedule, which gobbles up most of prime time as well as some other spaces. This is called common carriage—and it's the reason viewers see *Masterpiece Theater* and *Frontline* on all the primary PBS stations at the same time, regardless of what market they're in.

But not everything you see on public television is distributed by PBS. Although all sorts of nooks and crannies are left empty when PBS releases its primary schedule, there is a lot of competition for each precious space. The key to dealing with the competition for these spaces is to have either a great film or the right film for a particular moment.

Just as films have animal wranglers and child wranglers, documentary filmmakers and producers often have publicists behind the scenes working to get their films (and other shows) on public television. I had found my niche filling those empty spaces with the films I was hired to get on the air. Instead of calling myself a publicist, I called myself a "PBS station wrangler."

It's sort of like what a literary agent does. But instead of finding one publisher for each book, my task was to get the films I represented on several hundred PBS stations—and as simultaneously as possible to make them eligible for press coverage. In independent filmmaker terms, it's like submitting your film to more than 150 film festivals *at once*, which is a serious amount of work.

It was the foundation from which I launched a two-and-a-half-decades-long career in public television. Bill Baker could not have given me a better gift.

BLACK SMOKE ON THE HORIZON

September 2001 [excerpt from a letter to a friend in Denmark] . . . *Dear Jørgen, It is a horrific time here. The Pentagon is only 12 miles away from me. And, with my work projects these days, I could easily have been in New York that day. We Americans have so little experience with something of this sort and it made me think of how many people around the world have to live with this sort of hell on a daily basis. We have been very lucky until now, and certainly I feel we have been naive. I would hope that one outcome of all this tragedy would be to create more of a team spirit towards world matters. . . .*

I WAS STILL looking for the security of an actual *job*—one with regular paychecks, steady hours, hopefully health insurance and, if I was really dreaming, paid vacation days. I'd had so little of this since I left my earlier, pre-marriage career working in design. In the meantime, in the wake of the success of *The Face*, freelance projects began coming my way, starting me on a road to self-employment.

That summer, I'd been dating Charles

Oppman, the chef/owner of Café Marianna, my favorite eatery in Alexandria. He suggested I should protect myself by incorporating. He also suggested using his lawyer, Gregory Wade. It seemed like a good idea, so I booked a meeting with him for September 11, 2001.

The morning of our appointment, I was in my bathroom, listening to NPR as I put on my makeup. Staring into the mirror, mascara wand in hand, I paused.

Did I just hear someone say a plane flew into a building? In New York City?

I finished getting dressed listening to NPR's erratic and jangled news reports, trying to piece together what was going on. I thought I heard someone say people were jumping out of a building.

Confused, but needing to pull focus on my meeting with Greg, I made a mental note to call my friends and family in NYC later to get their take on what had happened.

As I drove north along the Potomac River on the George Washington Parkway towards Old Town, I saw an enormous cloud of dark smoke on the horizon. It appeared to be on the Virginia side of the river, the side I was on. Must be a bad fire, I thought, as I eased my car into a parking space on King Street. I walked up the path through the small garden and into the historic house that Greg used as his law offices.

"It'll be a minute!" I heard someone call out by way of greeting. "Why don't you grab a coffee across the street? For some reason, our coffee machine's not working this morning."

I walked back across the street to Starbucks and placed my order. I was waiting to pay when things suddenly got crazy.

A phone on the other side of the counter rang and one of the baristas answered. The buzz and hiss of the coffee machines suddenly stopped, as if someone had pulled the plug. Then the lights went off. The barista put down the phone and turned to face us, panic in her eyes.

"Get out!" she shouted at those of us waiting for coffee. *"EVERY-ONE! GET! OUT! We're closing IMMEDIATELY!"*

I was confused. This was all very unfriendly. Was she yelling at us because the power had failed?

"But I haven't paid for my coffee yet," I said, as the others headed for the door. "Should I just leave the money?"

"No! *GET OUT NOW!"* she yelled, flinging things around behind the counter.

Feeling a little ruffled and confused by her behavior, I did as I was told and followed the other customers out the door. Happy with the free coffee, I walked back across the street to Greg's office to tell him the strange thing that had just happened over at Starbucks.

Weirdly, all hell had broken loose inside *his* offices, too. Everyone was scrambling to find phones, purses, keys, papers, belongings. Once again, I felt like a character without a script on the set of the wrong film—with a cup of coffee as my only prop.

A moment later, the lights went out here, too. Then Greg's computer shut down. As his staff began making their way out the door, he apologized, then began hastily gathering up his own papers, saying it would be better if we met another time.

"One of the Twin Towers in New York was hit with a plane this morning," he explained, as he ushered me out the door. "And now also the Pentagon, apparently!"

The Pentagon? It was only a few miles north of where we stood. That was the smoke I'd seen driving into town.

I started my car and nudged my way out into the traffic. Wanting more information (and a comforting hug), I turned down a side street instead of going home and headed over towards the river and Charles' restaurant. The lights were still on there.

Inside, in the middle of what should have been a busy morning prep, Charles and his kitchen staff were huddled together in a small cluster, staring silently up at a television mounted on the wall. When he heard me come in, Charles came over and put his arms around me. We watched in silence as the newscast showed footage of a plane flying into the second tower and bursting into flames. I heard someone crying. No one spoke. No one understood what was happening.

And then came the news that a fourth plane was headed to Washington, DC. Café Marianna was close to the Pentagon and not far from Capitol Hill. Charles decided to close the restaurant. He began almost pushing everyone out the door, including me, promising to call me later.

The phone was ringing as I walked into my house. It was a robotic call from the elementary school telling me to pick up my child immediately. Moments later, it rang again. It was the father of one of Leif's friends, asking if I could pick up his son and keep him at my house until he could get home. Of course, I said.

I walked the few blocks over to the elementary school, trying to guess how much the boys had been told, and what I should, or should *not*, say to someone else's son.

Neither seemed to comprehend the shocking horror of the situation; they were just ten years old. But they did at least have an awareness that this was a national emergency. At one point, Leif's friend Sandy stopped walking and looked at us.

"Hey," he said. "This happened on September 11th! That's 911—just like the number you call for emergencies!"

He was right. I hadn't put the two together. How weird and strange the coincidence—if it was, in fact, a coincidence.

Because of my work on *The Face: Jesus in Art*, both Zoë and Leif had experienced New York City themselves for the first time just months before September 2001—and I felt part of the WNET family.

The New Yorker Hotel, where Zoë and I had stayed for the premiere of *The Face* just six months earlier, donated 10,000 free nights to volunteers in the aftermath of the 9/11 attacks.

WNET suffered a personal loss. Exactly two months earlier, on July 11, 2001, they had celebrated the installation of a state-of-the-art digital transmitter on Tower One of the World Trade Center with a party at the famous Windows on the World restaurant. Rod Coppola, the engineer whose responsibility it was to maintain the transmitter, was among the nearly 3,000 people killed when the towers collapsed.

As general manager, Bill Baker responded immediately. The day after the attack, WNET donated its dozens of phones and available space, including the corridors, to the Mayor's Office of Emergency Management and the Red Cross.

"Hotlines were set up for families trying to locate their loved ones. For weeks, volunteers took up residence in the hallways and the Boardroom of our former offices at 450 West 33rd Street," Baker said, "And two volunteers, whose wedding had to be postponed, got married at WNET a few days later."

As a result of working on *The Face*, the kids and I now had a more personal comprehension of the impact and losses of 9/11 than we would otherwise have had. Strangely eerie as that was, I appreciated the fresh personal connections it had given all three of us to the city, as if something had been calling us to come and experience New York City—before the world was forever changed.

HEY MIKEY!

AFTER THE SUCCESS of my work on *The Face*, Anne and Lisa, the program marketing team at WNET, handed me another project they didn't want to work on themselves.

Who Cares was a one-hour special produced by the Fred Friendly Seminars, a production team housed at Columbia University's Graduate School of Journalism in New York City. Founded in 1912 by Joseph Pulitzer, it's one of the oldest journalism schools in the world.

In 1966, Fred Friendly, former president of CBS News, was appointed to the tenured faculty at Columbia as the Edward R. Murrow Professor of Broadcast Journalism. For the next thirteen years, he pioneered the university's threadbare broadcast journalism program.

Inspired by his classroom discussions, Fred had the thought to create seminars on media, law, and public policy. These eventually evolved into PBS's long-running *Fred Friendly Seminars,* a collection of more than one hundred PBS programs.

Using the Socratic method—a dialogue based on hypothetical situations—to stimulate problem-solving conversations, the seminars invited PBS viewers to ponder solutions to hypothetical dilemmas drawn from real scenarios facing Americans. They covered topics including affirmative action, health care, end-of-life issues, energy policies, bioterrorism, and ethics. Fred was famous for saying that the only escape was to *think* your way through these problems.

The latest one, titled *Who Cares,* was moderated by journalist John Hockenberry and featured a group of individuals, each of whom had experience in some aspect of chronic illness—from doctors and insurance professionals to patients and caregivers. Through a series of hypothetical scenarios in which each panelist was asked to play a particular role to get conversations going and people thinking, the program was written to raise provocative questions about the way America's fastest-growing health care challenge was financed, managed, and delivered.

Are you still with me?

Who Cares was a wonderful opportunity to work on an iconic series with a legendary production team. Especially for someone currently unemployed, it was a dream come true.

The problem was I nearly fell asleep watching it.

I wanted to work with everyone involved and I certainly needed the work, but the program (in my mind, at least) didn't have the compelling energy needed to capture a television audience's attention.

It turned out I was not alone in my opinion. Nobody on the WNET staff was in a hurry to jump on the phone and ask their colleagues at PBS stations all over the country to air this. So, they passed it down the metaphorical table to me.

Back in 1972, the Quaker Oats Company came up with a commercial designed to re-energize sales for Life breakfast cereal—the little brown squares of cereal they'd created eleven years earlier. In the commercial—now considered a classic of American advertising—two little boys are discussing the contents in a bowl set in front of them.

"What's this stuff?" one asks.

"Some cereal," his brother responds disparagingly. "It's supposed to be *good* for you."

"Are *you* going to try it?" the first brother asks.

"*I'm* not gonna try it!" the second brother responds. "*You* try it!"

They push the bowl back and forth, each refusing to eat the cereal. Then they come up with an idea.

"Let's get Mikey to try it!" one says, as he passes the bowl along to the youngest of the three, thinking he won't eat it either. The two watch closely as, to their great surprise, little Mikey begins spooning the cereal into his mouth.

"He likes it!' they shout. "Hey Mikey!"

I had the feeling I had become "Mikey."

I could just imagine Anne and Lisa watching *Who Cares* and saying back and forth to one another, "*I'm* not gonna promote it—*you* promote it!" At some point, a light bulb went off and one of them said, "I know, let's give it to *Kristin!*"

I had no work or income at the time. The mortgage and all my other monthly bills were due. I needed this project, and I very much needed it to be a success—not only for the program itself, but also for my fledgling consulting gig in public television.

And so, I said, "Sure, I'll give it a try."

The content was important and being offered free of charge (as many programs are) to all the other PBS stations. It was also coming from three reputable sources: WNET, the Fred Friendly Seminars, and Columbia University's J-School.

The previous seminar, however, had reached just 18 percent of the U.S.—a low bar indeed. I figured I could at least improve on that number, even with this program.

But what would it take to pull that off?

I reminded myself of my "Kissing the Leper" mantra. Here I was again, being asked to work on another PBS project no one else wanted to work on. And how ironic was it that it was called *Who Cares?*

What it would take, I soon realized—channeling my sideways thinking—would be for the decision makers at PBS stations *not* to watch the program.

From previous project marketing experiences, I was already aware that many programmers, faced with more content to air on their stations than they had room for in their schedules, often made a decision based on screening just the first five minutes of a program.

That could work to our advantage, I thought. But *not* the first five minutes of this program. I had my work cut out for me. But I also had an idea.

I suggested that rather than sending out the usual copy of the actual program on a VHS tape to all the PBS stations, we instead produce a special screener. One in which the first five minutes would be carefully crafted to be more interesting than the program itself.

I don't know what Anne and Lisa thought of my idea, but they supported it enough to set up a meeting with the production team. I was introduced to Fred Friendly Seminars' president, Richard Kilberg, executive director Barbara Margolis, and Ruth Friendly—Fred's widow and the director of the seminars.

Outlining my concept, I suggested the producers bring the show's moderator, John Hockenberry, back into the studio to tape what is called a stand-up.

Stand-up is when a reporter appears on camera and delivers information speaking directly to the audience. (Although this is a normal television term, I tried to use it as tactfully as possible, given Hockenberry would be doing it while sitting in the wheelchair he's used ever since an automobile accident at nineteen left him unable to walk.)

I also suggested he break what is called the fourth wall by looking at the camera, therefore appearing to speak directly to the viewer, in this case our PBS colleagues. It's a technique often used to engage and connect to an audience (one that would be used very effectively in the American version of *The Office*.)

Hockenberry himself would appear to be speaking personally to each PBS programmer, telling them why the content of this special was vitally important to their viewers.

Following his appeal, Hockenberry would then invite the

programmers to let the tape roll to see a compilation of the highlights so they would get a quick idea of the content. Strategically, these would be the best and most engaging bits carefully selected from the program. (But of course, we didn't say that.)

"If you'd like to watch the full program start to finish," Hockenberry would then say, "you can fast forward to minute 7:35 and watch from there."

I was hoping few people would do that and would instead watch just the highlights.

To my surprise, the production team agreed to the plan. They asked me to write the Hockenberry script and come up with an edit plan for the highlights complete with the relevant time codes.

Both pleased and nervous they were going with my idea, I wrote a draft script. Hockenberry came back into the studio for the taping while Ruth and I worked on the highlights reel. Eventually, everything was edited together in the new format. VHS tapes were produced and sent out to PBS stations all over the country and *Who Cares* was launched.

Two weeks after the tapes went out, I held my breath as I picked up the phone and began calling PBS stations to see how the program was being received.

"Well, if *that* isn't the most appropriate title for a public television show," a program director in a top market responded sardonically.

Others were kinder, however, and despite its lackluster title, the unusual presentation and format worked. To my great relief, I was able to get *Who Cares* on the air throughout more than 65 percent of the U.S.—a huge improvement on the previous Fred Friendly Seminars program's disappointing 18 percent.

Key to this success was making it about others, however, not myself. In addition to what I thought was a more effective strategy for the film, uppermost in mind for me was having the producers' backs. The strategy had to be more than just a good idea, it had to be one that would support their vision; one that would make *them*—not me—look good. After all, it was their names on the broadcast, not mine.

Paying attention to my instincts and having the courage to voice them resulted in a successful national rollout, which in turn led to more work with both WNET and the Fred Friendly Seminars, as well as lasting personal friendships with Barbara, Richard, and Ruth.

Unlikely as he was as a role model, little Mikey has stayed in my head ever since as a reminder to try projects nobody else wants and find something tasty and appealing in them.

Even at the age of three, Mikey had his own opinions. I wasn't three, but I was the most junior person, experience-wise, involved in this project. And like Mikey, I had my own thoughts and opinions. Had I not voiced them, it's quite likely this program would have underperformed and my career in public television would have ended with it.

The House in Teakettle Village: Adventures on the Mosquito Coast

BELIZE, APRIL 2002

The kids and I were the last ones to leave the plane after it touched down at the small airport in Belize, Central America.

Months after 9/11, I couldn't shake off the terrifying awareness that there were angry people in the world ready to kill themselves in order to kill us and I was constantly worried the kids and I were sitting ducks, too close to Washington, DC. I decided to tap into the little trust fund Karen had left the kids to help cover their expenses and take them far away to visit their Uncle Lou. Even though it would only be for eight days, any reprieve was welcome.

I had it in mind that Zoë and Leif should experience life in a culture other than their own. After two and a half years of consulting, work projects were now coming in steadily and we were okay financially. But I wanted them to see a world where people lived for an entire year on less than what I earned in a decent month—which was about $4000. I also wanted to keep Lou tightly in the family's embrace.

This was a real holiday, an escape to a different world. For once, we weren't going somewhere because of a film project. Nevertheless, films seemed to follow along with us throughout our days there as if we'd packed them in our suitcases.

Filmmaker Francis Ford Coppola visited Belize in the early 1980s, fell in love with the location and bought the abandoned Blancaneaux Lodge, which he then renovated and used as a family retreat before opening his tropical paradise to the public in 1993. Over the years, two more extraordinary Belizean properties would also become part of the Family Coppola Hideaways.

In another film connection, we were heading to one of the locations featured in *The Mosquito Coast*, a 1986 feature film starring Harrison Ford and Helen Mirren as a married couple, based on Paul Theroux's 1981 novel of the same name. It's fun to see that Jason Alexander played a hardware clerk and Butterfly McQueen (Prissy in *Gone with the Wind)* had a role as Mrs. Kennywick.

Told from the viewpoint of 12-year-old Charlie (River Phoenix), the story centers on Allie Fox (Harrison Ford), a brilliant but stubborn inventor fed up with the American Dream and its accompanying consumerism. Believing a nuclear war to be looming as a result of American greed, Allie packs up his family and moves them to Central America where he purchases a small village along a river in the rainforests of Belize. Everything soon goes awry.

The Mosquito Coast was a critical and commercial success, attracting Academy Award nominations like fruit flies to a forgotten glass of wine.

The kids and I weren't on the run from the U.S., we were just desperately in need of a mini break from it.

After our plane landed, I stepped out onto the disembarking stairs that had been rolled into place next to our plane and caught sight of my brother-in-law standing on the airport's terrace. Lou's trim white beard and old safari hat were unmistakable. Even in the nearly blinding glare of the sunshine, I could almost see his bright blue eyes. I raised my arm to greet him, and in response he gave a sweeping 180-degree wave back and forth over his head.

The kids and I collected our bags, then piled into Lou's beat up old Mazda for the two-hour drive west across the scorching jungle landscape of Belize to his farm in Teakettle Village.

Before getting on the road, Lou told us he needed to make a quick stop in Belize City to get a part for his water heater.

"Unless you want to take cold showers," he said laughing.

"Not really," I said.

We detoured into the largest city in the country, founded in the mid-seventeenth century by British timber harvesters who liked its coastal location and confluence of rivers and streams. Over time, the British brought thousands of slaves from Africa to Belize to toil in the forestry industry.

Belize City in 2002 was not lovely. The buildings lining the streets—a fanciful mix of mostly homegrown, thrown-together architectural styles—were modest and ranged from shabby to run-down. There was nothing more than two or three stories high. Many had shades rolled down across their storefronts against the afternoon heat.

Lou parked the car on a side street and got out. I started to open my door to join him, but with an uncharacteristically stern expression he told me and the kids to stay put. And so, we sat in the car with the windows down (his air conditioning didn't work), sweating in the tropical heat, quietly taking in the scene around us.

We were parked near a small storefront that opened onto the street and was doing a brisk business selling liquor. Several men, in various shades of intoxication, passed by. One, a shirtless Rastafarian, stopped and stared at the three of us in the car. His dreads, thick and knotted, tumbled down his black-skinned back in a slow race to the sidewalk. The three of us watched silently as he leaned in closer and raised his arm. I smelled the stale liquor on his breath as he stared at me, eye to bloodshot eye, but it was too late to close the window.

Because why, I asked myself—*I don't want to be rude?*

He opened his mouth and a torrent of words streamed out, of which I was only able to make out "Book of Revelations" and "de Bible says."

Not knowing what to do, hoping this was nothing more than a drunken blessing, and that he was not going to harm me or the kids, I thanked him. He stared back at me for a long moment as I sat there sweating and willing Lou to reappear. Zoë and Leif watched wordlessly from the back seat. We played this weird and silent game of Blink until, muttering to himself, he moved on.

"Welcome to Belize, kids!" I said brightly, wondering if I'd made a huge mistake bringing them here.

Eventually, I caught a glimpse of Lou in the rearview mirror as he carefully stepped around the body of a man sprawled on the sidewalk. From where I sat, it was hard to tell if the man was dead or just sleeping. Yeah, perhaps coming here *was* a mistake.

Lou got into the car, started it and shifted into gear. I told him about the Rasta's speech.

"That's why I told you to stay in the car!" he laughed, his Arkansas accent shining through.

Lou turned down a side street, past a man urinating on the sidewalk. He checked the kids' faces in the rearview mirror and seeing their shocked expressions, laughed again, both amused and perhaps also hoping to put them at ease.

Moments later, we were out on the Western Highway—one lane in each direction and mostly paved—on our way to the farm in Teakettle Village. Initially, the country was flatter and less jungle-like than I had expected. But the farther west we drove, the more interesting the scenery got. Small hills began to emerge from the ground smothered with trees and vegetation unfamiliar to me. The occasional smattering of dwellings we saw seemed to be randomly tossed by the side of the road, like dice rolled from a shaken cup. Or litter thrown from a passing car.

Many of the houses were propped up precariously. Or leaning. Some were half-empty shells, only partially built.

"It takes a long time for most people to save enough money to build even a cinder block house," Lou explained. "So, they just add to the house they're working on when they have the cash."

No particular style of architecture dominated, but I saw touches of Moroccan arches, Spanish wrought iron gratings covering windows, and occasionally Cuban or Caribbean colors brightening up the monotony. This description makes it sound lovelier than it was, but I was looking for any signs of beauty. Few homes had doors. Windows were covered by screens or lattices or louvered shut. Small wooden houses balanced precariously on stilts. Most seemed to be assembled from an assortment of salvaged or scavenged building materials.

"What's the speed limit here?" I asked, not that Lou was speeding, but because I didn't see any signs.

"There isn't one," Lou responded. "And there are a lot of bad accidents."

"It's so desolate along these stretches of highway—how would anyone know if there was an accident at night?" I asked.

"Oh, they find them in the morning," he said with another one of his easy going, accept-the-world-as-I-find-it laughs that made him such a pleasure to be around.

Just as I was beginning to relax and feel a little less judgmental, we passed the remains of a small blue car in pieces by the side of the road.

"That one was two or three days ago," Lou said. "Three people killed. They hit a bus."

Lou pulled off the highway at mile marker 31-1/4 and parked in front of a modest looking building with the sign *Cheers!* on it.

"Hungry?" he asked the kids. We'd been up since 4:30 a.m. for our day of travel and yes, we were.

Cheers opened in late 1995 when the Tupper family left Vancouver and came to Belize to open a restaurant in the middle of nowhere. Lou, who loved good food, had probably smelled it from his farm, which was miles away.

The kids liked the name and went inside expecting it to look like the television show, which of course it didn't. We were a long way from Boston.

Lou ushered us to a table in the large, open air back room. Scores of potted bromeliads created a natural and colorful barrier between the tables and the garden beyond. Photographs and small pieces of handmade art adorned the walls. Above, hundreds of T-shirts with handwritten messages on them hung from the ceiling. The kids ordered nachos, then passed the time waiting for them by looking at the T-shirts to see if they recognized where any of them were from.

In preparation for the trip, I'd gotten Leif a couple of disposable cameras and Zoë two or three rolls of film for her camera. Back at the table, Zoë fretted that the airport x-ray machines might have ruined hers.

Lou listened to her, then said, "Zoë, can I give you some advice?" She nodded.

He smiled and said kindly, "There's big shit and little shit in life. And that is in the little shit category."

Zoë looked a bit miffed—not the empathetic response she expected from her good-natured uncle.

But watching Lou, I blinked back tears. Before leaving for this trip, my mother told me Lou's son from his first marriage had taken his own life just a few weeks earlier. Watching my own two kids tuck into their food when it was placed in front of them, I couldn't imagine Lou's pain. And yet here he was, in the midst of fresh grief, putting his personal feelings aside, smiling at his niece and nephew and generously welcoming all three of us into his world for a week. This was someone who knew only too painfully the difference between big shit and little shit. I'd been wondering if I should say something to Lou but could find no words. In the end I decided not to unless he brought it up himself during our time together.

Back on the highway, Lou and I passed the rest of the ride with idle, catching-up-on-the-family chatter, never veering to the dark side. Leif and Zoë listened quietly from the back, staring out the windows at the strange new world they were passing through.

We'd traveled more than halfway across the country by the time Lou slowed down and turned north onto Young Gal Road—a dirt and rock-strewn road that took us up through the hills and past a dozen more ramshackle houses, each with its own assortment of rusted cars, hammocks, cows, chickens, goats, and barking dogs.

Colorful wash hung neatly from a line on almost every porch. Now and then we caught a glimpse of a Belizean sitting quietly in the shade, an occasional dark arm raised in greeting as we jolted by, bouncing between the rocks and the ruts.

Eventually we turned onto a dirt lane that ran through a hundred-acre orange grove that had originally been part of Lou's property until he sold it the previous year "to the Chinese," he said. The orange trees gave way to groupings of tall palm trees, changing the scenery dramatically from clusters of little orange balls to dark green, frondy giants welcoming us into their cool shadows.

We had arrived at the farm.

As Lou's car lurched to a stop in front of his house in a clearing in the jungle, a skinny, brown-skinned waif of a girl in a colorful frock ran out to greet us, hopping up and down in excitement. This was Sylvia, one of two Belizean kids Lou had informally adopted and whose private school fees he was paying. In anticipation of our arrival, she had been busy with her machete; she greeted us with a big smile and two large bunches of green bananas, each half as tall as she was.

There was just enough time for a quick tour of the house and surrounding gardens before Sylvia threw off her dress and, wearing nothing but her knickers, took Zoë and Leif down through the jungle gardens to the river to wash off the heat and travel dust. There, she taught them how to catch tiny fish with their hands and collect them in an old plastic bucket. Lou's Belizean housekeeper Anna fried them all up later for a tasty meal.

By Belizean standards, Lou's house was quite large. My sister had designed a series of simple but spacious and airy rooms with high ceilings and suspended fans. A cool breezeway divided parts of the house. As I wandered through the rooms, I tried to picture my sister, who was more of a city dweller, living here.

A veranda, painted white, framed and supported by dark brown stained tree limbs, ran the entire length of the backside of the house. With its sheltering eaves, surrounded by enormous tropical plants overlooking the Belize River and the jungles beyond, this is where we would spend many peaceful and cool hours in the days to come—ending each with five o'clock rum and cokes for me and Lou.

Mornings also began on the veranda.

Our first morning, Anna served up biscuits with banana jam, tortillas, scrambled eggs with onions and tomatoes, refried beans, and juice. The kids were in jungle heaven.

After eating, Leif established himself on the porch swing while Zoë, her long blonde hair swept up against the heat in a knot on top of her head, perched in an old Adirondack chair next to Cheyne, Lou's snoozing dog. Both kids were under strict orders to spend an hour each day on the homework they'd promised to do in return for getting permission to take a holiday during the school year. Much as they tried to comply, they were easily distracted by the exotic new world all around them. I caught Leif with his book open, but his head turned down to the river where Sylvia and Lee, Lou's adopted son, had set out in a canoe. Sylvia turned and waved a skinny brown arm up at us, a tiny twig fluttering in the breeze.

After the homework hour, Lou decided to take us to the Belize Zoo, thinking the kids would like to see the animals and that I would appreciate learning how it came into being. The zoo would likely not exist had it not been for, of all things, a documentary film.

Twenty years before our visit, Sharon Matola, an experienced big cat trainer and wrangler, was hired to manage twenty animals for a wildlife documentary shot on location in Belize back in 1982.

Matola had received jungle survival training during her stint in the U.S. Air Force. She'd worked as an assistant lion tamer at the Circus Hall of Fame in Sarasota, before going on to study fish taxonomy in Belize. She left graduate school for a job as an exotic dancer in a traveling circus in Mexico, hoping to do biological field work as her day job. It was her work in Mexico—and likely the fieldwork, not the exotic dancing—that brought her to the attention of filmmaker Richard Foster, who hired her to care for the animals used in the making of his wildlife documentary film.

At the end of the shoot, the director and crew packed up and left, leaving Sharon with the animals. Concerned about rewilding them, Sharon decided instead to create a home for them. With few resources, she put together animal enclosures and put up a Belize Zoo sign by the side of the highway, hoping people would pay to see them.

Over time, Sharon learned of the myths and superstitions Belizeans harbored about the native animals now under her care. She also discovered that many Belizeans had never seen these animals in the wild before. She was especially moved by the experience of seeing an elderly man brought to tears while looking at the jaguars. "They are so beautiful," he said. He'd lived in Belize his whole life and it was the first time he'd seen his country's animals up close.

This and other experiences motivated Sharon to expand her makeshift little zoo into a living classroom and educational facility where both children and adults could learn about their natural heritage. From lion tamer to exotic dancer to zookeeper and animal advocate—Sharon had finally found her calling.

Over time, the Belize Zoo attracted international support. By the time of our visit, it had grown to include more spacious habitats for the animals; a visitor center; charming, black-and-white, hand-painted informative signs telling visitors about the animals; and a commissary for food preparation and veterinary care. In her spare time, Sharon created children's books, developed radio programs, and wrote newspaper columns. Eventually her outreach efforts included school visits for those unable to travel to the zoo itself.

"If we can reach the children," she said, "we've won half the battle."

Her nearly 40 years of work has had a long-lasting impact on the conservation field. It's fascinating to think all of this began with a single documentary and the animals left behind once the cameras were packed up.

But, of course, this was Central America. Not all the animals were in a zoo.

During our first night there, I was wrenched from sleep by the most surreal, skin-jarring screaming. I sat up in bed, scared out of my wits, trying to understand what was happening. I looked for the kids. Amazingly, they slept quietly, Zoë next to me and Leif in a makeshift bed next to Lee out in the great room.

I pulled on a robe and walked out onto the veranda. The screaming was coming from the jungle on the other side of the river. It sounded like a bloodbath was happening somewhere out there. I was happy there was at least a river separating us.

Gradually it calmed and I went back to bed, still mystified. In the morning, I mentioned it to Lou over breakfast. He burst out laughing.

"Those are howler monkeys you heard!" he exclaimed delightedly. "They don't always perform for visitors. I'm glad you got to experience them!"

I didn't quite share his enthusiasm but read up on them later and discovered they are vegetarians who hang out at the very top of the forest canopy. Although the turf-protecting sounds they produce can be heard for miles, they're actually quite small for monkeys. Their shrieks have been described variously as a "zombie apocalypse" and "a combination air raid siren and heavy metal guitar solo," in the words of a National Geographic writer. And of course, once one gets going, it provokes a call and response with others. Which makes it difficult—at least for me—to sleep through.

> *Belize, Day Two . . . We have no watches and for the first several days, we don't even look at clocks. We use nature to tell time. At night, we sleep like Belizeans, with all the windows open. The jungle starts waking up around 4 a.m. with lots of insect noises. Dawn comes an hour later, and with it the birds and their exotic calls to one another. It's hard to stay in bed much beyond 6 a.m., at least for me and Zoë. It takes us just five minutes to get dressed. Then we join Lou on the veranda for coffee, which is served very hot and sweet.*
>
> *"Just another day in paradise!" he announces joyfully each morning, surveying his domain happily.*
>
> *Breakfast is at 7 a.m. We wake Leif. Lee and Sylvia appear in their dark blue school uniforms. The farm workers have already stopped in to talk with Lou about the day's chores.*

Retired from a career as a computer specialist working U.S. government contracts, Lou now devoted himself to being a wholesale grower and distributor of ornamental plant seeds, specializing in palm and cycad seeds. His company, Teakettle Enterprises, shipped seeds to resorts, nurseries, and clients all over the world.

He was a member of the International Palm Society, an organization devoted to the study of palms, their culture, conservation, and natural history.

I had always thought a palm tree was a palm tree, and was surprised to find out palms are a vast plant family made up of around 2,500 tropical and subtropical species. During a tractor tour of his 300-acre farm, I asked Lou how many kinds of palm trees he had.

"Right now, I have about 123 species. But we don't sell them all. Some we just keep as pets," he said, laughing.

Selling palm tree seeds was not a hugely profitable business. But

Lou was living his dream and it's a wonderful thing to spend time in the company of someone doing that.

Each evening, we sat in the Adirondack chairs on the veranda, sipping our rum and cokes, watching the twilight silhouettes of the trees after the sun sets, Lou with his feet propped up on the veranda railings.

"Just another day in paradise," he said again, almost reverently, looking out over the jungle and the river, followed by a quiet remark on the beauty of this time and how quickly it passed.

As Lou was busy with the daily workings on his palm tree farm and wouldn't be able to be our tour guide around Belize, I asked if I could borrow one of his vehicles.

"Sure! You can take either one, it doesn't matter to me," he offered generously.

I surveyed my choices: 1) a very beat-up Toyota truck used to drive around the farm; or 2) a beat-up Mazda 4-door.

"I'm not a believer in preventative maintenance," he said, cheerfully stating the obvious.

Was it really okay for me to be driving my kids around Central America in unreliable cars? I wondered.

But there was no choice. I alternated between them during our days there. The Mazda had, for reasons that mystified Lou, trouble staying in gear. I found going forward was usually okay, but reverse had its own personality, mischievously playing hide and seek with me. Sometimes I found it in neutral, sometimes it was in park. And once or twice, I actually found it in reverse—something that never failed to take all of us by surprise.

The kids thought this was hilarious and offered suggestions from time to time, making bets on who could guess it correctly.

The Toyota truck had a tricky third gear; sometimes it was there, sometimes it wasn't.

"Why don't you skip it and go from second to fourth?" Leif suggested pragmatically one day when I was particularly frustrated with it. I tried that and it worked.

Quite by accident, I discovered third gear snugly slotted against first, and with a gentle two-finger maneuver, it slipped right in.

In this manner, we lurched around the country, adventure to adventure, only resorting to hitchhiking once when we crossed into Guatemala for the day to check out the markets on foot, leaving Lou's vehicle in a parking lot on the other side of the border.

"I've been looking for a used Volvo station wagon," Lou remarked one evening.

"I'll help you find one when I get back to the States," I replied.

Belize, Day Three . . . Leif is less comfortable here than Zoë and I are, something Lou clearly enjoys teasing him about. When Leif described the scrambling footsteps he'd heard on the wall of the great room where he slept, Lou told him it was probably just rat bats.

"They get in between the walls sometimes and you heard them trying to get back out," he said playfully, eyes twinkling. "Sometimes, a bat will get in the great room, get disoriented and get hit by the ceiling fan.

"But don't worry, Leif," he added. "You chose the right bed. When they get hit, they usually land on the bed Lee's sleeping in!"

Leif's unhappiness at hearing this was plain to see on his slightly sunburned, freckled twelve-year-old face.

"I wish I had a picture of that cockroach we found last week," Lou continued, spreading his two forefingers about six inches apart.

Out on the veranda, the geckos chortled to one another.

Our third day in Belize, Lou told us we were invited to visit Lee's private school where he was in fifth grade. It was a small campus of one-room white buildings, spotlessly clean and cheerful, and run by a principal from Scotland. Lou had promised to bring a case of cold Fantas to the classroom if we were permitted to sit in on a class, so everyone was very happy to see us.

Lou tried to introduce us to Lee's teacher, but stumbled over our relationship, not knowing how to describe me.

"What do you call the sister of the wife you are divorced from and who has died?" he said. The teacher smiled but offered no response.

"Well, anyway," Lou said cheerfully, placing a hand on each of Zoë's and Leif's shoulders. "I don't know what you call *her,* but I'm definitely *their uncle!*"

That he claimed my kids made all of us very happy.

After the introductions, the teacher asked the class to vote whether they would like to do a report on birds or reptiles. Reptiles won. Each child called out which one they would do. Two girls near us argued over who would get geckos. Lee chose a boa. One boy, who'd voted for the birds, approached the teacher's desk with a plea bargain; instead of a reptile, could he do *all* of the birds? Leif and Zoë looked at each other in astonishment. That would *never* happen in their schools, they said laughing. The teacher turned down the boy's offer and told him to choose just one bird.

Belize, Day Four . . . In the evenings, the kids play jacks together on the floor of the great room. Sylvia is the reigning queen of the game. At ten, she is also the youngest of the four kids. Sylvia speaks in her own special vernacular.

"I am winning she!" she announces proudly, pointing to Zoë, when I came across a match earlier. Zoë tells me Sylvia got up to 15s while she was still on 2s.

"Doan be watchin' on me!" she scowled at Lou one afternoon as she wielded a mean old machete that was at least half as tall as she is. We were sitting inside the thatched gazebo watching her as she squatted on the floor in front of a row of coconuts.

The machete pinged as she swacked it into the end of one of its intended victims.

"Don't you give me that snarly face, Sylvia," Lou laughed. "I don't want you to lose a finger!"

Still, we can't take our eyes off her, fascinated by this skinny little girl with the warm brown eyes and dimples and the constant energy she carries around with her that propels her impulsively from one idea to the next.

Whack. Whack. Whack. The machete flies as she cuts off the ends of the coconuts and dumps the white coconut milk into a bucket. Whack. Whack. Whack. Sylvia splits open pieces of the shell, all ten fingers intact, and carves out the coconut meat impatiently. Lee passes by and grabs a piece of coconut, then walks away.

"Did he ask if he could have that, Sylvia?" asks Lou.

"No-ah," she says with another scowl.

Zoë and Leif each try the scooping out but not the whacking. It doesn't hold their interest and soon they, too, drift off. Sylvia finishes off another eight coconuts by herself.

Whack! The machete comes a little too close to a drowsing Cheyne who startles, jumps up and starts running at the same instant. Lou has laughed a lot during our visit, but Cheyne's reaction keeps him laughing for almost ten minutes. Each time he plays it over in his mind, his shoulders begin to shake again.

The sun was so hot that each day was planned with a dip in the water—a swimming hole with large boulders to jump from, a river, or waterfalls—somewhere, anywhere. After watching Sylvia butcher the coconuts, Lou decided to take all of us out to Clarissa Falls. Sylvia got into the car with the precious coconut milk carefully poured into two empty Fanta bottles—one for her, one for her adored big brother, Lee.

I watched all four kids splashing deliriously in the short waterfalls for an hour before Lou gathered everyone up. We stopped for pizzas on the way home.

Belize, Day Five . . . It's our last breakfast together on the veranda. Zoë finishes first and asks to be excused. Sylvia, meanwhile, is still cutting off chunks from a messy piece of cheese.

"Excuse," she says, tapping me on the shoulder and pointing to Zoë's unused napkin. "May I please have the Zoë paper?"

At the time of our trip, Zoë was fifteen and already thinking she would study marine biology at university, leading to a career saving the manatees. That gave Lou an idea. He made a phone call to a friend of his, whose name also happened to be Karen—a good sign. Karen was the manager of Manatee Lodge, located at the tip of the peninsula just past Gales Point Manatee Village. Lou told us it was popular with marine biologists and researchers. Seeing Zoë's interest, he booked us a room. From there, he said, we would be able to take a boat ride out to see the manatees.

It was a perfect idea. Lou dropped us off. After tearful farewells (mine), we dropped our things in the large room we would share before setting off to explore our surroundings. A two-and-a-half mile stretch of land that reaches out into the middle of the Southern Lagoon, Gales Point serves as a protected area for the endangered West Indian Manatee and is also home to an abundance of birds, plants, and animals.

It was a good thing we explored on our first evening. Whatever nasty little creatures we'd ingested over the previous days staged a midnight attack on our bodies. The following morning, all three of us came down with wretched intestinal troubles. None of us felt comfortable being more than a few feet away from a bathroom.

Were they in the ice cubes in our drinks? Or did they latch onto us as we splashed in the river beaches before we knew about the many potty shacks at the end of the piers behind houses, each of which deposited their contents directly into the Belize river.

Whatever it was, the damage had been done, leaving us to waste our last precious last full day in Belize—the day I'd promised Zoë we'd take a boat tour to see manatees. In the afternoon, we tried a short boat ride, but even that was too much.

Although Manatee Lodge offered Creole and Continental cuisine, Karen kindly made us simple grilled cheese sandwiches and toast with a side of saltines, which was all we could manage.

Belize, Day Seven . . . The kids are being good sports about it all. Leif and I sprawl in hammocks strung up on the breezy veranda of the Manatee Lodge. He dozes with a cold cloth on his fevered face, his journal and a bottle of water next to him. With water and palm trees on three sides, we are our own peninsula.

I write in my own journal, waiting for my stomach to find normal. Zoë prefers the peace of our empty room inside and being closer to the bathroom. She, too, tries to doze away her nausea.

Curled up in his colorful sling and suddenly awake, Leif hums and fusses with the cold cloth I'd put on his forehead. "I don't have a tan anymore," he announces sadly, surveying his outstretched arms from the depths of his hammock.

Moments later, he is laughing at the whistles and shrills the bow-tailed grackles make.

After 24 miserable hours, we rallied for our last evening in Belize. Karen walked us down the road from the Lodge and into the tiny little village that is home to the Garifuna—a people of mixed indigenous Caribbean and African heritage. Many of them are likely descendants of the slaves from Nigeria that two ships were carrying to the American colonies when the ships were wrecked off St. Vincent. The survivors took refuge on this peninsula and created their own unique culture.

Karen introduced us to Ray McDonald, a drummer and former dancer and singer for the Belize National Dance Company and owner of the Warasa Drum School. We walked single file up the long rickety stairs to a house precariously balanced on silts to find it filled with dozens and dozens of drums, most of which he'd made himself. He treated us to a small private concert after which we made our way slowly back down the lane, through the palm trees to Manatee Lodge.

Belize, Day Eight, our last morning . . . I wake after a peaceful night during which no one got sick. I love the sunrise at 5:30 and the easiness of living here. There are a few clouds on the horizon as I sit on the veranda to dry my hair in the soft trade winds which never seem to stop lofting gently around us. Breakfast is at 7, after which the water taxi will arrive to take us up to Belize City and the airport.

I am not ready to let go of this peacefulness, but it's time to go. . . .

Looking back now, the memories and images come spilling out of me. As I'd hoped, our time in Belize was filled with adventures and life lessons for Zoë and Leif—places and people none of us could have dreamed up in advance. From swimming with iguanas and nighttime canoe paddles on the river, to jumping into waterholes and splashing in waterfalls. From trying to get around in Lou's beat-up old vehicles, to trying to drive a four-wheeler on the farm, to hitchhiking in Guatemala and exploring the Mayan ruins at Xunantunich. From eating local food and what grew on the trees on Lou's farm or was caught in the Belize River, to memorable shrimp dinners at a nearby Sri Lankan restaurant, the whole scene in Belize was beyond any of our imaginings. It was just the kind of adventure to open their minds. And mine.

And the stories Lou told me about Karen that I'd never heard before, all of which were accompanied by his good-natured laugh. How, after he had his wonderful tiki hut built in the garden, the one where Sylvia had chopped coconuts, my sister discovered a snake in the thatch. After that, she refused to go back inside the structure he'd put so much work into. Scared of scorpions, she'd woken him up countless nights while the house was still under construction and made him hold the flashlight so she could pee in the garden in the dark. She'd been a good sport about everything, he told me, until one day it was suddenly too much, and she decided to move back to Florida. Everything he said told me how he still loved her.

Back home, I got our film developed. As we looked through the photos we'd taken, Zoë and I were already planning our next trip back. Not so, Leif.

"Please, Mom," he sighed as I tucked him into bed our first night back. "No more third-world holidays!"

The last photo from my camera roll is one Zoë took of me during our last hours in Central America, aboard the Mexican skiff taking us up the coast from Belmopan to the Belize airport.

In the photograph, my short-cropped blonde hair is blown back in the wind. I'm wearing a long blue and green print cotton dress with the beads I bought from a small vendor at Xunantunich strung around my neck. My left hand is gripping the side of the boat. It is May 5th, my birthday, and there is a fiercely huge grin on my slightly sunburned face.

A lot of parents take their kids to Disney World. I had taken mine to Belize. I had taken them on an unusual and, at times, not very easy international adventure. We'd all survived. And hopefully, I'd put something inside them they would never forget.

Mission accomplished.

Sidenote: In the wake of our visit, change was already coming to the scruffy little Belize City. And it was coming in the form of—of all things—a film festival.

The Belize International Film Festival was launched in Belize City in 2003, the year after we were there, with a focus on films made in Central America and the Caribbean, in addition to a selection of films from around the world. The festival now focuses on relevant contemporary issues, such as poverty, abuse, and poaching, with a special category for the Best Environmental Film.

Sharon Matola would have liked that.

BILL MOYERS AND THE MYSTICAL MONK OF CAPITOL HILL

ONE MORNING, I heard a knock on my front door. I got up from my desk and opened it, never suspecting that perhaps I shouldn't. We lived in a neighborhood where that kind of thing wasn't something I worried about.

There, on my front doorstep, stood a large man in dark clothes, perhaps in his fifties, a glowering expression on his beefy face. He looked like a bouncer from a dodgy bar. What he was doing on my front steps, I couldn't fathom. I guessed he had the wrong address.

"Are you Kristin Fellows?" he asked. I confirmed I was.

He then pulled out a billfold and held it up for me to see his identification. I stared at it in disbelief.

Some effing collection agency had sent a thug to harass me in person at my home?!

It turned out to be for a debt that was on Steve's side of the financial responsibilities we'd divided up post-divorce. Like a carelessly tossed match on dried kindling, this man's presence on my doorstep ignited the pile of injustices and outrages always hovering on the periphery of my darkest thoughts. As if someone flipped a switch, I instantly ascended into whirling dervish mode.

"SERIOUSLY?!" I exclaimed, in all caps. "What kind of a *bully* are you to come and harass a single mom with kids *at her home?!* How DARE you! You should be ashamed of yourself!"

Although Steve and I had been separated and divorced for a handful of years, the IRS and the occasional debt collector still hounded us. Talk about low-hanging fruit—between the two of us, we earned so little we barely had to pay taxes. Yet hound us they did.

Apparently, the goon felt the heat. Taken aback by my unanticipated ferocity, he stammered a few words I no longer remember and beat a quick retreat to his car. Shaking, and shocked I'd scared him off, I had a feeling this wouldn't be the end of it.

Strangely, it would be an obscure clause in the North American Free Trade Agreement, otherwise known as NAFTA, that would provide—after a few unexpected plot twists—the key to my release, at least from the grips of the IRS.

Of course, I had no way of knowing at the time that another story frame was sliding into place.

Trading Democracy, a wonky, legislative television project, turned out to be one of the most important programs I worked on, not only for its geopolitical content, but for whom it introduced me to. Yes, it was intellectually pleasing to work on a Bill Moyers special, but it was heart expanding to meet a man—via that project—described to me as "the mystical monk of Capitol Hill."

It had been two years since my departure from Martin's workshop. And while the security of an actual *job* had yet to materialize, a different path was unfolding before me. At first the roadmap felt somewhat blurry and indecipherable. But as I leaned into it, making my way along, various directions seemed to gradually come into focus. In my imagination, it looked like a whole network of paths and offshoots branching out from that Baryshnikov phone call I'd made ten years ago, like branches from the trunk of a tree that just kept budding, then dividing, then forking, each in its own beautiful and unique way, each one a pathway to the sky.

This latest freelance gig would have me working on behalf of veteran journalist and political commentator, Bill Moyers. Moyers had been the White House Press Secretary during the Johnson administration, followed by a long stint as the director of the Council on Foreign Relations. From there he segued into television; his programs on PBS had been a mainstay for years.

His latest PBS special was *Trading Democracy*—an examination of NAFTA and the smoke and mirrors inherent in the agreement.

Although there had been a lot of hype about how it provided jobs for Americans, according to Moyers there was one obscure section of NAFTA—Chapter 11—that the public was not aware of. *Trading Democracy* revealed how foreign corporations were using it to challenge democracy, attacking public laws that protected our health, environment, and even the American judicial system. Moyers revealed how NAFTA's Chapter 11 provided what amounted to an "end run around the Constitution."

Having heard about my work on *The Face: Jesus in Art* through WNET and the Fred Friendly Seminars team at Columbia University's J School, I was hired by Kelly & Salerno—a two-woman, high-energy publicity team—to figure out how to get a viewing audience for *Trading Democracy.*

How to get viewers to tune in to a program about NAFTA's Chapter 11?!

This did not sound like a must-see, let's-stay-home-tonight-and-watch-this-instead-of-going-out kind of program to me.

Nevertheless, I of course took the project on because: 1) it gave me the opportunity to work with Bill Moyers; and 2) the IRS and other debt collectors were literally on my doorstep, hounding me for money.

Once again, I was Mikey. I most likely got the gig because nobody else wanted to do it. I had no idea what I was getting myself into, much less how to pull it off.

Back in 2002, social media didn't exist. The Internet was still in a very nascent stage. Entities had basic websites, but it wasn't much of a communications tool. That left phone calls and emails.

Guided by Kelly & Salerno, I designed an email tree. I researched and identified the kind of organizations that would most likely be impacted by this hidden clause in NAFTA. From environmental groups to labor interests, we came up with a list of more than 100 organizations. Then I got to work contacting their communications directors, one by one, introducing them to the Moyers special and asking if they would share our press release on *Trading Democracy* with their members and email lists.

At the suggestion of one of my contacts, we hosted a pre-broadcast screening and pizza party at his apartment in Washington, DC, for dozens of these communications specialists. It was a success. At the end of the screening Colby Kelly and I did a Q&A. One person asked if he could get 535 copies—one for each member of the House of Representatives and the Senate. It was the exact reaction we'd been hoping for.

I created a spreadsheet to track each organization's efforts, trying to keep tabs on the reach of this word-of-mouth-via-email campaign as best I could.

I worked on this for weeks until one day when I got a phone call from the director of communications for Friends of the Earth, a Washington, DC-based federation of grassroots groups in seventy-six countries.

"I think you can stop now, Kristin!" he said laughing. "I just got a copy of my own email this morning. When I look at the chain of forwards, I can see it went from me through 18 other organizations around the world, one by one, until someone forwarded it on to me, not realizing I had initiated the message in the first place!"

It's weird to think back at how labor-intensive our get-the-word-out campaigns were back then. We didn't know it at the time, but efforts like these were laying the groundwork for what would soon blossom into social media.

In the course of cold-calling numerous environmental agencies, telling them about the documentary and asking if they would spread the word with their mailing lists, I had reached out to a woman affiliated with a labor organization headquartered in Gaithersburg, Maryland. She listened carefully to what I had to say, then gave me some life-changing advice.

"If you haven't already," she said, "you need to reach out to a guy named Anden."

"Who's that?" I asked.

"He's the mystical monk of Capitol Hill," she said with a laugh. "He knows *everybody* and therefore you need to know *him*. I'll introduce you."

COFFEE AND CONFESSION

OVER THE YEARS, I have kept nearly every letter I've ever received, along with copies of emails, and far too many photographs. I cling to things likely meant to exist or be enjoyed for only a short period of time. My rationale has always been that, as the youngest, I'm the family archivist. And also, like my father and grandmother, the one in my generation inclined to storytelling.

I know I've kept too much. *Why have I been hanging on to the past when there's the whole future to look forward to?* Part of me thought I might use them someday to tell stories. And that's exactly what has happened. Pulling together the stories for this book has given me the opportunity, however, to make choices and cull some of that ephemera—a process that makes me feel like a little kid with a flashlight wandering through the dark recesses of a huge library alone at night.

In the process, a lot has been tossed. I even burned a few. And each time I put something into the shredder or recycling bin or fire, I felt myself getting lighter and happier. But, hidden in these piled up boxes, binders, and folders, there have also been some keepers, waiting like buried treasure to be redis-covered and appreciated all over again.

Anything that makes me smile, I keep—including some from a mystical monk I have nicknamed "Anden." Once again, had it not been for a documentary film, I would never have met him.

Anden grew up with his heart set on entering a cloistered order of monks. Partway through the process, however, he had an epiphany that took his life in a diametrically opposite direction. Anden left his cloistered order for law school, having decided he could be more helpful to people by representing their welfare against corporate interests. In time he became a skilled government relations professional with a broad knowledge of international legislative strategy. Anden's transformation from monk to the madness of Capitol Hill made him quite special. Who else has a backstory like that?

I reached out to contact him about the Bill Moyers' *Trading Democracy* special, and we arranged to meet for coffee at what was then a brand-new Starbucks on Capitol Hill so I could give him a copy of the program. The location was Anden's suggestion. He liked it because it had a room upstairs, filled with writers and slow coffee drinkers, a space where we could talk quietly for an hour or two, bothered by no one.

He loved the opportunity for conversation, as did I. And so we tried to get together once a week to talk over coffee. Our conversations were deep and soul-filling, covering a wide range of topics. Gradually the barriers came down and we confided all manner of things to one another—from each other's laugh-out-loud funny first dates to matters of faith and world affairs.

Of course, there were times when work kept him from getting together. When that happened, Anden let me know via playful and irresistible emails.

One of them told the story of how the Supreme Court had just delivered "a stunning opinion" stating that "any deprivation of Kristin Fellows' sought-after company" was "contrary to due process considerations" and that the absence of Ms. Fellows for "a weekly coffee klatch with any gentlemen who are former monks" working in international trade will forever be "deemed unconstitutional."

Another was more poetic. Anden wrote that although he was unable to get together at our appointed weekly time, he hoped the following week he would get a chance to hear my thoughts on "life, love, death, and the changing of the seasons."

"You have a truly impressive mind," he continued. "It is a joy to listen to you…. I wonder whether my withdrawal symptoms from our Friday talks can be alleviated by a much-needed Kristin fix."

Now you can see why I have hung onto his emails for more than two decades!

These conversations over coffee were a lifeline during some tough times. Even though he was no longer a monk, Anden became a sort of father confessor to me, giving me perspective on issues when I felt I needed spiritual guidance. Like a stranger in a foreign land who clings to someone able to speak their native language, I clung to the emotional lift our meetings and written exchanges gave me.

Eventually, I told Anden about the IRS situation and the stress it had caused me—not expecting him to be able to do anything about it, but just to get it off my chest. He listened thoughtfully before replying. And when he spoke, what he said surprised me.

"I have a friend," he said, looking at me kindly. He took out a small piece of paper and wrote down a name and phone number on it. It was a lawyer he knew in New York City, he said, who had a lot of experience working with the IRS, having once worked there herself.

I looked at the note in dismay.

"But I can't afford a lawyer," I said, sadly.

"Don't worry," he said. "She's a close friend of mine. She will understand and I know she will want to help a special friend of mine, regardless of what you are able to pay her."

Not really believing him, I thanked him and put the note in my pocket. We went back to discussing religion and politics and world issues. It would take another three years, but Anden was right—it did happen, just as he'd promised.

The Heartbreak of Losing the Muses— and a Danish Cure

IN THE WAKE of Karen's death, my mother decided to leave Florida. She packed up and moved to Alexandria to be closer to us and away from the memories. This was nice for the kids. And having her nearby meant she and I often went out to art museums or the movies together, after which we'd enjoy a nice glass of wine and a meal and conversation at a small, cozy restaurant.

We took turns choosing the films we'd see. She could be relied upon to pick anything by Woody Allen or starring Jeremy Irons, like *Stealing Beauty*. The only one I can remember choosing was *Love Actually*, which I loved but she didn't see the point of—*at all*.

Despite differences in taste, it was nice to have this interest in common. Even though I worked in documentary film, and not feature films, I felt like I was sharing a little bit of my world with her. I looked forward to these evenings—until that one night when I may have silently cried in the darkness throughout an entire film, even though it wasn't a sad one.

Earlier that afternoon, I'd arrived at my mother's flat in Old Town to pick her up as usual. When she opened the door, she didn't look happy to see me.

"Oh, just a minute, honey," she said, hesitantly, before turning her back on me. It wasn't the cheerful greeting I usually got from her.

She went into the kitchen, then returned a moment later holding a newspaper clipping in her hand. Wondering what news could possibly upstage a cheery hello, I scanned the torn fragment she handed me.

As I read it, I think my heart stopped beating.

It was a *New York Times* review of the book I had been working on for several years—a *New York Times* book review of *my* book about the muses!

"Smart, sympathetic, and keenly observed," the reviewer wrote. This was the review of my book I had long dreamed about!

But wait a minute . . .

Someone else's name was mentioned as the author—not mine. Also, I hadn't actually finished writing the book yet.

The non-fiction book about muses I'd been working on was, I thought, a unique take on a rather obscure topic. To write it, I'd put my degree in psychology to good use and woven together my passion for the creative process, my own career experiences, and a fuck-ton of research.

Glancing over the *New York Times* review, the themes and characters felt uncannily familiar to me. They included a number of the same characters I'd had in my original proposal. I didn't know the facts, of course, and I didn't know what happened in that publishing house. It may all have been just a crazy coincidence, but its resemblance to my own book concept and proposal hit me hard, especially having worked on it for so long. I felt crushed, devastated, and breathless.

After losing my literary agent two years earlier, I'd been preoccupied just trying to earn a living. Anything else seemed like a luxury.

But I still had all my research and writing. I'd always planned to get back to it just as soon as I was financially stable.

Over the following days, I received phone calls and emails from friends around the country who'd seen the review—all of whom were well aware of what I'd been working on and who were now wondering—hey, isn't that *your* book?!

My dream of being a published author was shattered. This was far more devastating to me than any romantic breakup. This was not the cleaving of myself from another individual, this was the searing pain of being torn asunder from my own identity, ideas, and creativity.

In the weeks that followed, I took long, solitary walks with the dogs along the river, trying to reconstruct what could possibly have happened, trying to staunch the flow of tears, trying to start breathing normally again.

I berated myself for being too thin-skinned and not continuing to work on the book I believed in, despite the critiques I'd received. *The Muse Factor* was *my* concept, inspired by my own life. So, why hadn't I kept writing it, regardless? That was the question I needed to face head on and answer.

As time receded and the stinging heartbreak began to ease ever so slightly, another thought occurred to me: My idea *had* been good enough to land a literary agent, and apparently a publisher! Just not with my name on it. Okay, here was a painful lesson learned: *Never give up on my ideas.*

The Danes have an expression, "to stand up where you fell down." This refers to the ritual of taking a shot of *Gammel Dansk*—or bitters—the morning after they've drunk too much the night before.

Being a half Dane, I gradually came to the realization that the only way to deal with a loss of this magnitude *was*, in fact, to stand up where I had been knocked down. I needed to begin writing another book.

Fortunately, a new idea for one would soon fall into my hands. Literally.

INTRODUCTION TO THE THIRD DIMENSION

DURING THOSE YEARS, whenever I was feeling especially low or depressed, I sometimes wandered through one of several former munitions buildings on the banks of the Potomac River in Alexandria.

That's right, I found comfort in century-old munitions buildings. Why? Because in a stroke of genius twenty years earlier, one of them—the Torpedo Factory—had been turned into a hive of artist studios.

Once upon a time, the complex had 5,000 employees and was responsible for the manufacture and maintenance of Mark III torpedoes. After World War II, it was converted to the Federal Records Center and became a repository for congressional documents, German war films, Nuremberg War Crimes trial records and, weirdly, dinosaur bones.

In 1969, the City of Alexandria purchased some of the old buildings from the federal government for $1.6 million, giving them five years to empty out all their stuff, including the dinosaur bones, from the buildings. A few years later, the editor of the *Alexandria Journal* suggested to the city's Art League that they consider the old torpedo plant for their headquarters. Funding was approved, fire hoses were used to power wash the building's interior, and forty dump trucks of the remaining debris were removed.

At the time of its opening on May 21, 1983, there were 225 artists with working studios in the former Torpedo Factory.

Just being in the atmosphere of artists, paint fumes, studios, and all that rampant creativity was like a drug—providing that addictive little buzz of happiness—and strangely therapeutic at a time when I needed it most.

Whenever I wandered through the studios, I picked up the Art League's seasonal publication about their studio classes. Karen had left some money to the kids with the instructions to use it for education and travel. Zoë's portion sent her to Denmark for half a year during high school, and I used part of Leif's portion to pay for him to attend Art League classes in stop motion photography, video animation, cartooning, and theater.

Throughout my entire life, I have gravitated to the company of artists. Lacking my sister's unflinching self-confidence, however, I'd always chosen to remain on the periphery—near artists but watching from the edges, a shy outsider.

That didn't mean I didn't have anything to express in a creative form, but I wasn't sure which medium to use to make something tangible out of the emotions swirling within me. I wanted to *release* much of what I'd internalized over the past years: disappointments, divorce, and death. Broke and brokenness. Documentary film helped, but in addition to storytelling, I also wanted something more tangible, something I'd made and could hold in my hands. And I wanted to tell my *own* stories.

It was while filming in Italy that I realized that I wanted to carve. And I wanted to carve *marble*.

So, when I noticed a class in the Art League's fall catalogue called "Introduction to the Third Dimension," I decided to treat myself to some art therapy and signed up for a nine-week evening art class.

Taught by Mike Abrams, a graduate of the Corcoran College of Art & Design and teacher of sculptural media, it felt like a fit. Plus, I loved the name.

Pietà

A disparate group of us—male and female, of various ages and abilities, gathered on the sidewalk outside an old, converted building on a quiet side street in Old Town. There were mumbled introductions as we eyed one another, our new kindred spirits. Moments later, a tall thin man with dark eyes and dark hair, perhaps a handful of years younger than me, opened the door from inside, then beckoned us into a brightly lit, cavernous collection of large rooms. I walked in last, following the others, walking over paint splattered cement floors, staring around at spaces open to the rafters filled with makeshift shelving and pallet racks, welding equipment, bins of stone, easels and shelves of half-finished pieces of art. It smelled of impermanence, creativity, and potential. That's a wonderful smell and I immediately felt at home.

Anxious to work in stone, I was a bit disappointed when Mike told us our first piece would be clay modeling. In retrospect, it made sense, but not to someone anxious to learn how to whale away on a block of marble to release the stories within it.

But Mike knew what he was doing and, more importantly, what he was asking of us. I picked up a large lump of clay and brought it over to the rough wooden bench I'd chosen to work at. Once settled, I began working it like bread dough, thinking and thinking, and waiting for inspiration. With memories of my sister ever present, I wondered if I could create something that would be a tangible manifestation of how I felt about her loss.

Just as my hands and fingers were beginning to ache, it came to me. Still under the spell of what I had seen and experienced in Italy, I decided I would try to create a very raw and very rough version of Michelangelo's *Pietà*. Instead of Mary, however, it would be *me*. And instead of Jesus, I would be supporting the lifeless body of my sister draped across my lap. I wanted to try to express my grief—not just a portrait of her, but one of me *holding* her, holding what remained of her physical presence.

Keenly aware I was no Michelangelo, I was free to make it my own. Instead of a head quietly bowed like Mary's, the clay head of the figure representing me would hang back, as if wailing in inconsolable disbelief and grief at the enormity of the loss I was holding in my arms. There would be no fabric covering my head, just my hair flowing back over my shoulders. And no draped clothing, just rough, figurative representations of two female bodies.

I worked on it for the first few classes and as I pinched and shaped the orange clay, I began to feel a little lighter, a little brighter and happier. Gradually, a little sculpture emerged from my fingers, its message clear despite its roughness. I gazed at it in amazement, astonished I'd been able to mold a physical representation of my emotions; a little clay repository for grief—slight on talent but filled with intense emotions.

Rock Opera

For our second project, we were now permitted and encouraged to work with stone.

At last, marble!

Mike directed our attention to an old wooden crate holding scraps and rejects. I picked up a pale gray block—8" x 6" x 4". It had some hashes and grooves in it from where someone had started working with it. But as it had been discarded, it was free to use. Having spent what available money I had on the classes, that worked for me.

I stared at it, once again wondering what to make from it. Pondering Franco Cervietti's words at his marble carving studio in Pietrasanta, how he carved to release the story inside the stone, I sorted through the chisels I'd selected, spreading them out on the rough wooden surface of my carving stand. Tentatively I began to chip away, lacking any confidence in my hands.

I chiseled and shaped some of the grooves already in the stone into a partially visible man—just his muscular arm and a glimpse of his leg. As I worked, a rough but recognizable figure of a woman gradually took shape next to him, and I knew she was a younger version of me.

Over the coming weeks, what began to emerge took me by surprise. With Mike's guidance and encouragement, it became the story of my marriage—the beginning, the end, and the middle. The good parts and the painful parts. From each side of the block, a different stage of our relationship revealed itself from the inner recesses of the stone, like acts and scenes in an opera. The long haired, young girl kneels, her clasped hands cupping her smiling face, gazing raptly up at the man's muscular torso. The suggestion of a man. The thought or memory of a husband.

On the backside of the stone, an unclothed, somewhat older woman sits, leaning back, her knees slightly raised, her long hair flowing away from her, one arm stretched back around to another side of the block, reaching for the foot of a curled-up infant partially covered by the mother's hair, which hangs down, covering half of her face.

Mike thought I should reveal the mother's full face. But to me it symbolized that she was now hiding part of herself from the man who, on this side of the block, is shown in multiple postures. In one, he leans over to cradle her passionately and protectively, while another version of him raises an arm in the air. A third man, barely visible between the other two, represents his as yet unfulfilled potential.

On the last side, there is a strong woman rising up from the rock beneath her feet, one arm pushing away from what is behind her, the other arm raised in calm freedom, as if announcing: *This is me, independent and standing strong on my own!*

I called it my *Rock Opera*.

A Shattered Heart

Earlier that fall, I had entered into a new romance with someone I knew through work. But it wasn't going well and as I walked into the final class, my head was in a pretty unhappy place. Having finished the *Rock Opera*, I rummaged around in the freebies crate for another piece of stone to work with. I came across a lovely soft pink piece I thought might be perfect for what I had in mind to create that night: a hand holding a heart—*my* hand holding *my* heart, as if to protect it.

"You'll have to be very careful with that, Kristin," Mike cautioned me when he saw what I had selected. "It's alabaster. One wrong hit and it will shatter."

That's appropriate, I thought. I nodded that I understood and walked over to my work bench without speaking to anyone. Normally gregarious in class, I was quiet that night. I'm sure my studio mates and even Mike could feel the dark mood I was in. I put on a pair of headphones to further distance myself from any potential conversation or pleasantries. Frowning in concentration, I got down to work.

The fingers of the hand emerged fairly quickly for someone of my limited skill level, and I was pleased. Not looking for realism, I shaped them figuratively enough and after a few hours, stood back to regard my progress. Mike glanced over at me periodically, noting what I was doing but keeping a safe distance. The others cheerfully went about their own projects, ignoring me, giving me the space I so obviously needed.

Gradually, a small heart emerged from within the grasp of the fingers. I was astonished and delighted that I had managed to tease out a representation of my thoughts and feelings from this fragile little piece of soft pink alabaster. *It's perfect*, I thought, smiling for the first time that night. *Just one more tap and I'll be finished.*

I positioned the detailing chisel and raised my hammer, aiming it with care before bringing it down on the metal end of the chisel. Instantly, the alabaster shattered in my hands.

The piece I was most proud of now lay in crisp pink shards across my wooden work bench. Pulling off my headphones, I stared at it in shock.

A hush fell over the large studio. Chisels and drills stopped in midair; collective breath was held. Everyone knew the sound of stone breaking when it wasn't supposed to. I felt rather than saw everyone turn to look at me in empathetic horror, knowing what had happened, not knowing what to say, and expecting perhaps a storm of tears and frustration from me.

Instead, as I looked at the pretty pink fragments of stone, I began to laugh. How appropriate it all was, this representation of my shattered heart. I saw the irony and felt a physical release from the swirl of negative emotions that I don't think I could have gotten any other way. I looked around at everyone and smiled.

"It's okay," I said. "It's all okay."

The buzz of chattering and hammering gradually resumed as I walked over to get a brush and pan to clean up the mess.

Much as I would have loved to have had that little sculpture, the accidental shattering of it actually made more sense to me. I floated out of the studio and into the dark winter night on an unexpected high.

My "introduction to the third dimension" was over, but it had worked its magic.

THE OLD SOLDIER COMES HOME

Morning journal, January 2004—At 48 years old, this is the mantra that runs through my head, this is what keeps me going: My health is good (so far.) I still have time to change careers when the kids are a little older, maybe when I'm in my fifties . . . My mother is looking good at 82, most people think she is only 70. I hope I have her genes. I think I've found a good home for Dad. I hope he doesn't topple over before I get him accepted there. I have a lot of small complaints: my house needs work and I should probably spend more time on how I look. But the bills are paid, there's food in the fridge and cupboards (maybe too much.) The house is clean (for the most part.)

Sometimes I dream that people think I'm older than I am. I don't like the term "middle-aged." Instead, I tell people I'm in my "middle ages"—I think that sounds more dynamic, as if there's still room for changes and flexibility and optimism.

SUDDENLY, THERE WAS my father to take care of. Now in his early eighties, his heart was beginning to falter.

A hard-charging, ideas-oriented,

problem-solving, adventure-loving workaholic, he'd been through open-heart surgery twice for a total of seven bypasses—a number he was weirdly competitive about—brought on by two massive heart attacks during the years he'd lived and worked in southern California.

He moved east after the second one, settling close to Philadelphia in a strategically optimal location. Nearby was his easygoing younger brother, Frank, with his charming and cheerful Ethiopian wife, Stella, and their grown daughters and grandchildren. His brother Larry, the retired *New York Times* foreign correspondent, lived three hours to the north with his German wife, Ruth. And the kids and I lived three hours to the south.

Together we rotated our visits to his townhouse, celebrating everything possible. Dad was always a convivial and happy host. Nothing was ever a problem. He delighted in each visitor and never minded how late the parties ran—and they tended to run well into the night when any of our Ethiopian family was involved.

By 2003, however, my father's health began to deteriorate. My long-distance visits increased to once, then twice a month—three- to five-hour long drives up and down I-95 in the midst of what too often seemed to be a dense and slow-moving scrum of traffic.

And then one day I got a call from my Ethiopian cousin, Gladys. She lived nearby and was the one who helped Dad the most.

"Kristin, your dad's in the hospital *again*," she said. "With the condition he's in, it's become too difficult for him to live by himself in his three-story townhouse."

She filled me in on the details of the latest incident.

"I think you need to find somewhere else for him to live," she said finally, with nothing but care and concern in her voice.

I sighed and started packing my overnight bag yet again. I'd only been home for six days. Fortunately, the kids were now thirteen and sixteen—old enough to manage by themselves, especially with their dad living nearby.

On my way out the door, I remembered a film I'd seen recently in DC at the Goethe Institute. It was called *The Price of Freedom: The Untold Story of America's WWII Prisoners of War.* The documentary featured a group of veterans who discovered one other in the later years of their lives. They met weekly to talk and help one another deal with their painful memories of being taken as prisoners of war in Germany. Directed by award-winning National Geographic filmmaker Bruce Norfleet, it was a semi-finalist in the Short Documentary category at the 2002 Academy Awards.

After the screening, I'd reached out to Bruce to ask if he might be interested in having me promote his film to PBS stations around the country. I knew it would do well with a public television audience. He sent me a DVD and we agreed to a small outreach plan.

Dad had not been a POW himself, but he'd served in the Army during WWII. He once told me he was classified as D6—a soldier who arrived at Normandy on the sixth day of the invasion, he explained. Thinking he might be interested in seeing the film, I grabbed the DVD from my desk and tossed it in my backpack. I always liked to bring him little surprises and I also wanted to hear more about his own experiences in France and Germany during the war. Perhaps watching the film together would trigger some stories I hadn't yet heard.

Despite everything going on in my life, I was in good spirits driving up to Philadelphia until I reached the hospital. Inside, it was a maze of confusion. When I finally located Dad, his appearance startled me. My sense of humor, inherited from my father and always my surest and most ready companion, fled the scene the moment I saw him, leaving me alone and unprepared.

It had only been a week, but now Dad's skin seemed to hang off his arms, his face was haggard, and his legs had mysteriously ballooned. Dark red and purple blotches covered his hands and forearms, reminding me of one of the kids' preschool paintings.

"Your software is great, Dad, but your hardware's letting you down," I finally said softly, uncertain of what to do or say and hoping the analogy might soften the news.

My father was not just an old soldier—he'd also been a pioneer in the world of computers. After serving in the Army during World War II, Dad got a job working on the ticket counter for Eastern Airlines at Washington, DC's National Airport. Always an ideas kind of guy, from that simple beginning, he rose to general manager for data processing. And after that, he was promoted to Eastern's VP of customer service where, in the early 1960s, he set up the first real-time computerized reservations center for the airline industry. The daily shuttle service between Washington, DC, and New York City was his idea, as well as the concept of curbside check-in. He loved having ideas and solving problems and was in his element when doing a combination of both. I've inherited that from him, too.

In 1964, Dad changed jobs again, becoming the London-based project manager for Univac's largest overseas client, British European Airways, or BEA. I was just eight when we moved to England.

Dad knew about the power of computers from his awareness of how NASA used them to process the information that kept guided missiles on course.

"How many little bits of information do you suppose are floating around this company?" he once mused to a reporter. "Millions? And how many managers need bits of the same information at the same time?"

Once the NASA information was declassified, he began applying it to the airline industry. From there, his career in the nascent field of computers took him from one interesting job to the next, from London to New York, then back to London, Chicago, and eventually California.

He retired in the mid-1990s and moved to Philadelphia to be near his family.

After the hospital released him, I took Dad grocery shopping, then back home to his townhouse. Over dinner, my resolve strengthened by a glass of red wine, I gingerly broached the conversation about moving to some type of retirement home—a conversation I'd been dreading, fraught as it could be with hurt feelings, depression, restrictions, and loss of independence, especially for someone like my father.

To my surprise, Dad was fine about discussing it. He even seemed to welcome it. But his end of the conversation consisted mostly of telling me where he *didn't* want to go. At least it was a start, I thought, and left it at that.

We turned our attention to dessert. He was delighted with the homemade pumpkin pie I'd brought from my mother and launched into a story of how he'd managed to keep two pies to himself on a crowded troop train during WWII by giving away all his sandwiches to the guys around him.

Although his appetite had been skimpy, he ate two pieces that night. Remembering the DVD, I retrieved it from my backpack, told him what it was about and asked if he'd like to see it.

"Sure!" he said, settling back in his rocking chair, a glass of wine by his side, always amenable to my film and television suggestions.

We sat side by side, watching wordlessly in his darkened living room. Then, as the closing credits ran, a thought occurred to me.

"Hey, Dad, *that's* what you need!" I said. "A collection of buddies who have the same shared experience!"

He nodded in agreement. But where to find them? His own friends from WWII days, if they were even still alive, were dispersed all over the world. I refilled our wine glasses as we pondered the idea. Suddenly, his eyes widened, and his dark eyebrows shot up.

"Hey, what's that place in DC?" he said. "That place for old soldiers?"

"The Old Soldiers' Home?" I said.

"That's it!" he said happily. "Is that still there?"

"It *is*!" I said, smiling back at him. Had it not been for working on *American Byzantine*, however, I wouldn't have even known about it. Four years earlier, Martin thought it would be cool to shoot some aerial footage of the Basilica, given its unusual architecture. While we were preparing to do this, we received a request to capture aerial shots of the land the Old Soldiers' Home had been forced to sell to the archdiocese—and that was my introduction to the facility with its storied history.

In 1851, "Congress used booty from the Mexican War to establish an asylum for old and disabled veterans," according to *Washington Post* writer Steve Vogel. "The elderly soldiers and airmen now at the home—most of them veterans of World War II or the Korean War—live in hotel-size dormitories amid a miniature city unknown to most area residents, complete with its own chapels, gymnasium, golf course, library, and fishing lakes."

Located high on a leafy and beautiful 350-acre expanse in northwest DC, it's possible to see the Washington Monument, the Potomac River and the dome of the Capitol from the upper floors of residence buildings at the Old Soldiers' Home.

Dad agreed it sounded like a perfect solution for him.

After I returned home, I began researching how to get him into what was officially called the Armed Forces Retirement Home. It was a community of 1200 soldiers from all over the country, both male and female, all of whom had seen active duty, from WWII, Korea, Vietnam, and Operation Desert Storm. Dad's Normandy service qualified him.

I booked a tour for the two of us, then drove back up to Philadelphia to pick up Dad and bring him back down to DC to see it. Driving through the gates felt like driving onto the grounds of a beautiful and well-established old university.

Abraham Lincoln used some of the older buildings on the campus as his "summer White House." Each spring before it got too hot, his staff would load up the White House furniture in a horse-drawn cart, retreating for each of the summers during the Civil War to escape the heat and humidity of the city. Lincoln wrote the last draft of the Emancipation Proclamation in a Gothic Revival-style cottage on the campus. Now called the Lincoln Cottage, it's a designated National Monument.

Each fall, as the temperatures cooled, the president's furniture would once again be loaded on the cart and moved back down to the official White House.

In addition to the nine-hole golf course, there was a state-of-the-art bowling alley, a 700-seat movie theater, a 40,000-book library, computers to use everywhere, a room full of jigsaw puzzles, and vending machines that sold beer as well as soda. (Dad *loved* that.) They even had studios for artists and woodworkers along with five or six kilns for potters. Pondering the unlikelihood of an old soldier's home having *pottery kilns* felt like getting a surprise thumbs up from Karen, as if she was there with us, putting her personal stamp of approval on this phase of Dad's transition. I could almost hear her laughing at our surprise.

Over the next few months, as I dealt with the paperwork to get him in, Dad rose to the occasion and was a good sport about all the changes. He gave away most of his treasures to relatives, pleased they were staying in the family. Everyone wanted something to remember him by. We sold his house to one of my Ethiopian cousins, saving us all from the cold thought of strangers living there where so many family gatherings had taken place.

In case he tried to change his mind, I did my best to scare him with unsavory options. But I needn't have bothered. Dad loved the idea of joining his own "band of brothers," and of going "back into the Army," as he told everyone with a grin.

Adding to that, Dad was happy to be back in his hometown, Washington, DC—the town where he went to high school and coached local teams, the town where his parents had lived for years. The town where he went to American University, where he met and married my mother, and where his first two children were born. He loved the idea of his life coming full circle. It felt right.

Best of all, though, the Old Soldiers' Home was filled with hundreds of potential buddies for Dad—guys he had stories in common with. The day I moved him in, I hung his WWII uniform on the door to his room as a conversation starter, to let people know who he was.

Dad was delighted with the greetings, welcomes, and conversations it attracted from the old guys walking by. Friendships were born.

The Old Soldiers' Home was just an hour away from my own home in south Alexandria. I visited Dad every week, often with the kids, sometimes taking him out somewhere, but usually just hanging out with him for a meal, often joined by one or two of his new buddies. Although there was a nice dining room, which Dad called the "mess hall"—his favorite place, not surprisingly, was the pub with its cozy atmosphere, friendly servers, grilled cheeses, and martinis. We'd hole up there for hours—him talking, asking a few questions about the kids and my work, and me listening to his stories.

That summer, my cousin Gladys had the inspired idea to throw a family reunion for him on the grounds of the Old Soldiers' Home. Dozens of relatives came, including all of our Ethiopian family.

It was a wonderful celebration—and the last time most of them would see him.

Azaleas and the IRS

ALTHOUGH HAPPY AT the Old Soldiers' Home, Dad's health gradually deteriorated. After his first summer there, he had to give up his studio in the independent living building and move to a room in the moderate care building on campus.

Throughout the fall and winter, my phone rang frequently with urgent requests from the staff doctors to come over and take him to Walter Reed Army Medical.

And then in February of 2005, a call came in from one of the doctors asking me to take Dad to see a nephrologist at Washington Hospital Center. His kidneys were beginning to fail. After the examination, Dad and I sat side by side across the desk from the doctor, waiting to hear the verdict. The doctor reviewed the paperwork before him, then looked up at Dad, studying his face for a moment. When he eventually spoke, it was to ask gently how much he wanted to know.

"Just tell me exactly what it is," Dad replied calmly.

The doctor paused for a moment. He looked over at me and I nodded. If anyone could handle getting hard news, it was Dad.

"To be honest, Phil, you don't have long,"

he finally said. "It's a race between your heart and your kidneys as to which one will do you in first."

Dad nodded, with what I could only describe as an expression of keen interest on his face.

"How long do I have?" he asked.

"I can't say for sure," the doctor replied in a quiet, but kind tone, "but it will be this spring. I think you have about five to seven weeks."

I turned my head away and stared out the window, realizing Dad might not live long enough to see the azaleas bloom in Washington, DC. Azaleas were his favorites and something I had always associated with him. When I was a child, he'd built a miniature greenhouse in our garden out in the country using old wooden window frames, then showed me how to grow azaleas from cuttings using a special root stimulating hormone that looked like Noxzema. Tears filled my eyes at the memory.

Dad, however, seemed to brighten up immediately, even sitting up straighter at these words.

"*Finally,*" he said. "Someone who tells me the straight deal!"

That was when my phone rang. I saw it was Anden's lawyer friend from New York City. Wiping my eyes, I excused myself and stepped out into the hallway to take the call.

"Good news, Kristin!" she said, not bothering with pleasantries. "It's all resolved. You are a free person; the IRS will not bother you anymore."

Over the past eighteen months, she'd compiled a case on my behalf, which included a letter from Dr. Peckar, the psychiatrist responsible for bringing the *American Byzantine* documentary film into my life. In it, he'd gently laid out the nature of the traumas I'd been through, including my divorce and Karen's death, asking them to show me some compassion.

Happy and greatly relieved as I was, I found it difficult to process this wonderful news within minutes of hearing what amounted to my father's death sentence. As I walked back into the nephrologist's office, I could not longer hold back the tears.

Dad thought they were for him. Which, of course, they were.

Driving back home that night, I gathered more and more anxiety around me, once again feeling pulled and torn about where I was and where I wasn't; what I *had* to do and what I *should* be doing—and even what I *wasn't* doing that hadn't yet occurred to me.

Looking at my phone, I saw a message from Stephen, my friend from my time at the documentary workshop. I pressed play and listened as I drove along the Potomac River to Stephen's voice reading me two poems he said reminded him of me at this moment in my life. After the first one, Robert Frost's *The Road Not Taken*, I pulled my car over by the side of the river to concentrate on the second one, which was Longfellow's *Psalm of Life*.

> *Tell me not, in mournful numbers,*
> *Life is but an empty dream!*
> *For the soul is dead that slumbers,*
> *And things are not what they seem.*
> *Life is real! Life is earnest!*
> *And the grave is not its goal;*
> *Dust thou art, to dust returnest . . .*
> *Lives of great men all remind us*
> *We can make our lives sublime,*
> *And, departing, leave behind us*
> *Footprints on the sands of time;*
> *Footprints, that perhaps another,*
> *Sailing o'er life's solemn main,*
> *A forlorn and shipwrecked brother,*
> *Seeing, shall take heart again . . . .*

Listening to these words as I sat in the dark watching moonlight dance on the water, I leaned my head against the wheel—and just sobbed like no one was watching. Because nobody was.

The next morning, I woke up with an idea. In case Dad didn't live long enough to see the azaleas bloom in the gardens of the Old Soldiers' Home, I would bring one over to brighten his room.

I drove to the local garden center. To my relief, they had half a dozen in flower. Unable to choose which one he might like the best, and unable to make a simple decision, I decided to buy them all. I filled my car with them. If Dad wasn't going to live long enough to see spring, the kids and I would bring it to him.

That afternoon, Zoë, Leif, and I arrived at the door of his room, each of us carrying two big pots of bright pink and red blooms. Dad was delighted. Over the coming days, whenever we spoke by phone, he would tell me how many people came to visit him—staff and friends—to admire the azaleas that filled his room.

A few weeks later, after the flowers had peaked, turned brown, and fallen from the plants, Dad was moved once again, this time to a nice room in the hospice wing of yet another building. I had his furniture moved there and hung up his art and photographs of family and the many places he'd lived so he could see his entire life on the walls around him during his last days.

Dad was "over the moon" (in his vernacular) to discover one of his doctors was Ethiopian. It was another affirmation—as if we needed it—that the Old Soldiers' Home had been the right choice for him. That connection inspired a lot of happy and animated conversations between them. The doctor even approved his wish for a daily dry martini.

Throughout that year, Dad kept a list of the tasks he wanted me to do on his behalf. One by one, we tackled everything until there was only one item left: his 2004 tax returns. I told Dad I'd put it off because I hated dealing with the IRS. But the real reason was that I was scared what would happen once there was nothing left on the list.

Sure enough, only a handful of days after he signed the completed return, he let go. His responsibilities finished, Dad slipped into semi-consciousness. He either wasn't able to speak, or he chose not to. His eyes were open, but I wasn't sure he could see anymore. Leaving the kids to take care of themselves, I moved into his room, watching over him by day, sleeping in his recliner at night, and leaving his room only for small breaks.

Sometimes I played Kris Kristofferson's songs to him. Sometimes I read his mother's letters to him.

(Remember when I said my next book project had literally fallen into my hands? I was referring to a binder of letters that had tumbled unexpectedly from the shelves in my father's townhouse and into my hands. Inside was a collection of letters written by his mother during the years she'd lived in Ethiopia where her husband, my grandfather, worked as an advisor to the late Emperor Haile Selassie.)

Sticking to my theme of the past few weeks, I snuck in a few mentions of azaleas, even though there were none in the letters.

In the late morning of the third day, desperate to see the kids and take a shower, I decided to slip home for a few hours. I brushed what was left of his thinning hair back on his forehead with my hand and whispered that I'd be right back. I told him his friend Frank—who had the same name as Dad's younger brother—would be stopping by so that he'd have someone with him while I was gone.

I drove home, hugged the kids, made sure they had enough food, and took a shower. Toweling my hair as I walked downstairs, I heard the phone in the kitchen ring. Once again, I somehow sensed it was *the call.* And it was. The doctor on the other end of the line told me Dad had hung on until Frank got there, then stopped breathing after he left. I wondered if he had thought his little brother was coming and had waited for him. I also wondered if he'd waited until I left before letting go.

Sadly, wearily, I put on fresh clothes, kissed the kids goodbye and headed back across town to the Old Soldiers' Home. I got to his room just before the undertaker arrived. Moments later, watching the gurney roll down the hallway with all that remained of my larger-than-life father zipped up in a black bag was the most alone I'd ever felt in my 49 years.

Mingled with the grief, however, was the huge sense of gratitude I felt for the past year of grace. Had it not been for an idea inspired by watching *The Price of Freedom*, I don't know how I could have managed to take care of my father long-distance. It certainly would not have been the wonderful and serendipitous bundle of experiences it turned out to be. Thanks to the thoughts and ideas triggered by Bruce's film, Dad's last year was spent in an atmosphere of high quality care, surrounded by a network of wonderful new friendships with WWII and Vietnam War vets at the Old Soldiers' Home.

It's hard to put into words just how meaningful that was to him. My father enjoyed a full and happy family life and a decades-long international career. Yet in his last months, he often thought about the war he'd fought more than sixty years earlier. As his life came to an end, he told me often dreamed he was back in France during the war, leading villagers across the mountains to safety.

I moved Dad into the Old Soldiers' Home at 2 p.m. on March 22, 2004. He died of congestive heart failure on March 22, 2005, at noon—having lived there just two hours shy of a year.

Dad would have appreciated the near symmetry of that—although he would likely have fretted about those two hours messing up a perfect year.

ANGEL WITH AN UMBRELLA

DAD'S MEMORIAL SERVICE was held at Oak Hill Cemetery, adjacent to Dumbarton Oaks in Upper Georgetown. It's where the Fellows family plot is; his father, mother and sister are all buried there.

It was Dad's idea that we plan everything together in advance; he wanted to see how it would unfold, at least in his mind. And so, a few months before he died, we spent an afternoon driving around Georgetown, looking at the house he grew up in and stopping to arrange renting a room at the Old Europe restaurant, where the grieving would gather for food and drinks after his service.

It occurred to me how fabulous it might be to have a New Orleans-style second line musical procession winding its way through the streets in celebration of Dad's life. A longtime fan of Louis Armstrong and Ella Fitzgerald, Dad loved the idea. Perhaps I could get away with it, I thought, if I pulled a film permit. I even spoke with my friend Richard Chisolm about filming it so it would look like a legitimate shoot.

After our day out, I returned Dad to the Old Soldiers' Home and, as usual, we stopped in at the lounge for an end-of-the-day conversation and drink—the customary dry martini for him and a coke for me, along with grilled cheeses with chips and a pickle, our favorites.

In between sips of martini, as we went back through the day's details and double-checked that I'd done everything he'd wanted, I saw an uncharacteristically wistful look come over his aging face.

"You okay, Dad?" I asked. "Is it too sad to make these plans?"

"No," he said. "It's all so great, exactly how I envisioned it. I just want to be there, too!"

I remember it rained slightly that day, misted really, as if weather were tears. . . .

On the day of the memorial, everything went as planned. In the end, I didn't pull off the second line. Instead, I chose a young saxophonist to play some of Dad's favorite songs by the side of the grave; mourners were able to follow the sound of his music as they made their way from the gates of the cemetery along the paths to the interment site.

I brought Dad's antique wooden rocking chair over to Old Europe and set it up in the corner of the room. Everyone who knew him, knew that rocker—and seeing it empty, without Dad in it, made a quiet statement. Friends, family, and work colleagues came from as far away as California. Drinks were had, stories and memories exchanged. Dad was right, he would have loved it.

Stephen came for the service and took photographs for me. Looking at them later, in almost every photograph, there is an immaculately dressed man, perhaps in his mid-fifties, with closely cropped graying hair, wearing a dark suit and standing either by my side or just behind me. There was a black umbrella in his hand, sometimes open, sometimes furled—depending upon the amount of precipitation. That was Joseph Pozell. Joe and his wife, Ella, were the caretakers of Oak Hill and had helped me with all the arrangements. I can't imagine it's an easy job, but together they struck the perfect balance—caring, thoughtful, and compassionate.

In all photographs, Joe stands like a guardian angel watching over me.

Joe was also a volunteer Metropolitan police officer. His regular beat was directing traffic at the intersection of Wisconsin Avenue and M Street in Georgetown, just steps away from where I had my first post-college job working for an importer of Danish and Italian furniture and textiles. Three weeks after Dad's memorial, while directing traffic Joe accidentally stepped into the path of an oncoming car that, for some reason, he didn't see.

And so it happened that just a month after Dad's service, hundreds of uniformed officers saluted as Joe's coffin was carried into Washington National Cathedral, a place filled with so many memories for me, now filled with more than a thousand mourners for Joe. He was there when I needed him most, at my father's funeral. And then, he was gone.

Dad was a lifelong keeper of letters—letters he received, as well as copies of letters he'd sent throughout his career. I keep the professional ones in a binder in chronological order. Together, they form an interesting memoir of the people and places in his life.

After he died, I hit upon the idea of keeping the ones he'd written to me in vintage cigar boxes. He'd smoked cigars for years—until his first heart attack put an end to that—and I've always associated the scent of a cigar with him. It seemed an appropriate and sensually rich solution.

Although by now they had been long divorced, my parents had stayed in touch with one another, if lightly. My mother used to say the two best decisions in her life were 1) marrying my father, and 2) leaving him—which never failed to irritate me each time she said it. It was, after all, *my father* she was talking about. Even though she was witness to how difficult this time had been for me—juggling kids, work, income, and caring for him—she chose not to help with Dad's care during his last years, nor did she come to the interment of ashes at the cemetery. She did, however, come to the party afterward at Old Europe.

A few days after the service, I was surprised to receive a card in the mail from her. On the cover was a painting by one of our favorite artists, Marc Chagall, *Flowers and Bird.*

Inside, the printed message said simply, *Peace.*

ON THE OPEN ROAD, DESTINATION UNKNOWN

She felt some measure of relief knowing that in the very least, on the open road she would have some time to think.

DAVE EGGERS

AFTER A FEW years of freelancing in various capacities in that invisible world between documentary film makers and public television, word-of-mouth about what I was doing started getting out and work was really picking up. More projects from Bill Moyers, WNET, and the Fred Friendly group at Columbia University came in, keeping me busy and funded. Even though it wasn't steady, I was earning a lot more than I'd been paid at the documentary workshop.

In the first half of the 2000s, two documentaries came my way with a similar theme but targeting different age demographics. Both involved life-changing road trips and that caught my attention. I love road trips!

Back in the early 1980s, my mother and I had a ten-day road trip in Denmark, merrily eating and drinking our way around the country. I introduced her to my colleagues at Kvadrat, the astonishing, contemporary Danish textiles company I was working with at the time, and she in turn introduced me to my Danish relatives, all of whom greeted us with open arms, welcoming us into their lives and their homes, apartments, and farms. We had such a great time that she sponsored another trip during the 1990s, this time with ten-year-old Zoë—a three-generation trip to see all our Danish family again and introduce the young cousins to one another.

I also took a road trip with my father in the '80s, driving from Chicago to San Diego. In the wake of my parents' divorce the previous year, I suggested the idea only after I heard he was planning to do the drive solo in an old station wagon. My father was not a keen driver. Often lost in thought, solving work problems, he got easily bored behind the wheel. Setting aside how upset I was over the divorce, I volunteered to drive so he would at least reach his destination. My father responded enthusiastically to my offer, which surprised and touched me.

Intuitive as he was about people and computers, Dad knew very little about cars. So, in preparation for our trip, I took a AAA course on basic car maintenance, including changing tires, oil, and doing battery checks. I also bought a basic toolkit with cables, etc. Not that I was sure how to use any of it, but at least I'd be prepared for whatever might befall us.

It was only after I arrived at O'Hare airport that I realized Dad had also been also thinking about the necessary preparations for our adventure. Opening the back of the station wagon so I could load in my suitcase and brand-new toolkit, he proudly gestured to the provisions he'd stocked up on for our 1730-mile cross country adventure. I gasped in astonishment. The back of the car was filled with Cheerios, Hires Root Beer, Tootsie Rolls, and red Twizzlers—my favorite childhood foods I'd missed during the years we lived in London. He'd remembered! I set aside my unhappiness about the divorce; our trip was already off to an amazing start.

Over the next four days, with nobody else to talk to, we got to know one another in an entirely new way. Dad always took the morning shift—driving west for the first three or four hours each day before he got too bored with it. Then I took over for five hours in the afternoon, stopping at nearly every scenic overlook to take photographs in Colorado, Utah, and Nevada.

It was the middle of the summer and as the old car had no air conditioning, we drove with the windows rolled down, country and western music (Dad's choice) playing on the radio whenever we were close enough to civilization to get reception. Driving west meant Dad's left arm was exposed to the sun in the morning while he drove, and his right arm was exposed to the sun in the afternoon when it was my turn to take the wheel. By the time we reached southern California, he had two nicely tanned arms and already looked like he belonged there—and I was still pale as a ghost.

My relationship with my father had entered a whole new phase. Many jokes were born of that trip, establishing memories we cherished and tossed back and forth at each other the rest of his life.

So, when not just one, but *two* documentaries involving open roads and road trips came my way, it seemed like more than a suggestion.

The Open Road: America Looks at Aging was an hour-long documentary that explored the possibilities and potential for America's 77 million baby boomers reaching the "Third Stage of Life." Rejecting their parents' version of retirement, boomers were instead charting a course of innovative and imaginative reinvention. It was a perfect fit for the PBS audience, and filmmaker Nina Gilden Seavey, director of the George Washington University Documentary Center, wanted my help getting it on the air.

Somewhere around that time, I also got a surprise call from Amy Wallens Green at PBS.

"I have a kind of rough but also kind of cool project, and so I thought of you," she said. That alone appealed to me.

"It's about these three guys who just graduated from Pepperdine

University. They don't know what to do with their lives, they only know they don't want to go the route of their parents' expectations.

"So, they set off driving across the country in an old RV they painted shocking green," she continued, "seeking out interesting and successful people to interview to try and figure out how to chart own their life goals. It's called *Destination Unknown*. Would you be interested in working with them?"

I liked the sound of it and asked her to send me a copy to watch.

Thinking it might be somehow inspiring for the kids—and always interested in hearing their reactions to films I was working with—I screened *Destination Unknown* one night with them. While they didn't latch onto the "what is life calling you to do" aspect of the documentary, they thought three guys living off a case of energy bars donated by one of their interviewees and sneaking into motel pools to rinse off (unable to afford a room) was hilarious.

I agreed to help get their documentary—and dreams—on the air.

A few weeks later, Roadtrippers Mike Marriner and Brian McAllister came to Alexandria to meet me and chat about working together on *Destination Unknown*. I arranged meetings at key PBS stations in the area, and in Florida, so programmers could meet and be charmed by the guys in person.

On the last day of their visit, I invited Mike and Brian over to our house so the kids could meet them. Zoë and I made tacos and chocolate chip cookies for dinner and together we watched the Grammys, laughing and joking our way throughout the show.

None of us had any way of knowing, but that night would be the start of a long journey working together that—along with their third partner, Nate—would last an incredible 17 years.

Over those years, Roadtrip Nation would grow into a collection of adventures featuring young Roadtrippers and successful and interesting entrepreneurs, visionaries, artists, scientists, businesswomen and men, becoming a huge international movement around the essential message of empowering young people to define their own road in life.

"There are so many voices out there telling you what to do and who to be," went the Roadtrip Nation mantra. "But your own voice is the one that matters most."

It was just what *I* wanted and needed to hear at that time. And so, it became my happy responsibility to get these road trip interviews on the air everywhere. Over our years together, I secured more than 100,000 broadcasts across 98 percent of the U.S.

Watching *Destination Unknown* steadied my nerves, convincing me that while my income would always be somewhat uncertain and precarious, I might be on what was just the right road for me. And *The Open Road* reassured me it was never too late for an interesting new phase of life.

In those days, my mother worried about my lack of what she called "a real job." But by now, I was learning to roll with the ups and downs of life as a freelancer—the flush times and the frightening times. Despite the lack of steadiness, it was always interesting with a continuously rotating cast of characters and mind-expanding ideas. And the films themselves continued to have a way of saving me.

I tried to rearrange her thoughts about stability, having had to do that for myself so many times.

"Yes, it's a bit unsteady," I agreed. "But at least I don't have a boss. I cannot get fired or laid off. Nobody can just change their mind and show me the door."

But my mother came from the husband-comes-home-with-the-regular-paycheck era. Much as I tried to tell her things had changed, she had a hard time letting go of that mindset, especially when it came to me. My creative interests and restlessness had always unsettled her.

And what I did next only confirmed that.

Ill at ease living in the DC area, I took the coincidence of these two films about the open road crossing my path as a needed push to hit the road myself again—this time, not with my parents, but with my kids. One doc wasn't enough, I needed *two* of them to take the hint and get my ass in gear. This wasn't just a nudge from the universe, it felt more like a full body shove to move on.

Our destination? The Blue Ridge Mountains of North Carolina.

"I may move to the mountains," I'd told Dad one evening while we were sitting in the bar over martinis and cokes at the Old Soldiers' Home. "After you no longer need me, of course."

That was code for "after you die"—words I could never bring myself to say.

"What do you think of the idea?" I asked, hoping for his approval.

He took a reflective sip of his martini, appearing to ponder the thought.

"That makes sense to me," he said a moment later. "After all, you were born in the mountains."

That was all the blessing I needed.

PART III

ASHEVILLE & THE MOST REMARKABLE THINGS

*I have learned, as a rule of thumb, never to
ask whether you can do something.
Say, instead, that you are doing it. Then fasten your seat belt.
The most remarkable things follow.*

JULIA CAMERON, *THE ARTIST'S WAY*

ESCAPE TO THE MOUNTAINS

OKAY, SO A slight explanation here regarding the "destination unknown" aspect of our road trip. In terms of a map, I knew *where* we were headed, but it was still a completely unknown world to me. This time, it wasn't a film guiding me there, but someone who *worked* in film who suggested our destination. But this next astonishing phase of my life wouldn't have happened had I *not* worked at the documentary workshop.

I'd first heard about Asheville in the fall of 2004 from my production crew friend, Stephen. At the time, we were both in the throes of plotting our escapes from big city life. For several nights, we'd sat on the phone with one another after Zoë and Leif had fallen asleep, scrolling want ads. I was looking for a small house with a garden in Seattle or San Francisco and Stephen was looking for a boat he could live aboard and ditch apartment life. It quickly became clear, however, that I could not afford to live in either of my West Coast choices.

"What about Asheville?" Stephen finally suggested.

"What's Asheville?" I said, having never heard of it.

"It's a small town—artsy and progressive—and it's in the mountains," he responded simply. "North Carolina."

Small. Artsy. Progressive. Mountains. He knew all my hot buttons. Each of the four words had an instant, visceral appeal. It was as if something inside me recognized this was the right answer—and I never second-guess that instinct when it sparkles to life. I took immediate action.

The next morning, I rang my mother and suggested a long weekend in the mountains around October 28th. It had been five and a half years since Karen had died, but we still celebrated her birthday each year by doing something special together in her memory. Always up for an adventure, my mother immediately agreed. A few weeks later, the two of us drove six hundred miles southwest to the Southern Highlands of Appalachia, overnighting along the way with old family friends in Charlotte.

The next day, we were in the car about an hour away from Asheville when my mother commented, "You know, your sister wanted to move to Asheville."

"*No,*" I said, startled. "I *didn't* know that. Why didn't you tell me?"

She just shrugged and turned to look out the window at the lush, green landscapes of North Carolina passing by.

Mom's comment turned out to be just the first of a few odd and surprisingly serendipitous happenings awaiting us in Asheville that weekend—*almost as if someone had planned them.*

When checking out prospective colleges with Zoë a few months earlier, we'd visited the University of North Carolina in Wilmington. After our trip to Belize, Zoë was still interested in saving the manatees and UNC-W was on the coast and had a biology program. When I told our Wilmington B&B owner that I had a trip planned to Asheville, 400 miles away on the other side of the state, she immediately suggested I stay at the 1900 Inn on Montford. So that's where I booked a room for our trip to Asheville.

Designed in 1900 by Richard Sharp Smith, an English-born American who'd been the supervising architect for the Biltmore House, the Inn's rooms and décor had a decidedly English feel to them.

The Inn took its name from Montford, a historic neighborhood filled with old homes built under the vision of the prolific Smith whose signature designs were an interesting blend of Arts and Crafts, Queen Anne, and Neoclassical styles. Mom and I liked it immediately.

When we checked in, the owners told us their weekly Saturday Social would be starting shortly, with wine and live music by a guitarist friend of theirs on the large front porch. That sounded delightful. After freshening up, we went outside and took seats in comfortable old wicker chairs. Mom sat at one end, next to the owners Lynn and Ron Carlson, and I found a chair at the other end of the porch.

I was speaking with someone when I heard my mother yelp. I looked up in time to see her throw both hands up in the air.

What on earth?

I got up and walked over to her end of the porch.

"Is everything okay?" I asked.

"You will not *believe* this!" she exclaimed. "Lynn and Ron lived in London around the same time we did. Ron was also in computers and knows Brian and Ed!"

She was referring to two of my father's closest work colleagues, Brian O'Heron and Ed Mack, both of whom I'd known since I was ten. It turned out Ron had been a computer developer and project manager at Unisys Corporation, the same global technology solutions company my father had worked for.

First an Asheville connection to my sister, and now one to my father....

Ron and Lynn invited us to carry on our conversation over dinner that evening at a small but charming eatery co-owned by Peggy Seeger, Pete Seeger's sister, and also a folk musician and songwriter. Pyper's Place was located in a converted old laundromat that Peggy and her partner had turned into what they described as a homey café-restaurant.

Inside, there was a nine-foot couch upholstered in leopard fabric in front of an orange 1960s wood stove.

The four of us had a delightful dinner swapping memories of London. Unfortunately, that was to be the restaurant's last night as Peggy and Irene had recently decided to close it down. *We got here just in time*, I thought.

The next morning, Mom and I walked into town to explore Asheville. Within minutes, I turned to look at her and announced, "This is it, I'm moving here."

"Now, honey . . ." came her typically cautious reply.

But I was head over heels smitten with the mountain town. Stephen had been right. Asheville felt like home. I understood this was where I needed to be.

The following spring, after Dad's memorial, I contacted a realtor in Asheville who sent me several real estate newspapers. I gave Zoë and Leif highlighters and told them to circle the ones they liked, each in their own color. I did the same. The ones with at least two or three colors around them became our wish list. We made plans for a May visit to see how the kids liked it.

Our first morning in Asheville, we got together with Allen the realtor, and began our search for a new home in the mountains. Zoë and Leif kept track of the ones they liked best, and after each stop, would recite the litany of their favorites by the sequence number in which we'd seen it.

"5, 7, 3, 4"—one would say.

Then the other would give their priority order: "*No*—6, 5, 4, then 7."

The numbers changed after each house we looked at.

At the end of the second day, having seen everything on our lists, Allen suggested a 13th house *he* thought might be right for us.

"We're too tired," I said. "I feel like Goldilocks—each one is not quite right. No more, please!"

"Just this one," he said. And just to be polite, I said okay.

The kids ran ahead of me and through the front door. I dragged my feet, looking at the unassuming little brick house, built snugly into the mountainside. At the foot of the property there was a bird sanctuary adjacent to a large lake. Another mountain stretched up on the other side of the lake. It was a lovely setting, but the house itself didn't do much for me.

Moments later, Zoë ran back outside.

"Mama, you *have* to see this one!" she said breathlessly. "Wait til you see the bathroom in *your* room!"

I followed her inside and room by room, I walked through the house, then out onto the decks overlooking the lake and mountains.

Back in the car, we went through the numbers again. I liked another one we'd seen better, but number 13 now topped both kids' lists. Allen the realtor smiled, kind of smugly, I thought. Of course, that's the one I bought.

The kids and I returned to Alexandria to put the house Mom and I owned together on the market. It sold in a whirlwind three days.

Three months after Dad's memorial, and a few days after Zoë's high school graduation, the kids and I piled into our Subaru wagon with suitcases and our two dogs and drove eight hours southwest through Virginia and down to the mountains of Western North Carolina, ready for a new life.

Keen to share in the adventure, Stephen followed us down a few days later, filling up his own Subaru with my houseplants, some breakables, and a few other treasures. A trip to the mountains, he said, was the perfect getaway for him from the stresses of DC. He was also about to literally set sail on a new adventure himself, the exact opposite of what I was doing. We'd looked at a few sailboats together before I left, and he ended up buying one of them.

Before leaving Alexandria, I had a phone call with Dr. Braddock, the lovely man who, along with his wife, had sponsored *American Byzantine*. We'd kept in touch over the years, and I wanted him to know I was leaving the area.

I thanked him for the opportunities he'd given me and Martin to create a documentary about a work of art so important to him, as well as the many social evenings he and his wife had included me in.

"Kristin," he said at the end of the call. "You have a remarkable combination of personality and moral fiber."

Astounded by the compliment, I wrote it down and have kept it ever since in my little notebook of emails, comments, and letters to reread when times are tough and I need some encouragement.

My sole concern about moving to Asheville had been whether or not filmmakers and producers would still hire me as a freelancer if I was no longer located in the nation's capital, just a train ride away from New York City.

But there was no need to worry; film projects would follow me down to the mountains like a flock of iridescent starlings.

THE ASHEVILLE FILM FESTIVAL AND DATING A GUY NAMED BOGDANOVICH

I'LL ADMIT THERE were times I took the whole film-themed-direction-to-my-life a little too far, sometimes with less than positive results. One such instance was my short-lived infatuation with a guy named Jack Bogdanovich, whom I briefly dated during my first months in Asheville.

Jack was a master craftsman luthier with a kind of rugged Mick Jagger-esque look I found appealing at the time. I've always been drawn to smart guys who work with their hands—designers, artisans, musicians, and writers. Men who *don't* wear suits. Men who *don't* smell like dry-cleaning. Jack had already made the transition from corporate life to being an artist.

His art form was crafting beautiful guitars from exotic woods—African mahoganies, Madagascar ebonies, and Brazilian rosewoods—which sold for thousands of dollars and were sought after by musicians all over the country. Of course, he also played guitar himself. Sitting in front of the fireplace, or out on the deck overlooking the woods, Jack segued effortlessly from Bach to the Rolling Stones.

Be still my heart . . .

Like my sister (Robert Redford, Rob Zombie, and Martin Landau), Jack was a graduate of Pratt Institute. His strong Staten Island accent made me laugh, and as a Northerner myself, I found it comforting in the sea of Southern accents now surrounding me.

His backstory was a fascinating one, and it didn't take long before I was writing a magazine profile on him. Jack liked the idea of this publicity.

From somewhere behind tidy stacks of paper-thin wood veneers and a dense but well-ordered architecture of rasps, lathes, and saws, four words slowly fill the air.

"Son. of. a. Bitch."

The accent is unmistakably that of a New Yorker—and as incongruous here in the mountains of Western North Carolina as the Empire State Building itself would be.

Guitar in hand, Jack Bogdanovich slowly stands up in the middle of his woodworking shop, sighs, and runs a surprisingly well-manicured hand through the thick mane of graying dark hair that falls to his shoulders. His expressionless pale blue eyes search the room restlessly for a missing tool. With his rugged T-shirt and faded jeans, weathered face and ornery attitude, Bogdanovich would not look out of place standing in for any one of the Rolling Stones.

He can bang out a rendition of "Street Fightin' Man" raucous enough to set empty shoes dancing, punctuated by the occasional gritty laugh whenever the correct notes fall away from his fingertips.

I also pondered the idea of making a documentary about him. One morning, I was sitting in his kitchen listening to him rattle on about the previous day's experiences.

"I went to Greenlife yesterday and man, it must have been Great Ass Day or somethin'," he said. "Everywhere I looked, there were just these *great* asses! I don't even know who I saw or what their faces looked like. I just saw *all these great asses*."

"I guess I'm an ass man," he continued. "That's how I build my guitars."

"Look at this one," he said, reaching for a guitar he'd made years ago. "The bottom's too big on it. I've changed the shape of my template now."

He ran into his workshop. A few moments later he was back, a plexiglass model in his hand.

"Look at this!" he said, holding it up triumphantly. "Now *that's* a Marilyn Monroe ass!"

His grin faded as he noticed the open notebook in front of me on the kitchen counter.

"What're you doin'?!" he asked, suddenly suspicious. But he already knew.

"That's *not* going in the film!" he yelled from across the room, jabbing his finger in the air at me as he walked back into his workshop. "I'm *not* saying that on camera!"

But he had to, I thought, smiling to myself. It was too good, too authentic, and too character-revealing not to include.

I pitched the feature article I wrote about Jack to *Rolling Stone* magazine and numerous other guitar and music publications but had no luck getting it picked up. We parted ways before I could make the film.

In all relationships, there is an unseen fault line which divides that which is acceptable from that which is intolerable. The trip wire lies hidden somewhere in our emotional baggage, tucked inside the leftover hurt feelings and disappointments from other relationships we cart around as if we're bag ladies, and these are our last and only possessions.

The equations between us didn't work. I was more interested in his story than he was interested in mine. I was more willing to put up with his erratic behavior than he was interested in being part of my life. When he was in a good mood, he was delightful and our times together almost magical. But when he wasn't—which was more often—it was a struggle. If only he'd played the guitar more and talked less, it might have worked.

At the time, Jack was in the middle of creating what would become a beautiful coffee table book about his craft: *Classical Guitar Making: A Modern Approach to a Traditional Design.* Ever autodidactic, he wrote everything himself and shot all the photographs. At one point, realizing he needed a better camera, he sold me the digital one he'd been working with. At the time, I was still using Karen's Canon AE1, a film camera. But it was 2005 and time to take the leap to digital myself. I'm still grateful to Jack for pushing me to make the transition. Working with a digital camera allowed me to take as many photographs as I wanted without thinking, *is this worth 75 cents?* each time I framed up a shot. It set me free.

If I'm being embarrassingly honest, though—in addition to the music, what I found most appealing was Jack's last name. Even though he was not related to actor and filmmaker Peter Bogdanovich, I sometimes daydreamed about how cool it would be, working in my wee little corner of the film biz, to have the name Kristin Bogdanovich. Not that I wanted to marry him—I didn't. I just liked his name.

A close friend of mine at the time, having listened to my tales about him over several wine-laced, long distance phone calls, told me quite perceptively that I was in love with his *story*—not him. And she was right.

It wasn't the first time I'd done that. I'm very susceptible to a good story and Jack had a great one. Eventually, however, I decided enough was enough. Working in my garden one fall afternoon, I was pondering how best to end the relationship when my phone rang. It was Jack.

"Hey, it's not workin' with us," he said bluntly. "I hope we can be adult about this and not argue about who's at fault."

And that was that. I hung up and, unsure what to do with myself, kept weeding.

Moments later, the phone rang again. This time it was my former husband, Steve. Wanting to be near Zoë and Leif, he'd also moved to North Carolina and had settled in a little cabin on a lake in the nearby town of Black Mountain, less than twenty minutes away from us.

"What's wrong?" he asked, hearing a few tears in my voice.

"Jack just broke up with me!" I told him.

He laughed.

"So why are you sad?" he asked. "Didn't you tell me *you* were going to break up with *him*?"

"Yes," I wailed into the phone. "But he beat me to it!"

A few days later, Steve called again.

"Hey, I have an idea," he said. "I know you're shy about going out to meet people on your own. Since we're both single, why don't we go out and do things together—not on a date—but just so you're not alone?"

Oddly, this made a kind of weird sense to me. At 6'3", Steve would also be a great bodyguard, should I need one.

"The Asheville Film Festival is coming up," he said. "Want to go together?"

I love film festivals and there was nothing I wanted to do more than to check out Asheville's very own, now in its third year. Normally I would have gone with Zoë, but she was more than 300 miles away at university.

I said yes to Steve's offer.

North Carolina had become a mecca for film production. Parts of *The Last of the Mohicans* (1992), *The Fugitive* (1993), *My Fellow Americans* (1996), and *Patch Adams* (1998) had been shot here.

Leni Sitnick, Asheville's first female mayor, decided to use the film industry to enhance the region's draw. What was needed, she decided, was something to help bring various industry components together and celebrate their accomplishments. She sent Asheville's Parks and Recreation director Melissa Porter to the Sundance Film Festival in Park City, Utah, for inspiration.

"I went out there and absolutely fell in love with the town and the look of it and what they were bringing to Utah, and the thought process behind it," Porter told the *Mountain XPress*. "This *so* could be Asheville, I thought. I could just *feel* that energy that we could do something really great."

She came back to Asheville and created a festival advisory board that included John Cram and Neal Reed of Asheville's Fine Arts Theater and local film critic Ken Hanke, among others. And *voilá*, the Asheville Film Festival came into being, preceding my arrival in town by just two years. Actress Andie MacDowell, who lived in Asheville at the time, helped get the word out.

Asheville was quickly building a national reputation for being cool. In addition to film, the local music scene was also booming. *Rolling Stone* magazine picked The Orange Peel, just down the street from the Fine Arts Theater, as one of America's top five rock clubs. New breweries, restaurants and art studios cropped up seemingly overnight like mushrooms.

The Asheville Film Festival attracted the attention of major film-makers. Director Ron Howard had attended the previous year. Ken Russell, the visionary and flamboyant British director of scores of films including *Altered States*, *Women in Love*, and *Tommy*, was featured the year Steve and I went.

We ended up sitting just behind Russell and his wife, Lisi, at the Fine Arts Theater for the festival's opening night screening of *Tommy*—the satirical surrealist operetta fantasy film based on The Who's rock opera album about a "deaf, dumb, and blind" pinball wizard. Film critic Ken Hanke, resplendent in a maroon shirt, brown velvet sports jacket, and luminescent pink tie, sat with them.

With his florid complexion, white eyebrows and white hair, Ken Russell was by then 78 years old and larger than life, quite literally. I was thrilled to be seated behind him where, like a curious bird on his shoulder, I could watch him watching his own film.

Afterwards, Steve and I went to the opening night party at the Diana Wortham Theater. Jack was also there but I did my best to ignore him.

What I couldn't ignore, however, was the bombshell redhead who'd stopped midway down the atrium stairs and stood staring at my ex-husband.

That was the night Steve met Nan, who would become his partner for the next two decades—and this while he was helping *me* try to start dating again.

So much for that idea.

GETTING NAKED IN DENMARK

Come to the edge, he said.
They said, we are afraid.
Come to the edge, he said.
And so they came.
And he pushed them.
And they flew . . .

GUILLAUME APOLLINAIRE

ONE CHILLY MORNING in the fall of 2009, I would find myself standing on the edge of Denmark, looking out across a dark sea of chilly water towards a distant Sweden. Dawn was breaking and I was naked. Why was I standing there with no clothes on? I blame it entirely on the Asheville Film Festival.

On Christmas Eve, Leif, Steve, and Nan—the redhead Steve met at the film festival—gathered at my new little home on the mountainside for a holiday meal and exchange of gifts.

Later, as we were relaxing around the

candlelit fireplace, I heard Nan say she wanted to go to a church service. Steve and Leif immediately expressed no interest. Tipsy on the spirit of Christmas and goodwill toward all mankind, I heard myself say I would take her.

What on earth?! my startled inner self exclaimed. *It's cold out there— just stay home, drink some more wine and fall asleep by the fire!*

But it was too late. As Nan's face lit up with gratitude, I realized there was no way to gracefully back out.

An hour later, I found myself inside a downtown church, along with dozens of others bundled up against the chill, trying my best to tune out the words of the legendary and charismatic minister of Asheville's Jubilee Church, Howard Hanger. He was going through the Christmas story and I'd heard it all before. Bored, I turned my thoughts to what people were wearing and whether or not there were any nice looking single men.

Preoccupied with these thoughts, I didn't hear any of the sermon until, clear as a bell amid the random clutter of my mind, I heard Howard Hanger say the words:

What if you were not afraid?

He had just gotten to the bit about the angels appearing and startling the shepherds.

That's crazy, I thought. *I can't imagine not being afraid.*

"Think about it!" Howard said, as if reading my thoughts. He paused to look intently at each person in the large circle around him, including me.

"What would your life be like IF YOU WERE NOT AFRAID?"

I thought about it and realized it would be refreshing and life-changing.

In fact, so captivating were those words and this different vision of my life, I missed the rest of the sermon. The idea of being not afraid, the *permission* to be not afraid, that it might be okay to *be not afraid,* was so alluring that I adopted it as my New Year's mantra for the coming year.

And that was how I ended up naked in Denmark.

My Danish cousin, Karen, whom I'd known since we were both seven years old, had a daily practice of plunging naked into the Øresund, the large strait of steel gray water that divides Denmark from Sweden. This was the true test of being a Viking, she told me.

When I visited her in 2009, each morning over cups of hot, dark coffee and fresh bread with cheese and jam in the kitchen of her cozy farmhouse—one of my favorite places in the world—she would look at me and say, "Okay, is *this* the morning you become a Viking?"

"Nope," I said each time.

Jumping into the cold sea in Denmark—*uden toj* (without clothes)—should not have been something a half-Dane would hesitate to do. But I didn't love the idea of immersing myself in freezing water.

"Can't I at least wear a bathing suit?" I pleaded.

"No," Karen said, laughing. "It is so cold here in the winter that if you wore a bathing suit, it would freeze to your skin the moment you immerse in the frigid waters, and the only way to remove it would be to cut it off."

Being the pragmatic people they are, the Danes had therefore decided long ago to do away with bathing suits altogether.

This did nothing to add to the appeal of the adventure.

And then one morning, Karen said slyly, "If you do this, Kristin, then you will be able to call yourself a *real* Viking."

My cousin knew me well. I sighed and, calling upon the mantra I had adopted back home in the mountains of Appalachia, said okay. And off we went to the edge of Denmark.

The Øresund was very cold that morning, but holes had thoughtfully been cut in the ice in support of this peculiar Scandinavian activity. I peeled off each layer of clothing as slowly as possible, placing them in a deflated little pile on the grass beside me.

Be not afraid, I whispered to myself. Then, in the midst of a small gathering of other naked Danes, I jumped into the water.

Ohmygod, was it cold!

In fact, it was something far beyond the parameters of cold—something so cold I'm pretty sure the word to describe it has not yet been invented, even in Danish. For what felt like a life-threateningly long time, I was unable to breathe. When I eventually realized I hadn't died, my breath came back to me in the form of gasps and sputters.

But as I emerged from the water, my skin felt astonishing, as if it was lit from within by a thousand fairy lights—a Scandinavian mermaid.

In the high that sometimes accompanies an unexpected flirtation with danger, it occurred to me that perhaps the magic lies in *not* feeling in control?

My new midnight mantra was the perfect antidote to the earlier years of worrying about paying bills, the late-night trips to the emergency room with Zoë or Leif, no "real" job, and keeping a roof over our heads. After all, I had made it through.

Not long after adopting the Be Not Afraid mantra, I traveled solo in Africa, tracking down that trail of letters my grandmother had written during the years she lived in the dusty highlands of Ethiopia, to research a memoir I was writing about her adventures there. Was I afraid? Absolutely, and for about 100 different reasons. But I went anyway.

Thank goodness Asheville had a film festival and that Steve had asked me to go with him. I don't think he would have gone without me. But thankfully he did because that evening he met Nan, who in turn introduced me to an evening with Howard Hanger and those adventure-inducing eleven words:

What would your life be like if you were not afraid?

The Unbearable Lightness of Being

AS I STOOD in the cold outside Greenlife, the natural foods market on the north end of Asheville, I stared in excitement at the newspaper I held in my shaking hands. Whether my hands were trembling from the February winds or the name I saw in the paper, I couldn't tell you.

Inside, stretching out over nearly four pages, was a feature article titled, "The Unbearable Lightness of Being: The Photography of Moni Taylor" by Kristin Fellows.

I had written it. *My* name was on the byline.

In a chilly state of bliss, I grabbed half a dozen copies of the paper, placing them in the passenger seat of my Subaru so I could keep an eye on them and revel in the moment.

At last, at last, at last, I thought. I've been waiting *years* for this!

Not long after moving to Asheville, I'd noticed an announcement in the *Mountain Xpress*, Asheville's cool, indie newspaper, saying they were looking for feature stories. Back then, *Mountain Xpress* was interesting, funny, irreverent, insightful, and very un-corporate. I devoured each weekly free edition, eager to get to know everything about my new town.

That fall, when I read the paper was looking for feature-length, interesting people stories, I knew exactly who to write about—a woman I'd met recently at a coffee shop.

Not long after arriving in town, I'd decided to treat myself to a morning coffee at Port City Java, just down the hill from my house.

It was an odd name for a coffeehouse in the landlocked mountains, I thought, hundreds of miles from the coast. (I would later discover it was owned by a small company in Wilmington, on the coastal side of the state where Zoë was now in university.)

I brought my laptop with me so I could linger if it wasn't too busy. Pretending to work, I was slightly distracted by two women at a nearby table, both of whom appeared to be close to my age. They were carrying on an animated discussion over what looked like a collection of artful black photo albums. Curious to know where in Asheville I might be able to buy similar artist journals for my photographs, I waited for a pause in their conversation before walking over and introducing myself. They were friendly and responded to my question.

After exchanging pleasantries for a few moments, I went back to my laptop. I was drafting an email, lost in thought, when I realized someone was standing near me. Looking up, I saw it was Moni, the tall blonde from the other table. She asked if we could continue chatting.

"Sure!" I said. And with that, a new friendship was born.

Moni (pronounced *mah-nee*) and I quickly discovered that in addition to art journals, we also shared a passion for photography, especially candid people photography.

In addition to being a photographer, Moni told me she worked as a nurse in the neonatal intensive care unit at Asheville's local hospital. At one point in our conversation, she mentioned she occasionally combined both professions by photographing the heartbreaking endings that sometimes are a part of a neonatal hospital ward—the fetal demises. She showed me a few of her photographs. In one, a woman gently grasps a tiny set of fingers, unbelievably fragile, between her thumb and forefinger. In another, a young woman leans her head on the shoulder of the man beside her, both of them gazing in tears down at the tiny, swaddled bundle in her arms. Cameos—both beautiful and heartbreaking—of families that will exist only for a few moments.

Moved by the unbearable poignancy of her photography, I felt an instant connection to her. And so, when I saw the announcement about feature articles in the *Mountain Xpress*, I called Moni to ask if I could write about her.

A week later, she was in my living room overlooking the mountains, perched on my sofa, her blue jean-clad slender legs tucked up underneath her, a cup of tea by her side. She told me the story of her life and showed me more of the black and white photographs she'd taken.

"When you tell them you're a Labor and Delivery nurse, people think, 'Oh, that's so wonderful!' That's the fun, happy place to be!" she said. "And it is. But it can also be the saddest."

"There's that magic moment," she said, her blue-green eyes narrowing with the poignancy of what she was trying to convey. "That little sliver of space where you just don't know. When you wonder, will the baby make the transition from living inside its mom to living by itself outside? People get light years' worth of experience in that moment."

For those who don't make it, Moni's photography offers an opportunity to pay tribute, not only to this "tiniest sliver of a life," but also to a fleeting tableau of a family that will soon exist only in those photographs. Over and over, she emphasized what an honor she felt it was to be part of a space in time that was, in the words of author and priest Henri Nouwen, "Arrival and departure . . . yesterday and today . . . all compressed in one blink of an eye."

Mountain Xpress editor Peter Gregutt published my feature story on Moni's photography in February 2006. Just seven months after I'd moved to Asheville, I could finally say I was a published writer—the kind that gets paid.

Landing a feature in the local newspaper was very affirming—not only of the move to Asheville, but also of my love for writing about people.

After I'd picked up my bundle of newspapers at Greenlife, I called Moni with the good news. And that morning, both of us drove all over Asheville, picking up a few copies here, a few copies there, amassing small stashes of them in our excitement.

Still high on the thrill of seeing my name in print, I phoned a local lawyer a few days later to handle the paperwork for starting my own documentary film production company. One week later, Asheville Productions was created.

My First Film:
A Woman Named Hello

Morning journal, March 1, 2006—It just occurred to me this morning, as I sit on the back deck looking out over the mountains on the first morning of the new spring season— coffee, oatmeal, paper and pen by my side—that my talent is not so much with words, but with story. Writing, film, music—it can all work for me, as long as I know my place, which is in recognizing the story. I'm not a wonderful wordsmith, although every so often I put words together in a way that pleases me. I think I'm more of a thought-smith.

I'm drawn to and want to work with stories, in writing or film. Luckily that's what's hot just now. When I look at what's happening at the Academy Awards this year— Brokeback Mountain, Murderball, and some of the others—I don't feel they are necessarily the best examples of the actual craft of filmmaking. They're being nominated for being a compelling tale or paradigm shift or vision, whether it's cowboys who fall in love or quadriplegic athletes playing wheelchair rugby.

IF I INCLUDED the documentary on Jack

Bogdanovich, *The Time Between* would be my second attempt at making a film.

After establishing Asheville Productions as a legal entity, my first thought was to make a documentary about Moni and her moving black-and-white photography of the little babies who'd had such brief lives.

I called it *The Time Between* in honor of that too little time between some babies' births and their deaths. I hired Leif to edit a trailer with Eva Cassidy's poignant "Songbird" as the underlying music track which, to me, felt like a mother's ode to her lost child.

Despite many efforts over many months, I was unable to get a grant or pull together any production funds. Which was just as well because not long after the feature I'd written for the *Mountain XPress* was published, Moni dropped a bombshell on me.

We were having coffee at the Dripolater in downtown Asheville when she told me she'd applied and been accepted to serve in the Peace Corps. Amid the happy morning buzz of coffee machines, chatter, and chill music all around me, I sat stunned and sad, the coffee in my cup turning cold as she told me all about her new adventure.

She'd been hoping to get stationed in Eastern Europe, she said. But instead, she'd been assigned to Malawi, a small country in Africa and one of the poorest in the world. Learning that Malawi was nicknamed "the warm heart of Africa," Moni turned it into an opportunity and embraced the idea of going there instead.

She was so excited, I tried to be happy for her. But I was also heartbroken that my first best friend in Asheville would soon be leaving to live and work on the other side of the world.

As Zoë and Leif were growing up, I tried to nurture in them the perspective of seeing how disappointments and bad surprises might be turned into opportunities—if seen from a different angle.

Of course, it's easier to give someone else that advice rather than act upon it yourself. It's not always obvious and sometimes you have to work hard to wrap your head around unexpected changes. But a few weeks after Moni gave me her news, I thought of a way to see it as an opportunity. Pivoting from the underfunded *Time Between*, I asked Moni if I could instead document her journey from Appalachia to Africa—and she agreed.

The narrative thread for this new documentary would be that it's one thing to join the Peace Corps in the early post-college years, before the responsibilities of a lifetime and family fall upon you. But what happens when you make a pledge to service at the age of 54, when the childbearing and child-raising years are behind you? What happens when you leave a life—everything and everyone you have ever known—and find yourself thousands of miles from home, in a culture that bears no resemblance to your own?

I particularly loved the idea that a nurse from Appalachia—an area which for so many decades has been associated with poverty and need—was shifting that old paradigm around by setting forth to help *others* in the world.

I would document her journey to Africa, I proposed. And along the way, we would discover what would be demanded of her in return after she got there. Moni said okay, and we high-fived our new adventure over cups of coffee.

Before setting off for Africa, Moni decided to get a tattoo. It would be her first and it wouldn't be just a little flower on her shoulder or a little Zen mantra. A devout Catholic, she decided she wanted a full back piece—an image of the Virgin Mary holding a ribbon with the names of her four children in script on it.

"That way the Blessed Mother will always have my back," she explained, smirking mischievously.

A back piece was a huge commitment in terms of tattoos and pain. I tagged along with her, photographing part of the process for our new documentary, watching her bite strands of her long gray-blonde hair, blinking back tears as Danny the tattoo artist inked the full color images across her backbone.

A few weeks later, I called cinematographer Richard Chisolm, and he flew down from Baltimore to help me with two days of shoots around Asheville. Local cameraman Jason Scholder shot a Peace Corps meeting at the Dripolator with Dave Schmidt running sound. To create a fundraising trailer, I licensed footage from Zygimantas Cepaitis to cover the Malawi part and requested permission to use West African musician Baaba Maal's "A Song for Women."

Putting the kids to good use, Zoë worked as my associate producer on the shoots and Leif edited another trailer for me. It still gives me chills—in a good way—to watch it.

At this point, however, nothing had really sprung to mind for the title of the documentary.

And then one day, over yet more cups of tea and coffee, Moni told me she was starting to learn some preliminary words in Chichewa, the primary language spoken in Malawi.

"And hey, how funny is this!?" she said. "My name in Chichewa means 'hello and welcome.'"

"That's it!" I said, smiling at her. "That's the title of our film—*A Woman Named Hello!*"

After Moni left for Africa, I busied myself writing and sending out more grant proposals to fund production. After that, unfortunately, nothing went quite to plan. . . .

WHAT'S BETTER
THAN A SHEEPDOG
IN NEW ZEALAND?

MUCH TO MY surprise, it turns out it's *me*—at least in the eyes of Joan Konner, Dean Emerita of the Columbia University Graduate School for Journalism.

That comment came about while I was promoting a documentary she'd made about the mystery of love. I thought her comment was funny, but it wasn't until I was immersed in the world of nanotechnology that it occurred to me how I could use it in my bio. That happened one morning as I was driving across North Carolina to a conference.

Immune to little modern luxuries, such as having a CD player in her car, my mother once told me she often hummed Big Band music from the 1940s to stay awake on the eight-hour drive between Alexandria and Asheville when she drove down to visit us.

Humming was not enough to keep me awake. I needed coffee and I knew, from my visits to Zoë in Wilmington, the location of each and every Starbucks along the route. I just had to take care to strike a balance between drinking coffee and the subsequent bathroom stops.

In early 2008, in search of marketing ideas and connections, I was on my way to attend the second annual NC Science Bloggers Conference in Research Triangle Park. I'd been hired once again by the Fred Friendly group at Columbia University—this time to promote a three-part series, *Nanotechnology: The Power of Small,* to PBS stations across the country.

Did I know anything about nanotechnology? Nope, not a thing.

I always tried to promote my projects in what I hoped was a uniquely counterintuitive way. It was never enough to simply say, "I've got a great documentary that I think you should air on your PBS station in prime time," and then rely upon friendships and goodwill for that to happen. That does nothing to distinguish you or set your films apart. It's an unimaginative approach and it certainly doesn't project: *This is a must-see documentary.*

I started each project pondering what aspect of it interested *me* and my restless mind. What surprised me? What got *my* attention? Once I figured that out, it gave me insights into how to make it interesting to others.

So when I came across an article on nanotechnology written by Steve Boggan in *The Guardian* titled "Once Bitten," I knew I'd found a great conversation starter to use with my PBS colleagues—food. To get their attention and offset any potential foot-dragging regarding what might appear to be a technical and wonky science series, I sent out a marketing piece with the caption "How Does Nanotechnology *Taste?*"

Quoting Boggan, I wrote: "If you have ever had concerns about genetically modified food, you will be either delighted or concerned by the implications for how nanotechnology could revolutionize the food you eat. Welcome to the world of nanofoods, where almost anything is possible . . . like bowls of ice cream with no more fat than a carrot . . . where smart packaging sniffs out and destroys the microorganisms that make good food go bad . . . From soil to supper, nano is set to become the next kitchen battleground."

And then, off I went to the bloggers conference to deal with the publicity aspect of raising awareness about this PBS series, for which I was also responsible.

Just saying the words "science blogger" made me oddly happy and I was looking forward to spending time in a whole room of them. While blogs number in the hundreds of millions these days, back in 2008, blogging had only been around for about a decade. Blogging platforms WordPress and TypePad were only five years old. The Huffington Post and Twitter, founded on the concept of microblogging, were both just toddlers.

For a full day, 200 participants talked about why they blogged, how blogs can be useful in teaching and learning, and how bloggers contribute to the public understanding of science. Topics so over my head and wonky, it felt stimulating and inspiring just to be in the midst of these scientific-minded people. In turn, I shared information about *The Power of Small* series, encouraging participants to write about it in their blogs.

Driving back to Asheville on I-40 the morning after the conference, I had a head full of ideas but hadn't yet had my morning coffee. Somewhere in the middle of North Carolina, I realized I didn't need coffee—I could actually *think* myself into a faux caffeinated state.

And for that, I could thank the experience of being called names by a couple of female documentary filmmakers!

I had recently worked with Joan Konner, the first woman to lead Columbia University's Graduate School of Journalism, on her documentary *The Mystery of Love*. Hosted by playwright and actress Anna Deavere Smith, it was one of the more than 50 documentaries and television specials Joan had produced on ideas and beliefs. She also wrote and edited books she described as "takeout gourmet food for thought"—and what's not to like about that? Joan's husband, producer

Al Permutter, had hired me to take care of the national PBS station wrangling for *The Mystery of Love.*

Renee Bishop, the other filmmaker, was the executive producer of *Farmers' Almanac TV*—an engaging series about rural America, practical wisdom, and environmental awareness I'd promoted in the early days of the farm-to-table movement.

Mulling over comments I'd recently received from these women, it occurred to me I should put them both at the top of the list of unsolicited feedback I sent to prospective clients. I've always liked using spontaneous, unsolicited comments, as they feel more genuine and sincere to me than quotes from clients who've been asked for their feedback.

Joan's note to me read: *Thanks again for your help and your powers of persuasion. You're better than a sheepdog in New Zealand rounding up this flock (of PBS stations.)*

And in response to my final project report, Renee wrote: *I am sitting here with tears running down my face. It means the world that this is happening, Kristin. Thank you for all your help! I have had a knot of anxiety that unwinds more and more with every email like this we get (from you.)*

Writing in my head as I drove west, I thought how fun it would be to use a mash-up of these women's comments at the top of the feedback page I send out to encourage new filmmakers to work with me:

"I've made filmmakers cry and been compared to a dog. And those are just some of the *nicer* things people have said about working with me!"

Smiling at these good memories kept me wide awake the rest of my drive.

Non-Fiction Nirvana

I LOVE GOING to film festivals. And whenever I can, I bring along at least one of my kids.

Ever the fun mum (at least in my own mind), when I heard the Found Footage Festival would be playing at The Grey Eagle, a live music venue in the heart of Asheville's River Arts District, I got tickets for me and the kids. I thought as a film studies major Zoë might enjoy it—a comedy film festival created by two dumpster diving dudes? Who *wouldn't* enjoy that? After all, it was the kids who'd insisted I watch the *Jackass* series (classified on IMDB in the "comedy/ stupidity/vile" genre).

Found Footage was the brainchild of Nick Prueher and Geoff Haas, childhood friends who'd created a comedy routine around discarded videos and tapes they'd discovered at yard sales and thrift shops. Initially put together just to entertain friends, their comedy routine was so well received they'd quit their day jobs the year before to go on tour and focus on producing a documentary, *Dirty Country.*

As expected, it was an evening of good fun, despite taking place in the dead of winter inside The Grey Eagle, which had not yet installed heating.

Most of the film festivals I went to, however, were on a more professional level.

If I ever needed affirmation that working with storytellers in film was where I should be, the first day at SILVERDOCS Film Festival—which I attended the year before moving to Asheville—confirmed that for me.

Watching interesting and often unusual stories with hundreds of other film lovers—this is what I love about film festivals. Red carpets, celebrity sightings, and champagne are pleasant distractions, but I go for the stories and to be in the company of like-minded individuals.

Founded in 2003 and centered around the old AFI Silver Theatre, a beautiful Art Nouveau indie cinema in downtown Silver Spring, Maryland, SILVERDOCS was a joint effort between the American Film Institute and Discovery Channel. With Nina Gilden Seavey as the founding director, the festival quickly became a major stop on the documentary film circuit. Nina's own documentary, *The Open Road,* was one of my inspirations to leave the Washington, DC area.

In its heyday, SILVERDOCS attracted thousands of attendees each summer from across the globe offering a diverse range of films and filmmakers representing as many as 60 countries. It was lauded as "Non-Fiction Nirvana" by *Variety* and "a premiere showcase for documentary film" by *Hollywood Reporter.*

I was on crutches following foot surgery the first time I attended, but even that did not stop me from being there. That year, SILVER-DOCS featured sessions that facilitated casual meetings between representatives from the World Bank and international distributors from all over Europe and Canada. It was kind of like speed dating for filmmakers looking for funding and distribution support.

That was the year *Born into Brothels* was on the film festival circuit—a documentary about Zana Briski's journey into Calcutta's underworld to photograph the city's prostitutes. In the process of making her film, Briski had the thought to buy a bunch of disposable cameras and teach the prostitutes' children the basics of photography and storytelling so they could document their own lives on the streets of one of the world's poorest cities. The resulting photographs were exhibited around the world.

The title alone scared me—kids living in India's worst slums and brothels? I felt I would surely be shattered by what I saw. But something nudged me to go ahead and see it anyway. It was both shocking and heartwarming and I walked out of the darkened movie theater wanting to tell everyone about it. Such can be the power of documentary film.

I wasn't the only one who left the screening feeling that way. Two days later, it won the audience award and later went on to win the Academy Award for best documentary feature in 2005.

I went to SILVERDOCS again in 2006, this time with Stephen, who was volunteering behind the scenes, and Zoë, who had just completed her freshman year at UNC-W. Stephen was able to smuggle Zoë into a front row seat during a special session so she could see and hear the legendary filmmaker and director Martin Scorsese talk.

After moving to North Carolina, I also decided to check out Full Frame in Durham. One of the oldest film festivals in the U.S., this one was founded by Scorsese himself.

Between sessions, I found myself standing in line in the ladies' room next to film director Mira Nair, who was part of a special panel discussion titled "Ten Filmmakers, Ten Films and Ten Years."

Scorsese, Cara Mertes, D.A. Pennebaker, Walter Mosley, Michael Moore, Mira Nair, and others each selected a film they felt marked changes in our culture and the documentary form.

While I'm sure everything they said was interesting to me at the time, what has stayed with me was Mira Nair's advice to filmmakers, which I feel applies equally to writers:

1. *Surround yourself with people who believe in you*

2. *Be fearless*

3. *Be foolishly optimistic*

4. *Have something to say*

5. *Be unique in your voice*

Of these, I'm pretty sure I have at least number three nailed—I am nothing if not foolishly optimistic. I also feel pretty good about numbers four and five—but that may be just my own opinion.

Despite my winter mantra—Be Not Afraid—number two continues to be a work in progress.

I added one of my own to Ms. Nair's list:

6. *Don't hesitate to be "Mikey," the person who takes on challenges nobody else wants to do and finds success pulling them off*

Whether it's getting improbable donations for an on-air auction, securing a personal interview with a sitting U.S. president, embracing a documentary no one else wants to work on, or saying "yes" to doing the national publicity for a public affairs special named *Who Cares*, where even the program's title telegraphs its lack of appeal: Take a deep breath and channel your inner "Mikey." Open your mind and figure out a way to creatively pull it off. Doing this successfully is the best investment you can ever make in your career, and your self-confidence.

THE FILM THAT NEARLY LANDED US IN JAIL

IN THE FALL of 2008, I found myself standing in front of an intriguing, quirky, and colorful dreamscape, lost for words.

The painting, by North Carolina artist Jane Filer, was hanging on the wall of Haen Gallery in Asheville. I'd come to the opening with friends and was stopped in my tracks. I couldn't take my eyes off it. I wanted to live inside the colorful, whimsical world I saw before me.

Chris Foley, the owner of Haen Gallery, and I had followed the same escape route southwest from Alexandria to Asheville. Trained as a painter and sculptor, Chris had his own connections to Old Town's collection of artists at the Torpedo Factory, where I'd had my "Introduction to the Third Dimension." But we hadn't known one another during our years there.

Noticing the look of helpless infatuation in my eyes, and perhaps my mouth hanging open, Chris walked over and side by side, we stared at the painting.

"*Like* this one?" he asked after a moment, a smile on his face.

"Like it?! I *love* it!" I responded—probably something you should never say to a gallery owner.

"It reminds me of Italy," I said, transfixed. "I *love* Italy."

Bracing myself, I asked the price. Chris walked over to check the little sticker next to the painting, as if he didn't already know.

"$2800," he said, watching to see my reaction.

Like a hat pin to a balloon, that number popped the trance-like state I was in. $2800 was well beyond what I should responsibly spend on a piece of art, especially now both kids were in college and I was their sole financial sponsor.

Nevertheless, I wanted it. If I couldn't live in that world, I at least wanted to hang it on my wall and escape into the magical landscape of its colors and buildings and trees and birds whenever I wanted to, whenever I *needed* to.

But being a responsible mother was woven into my body fabric, as much a part of my design and component parts as my freckles and blonde hair were. And although work was steady—the best it had ever been, in fact—I wondered how on earth I could justify the expense.

And then, a memory popped into my head and it took all of a New York minute to decide this painting would be a reward to myself for getting both kids safely through high school and on to university—despite what might be considered a recent lapse in judgment on my part.

Of course, a film was to blame for that lapse. But this time, not one I was working with.

Leif graduated from Asheville High School in the spring of 2008 and a few months later headed off to SCAD, the Savannah College of Art and Design, which was, ironically, where Karen once upon a time thought she might go for a master's degree. SCAD was Leif's first choice and well beyond what I could afford. But I decided, in the manner of Scarlett O'Hara, to figure that out another day.

That it almost didn't happen, however, was because of a film.

Just as films wove in and throughout my life, they often wove in and around the narrative of my kids' lives as well, usually passing through and doing no harm.

One evening the previous year, however, I'd thought it might be fun to watch *Saving Grace*—partly because it's a well-made, well-acted, and funny British film, and perhaps also to show what a cool mum I was (once again, at least in my own mind).

Directed by Nigel Cole and starring Brenda Blethyn, Craig Ferguson, and Martin Clunes (soon to be of *Doc Martin* fame) and set in Cornwall, it's the story of Grace Trevethyn, a small-town, middle-aged widow. The death of her irresponsible late husband leaves her with enormous debt, and Grace soon realizes she will lose her home and all her possessions unless she can come up with enough money to pay her dead husband's outstanding bills.

Grace has a greenhouse on her property. She's an expert in growing orchids. Aware of this, her young gardener, Matthew, offers to continue working without pay if she were to care for his own dying plants. Grace agrees to his offer, not realizing Matthew is growing cannabis.

Under Grace's green thumb, the plants flourish astonishingly, and she and Matthew soon realize they can grow and produce lots of cannabis in a short time. After further drama and misadventures, Grace eventually becomes financially solvent with the success of her subsequent novel, *The Joint Venture*.

Saving Grace premiered at the 2000 Sundance Film Festival, where it won the Audience Award for World Cinema.

[Interesting sidenote: I read that some of the plants used in the shooting were actually real marijuana plants. According to a note on the film site IMDb, the British government gave permission to the film crew to use 150 real plants, under the supervision of authorities. And it was somebody's *job* to guard the marijuana plants on set and watch over their transportation to a nearby storage facility for their safekeeping each night.]

Pleased I had selected a film to watch that we all enjoyed, I thought nothing more of it.

Leif, it turned out, found the film inspirational.

Several weeks later, I returned home from shopping and let myself in through the garage, which was on the lower level of our hillside home. Carrying my bags up the old wooden stairs to the kitchen on the upper level, I noticed glimmers of light coming from between the wooden steps.

I mulled this over while putting away my groceries. How odd, I thought—why had I never noticed that light before? Curious, I decided to find out where it was coming from.

Retracing my steps back down the stairs, I determined the light must be coming from the old closet underneath the steps at the back of the garage. I knew the closet was there but had never used it as there were plenty of wooden shelves in the garage itself that were easier to access.

Opening the door, I was astonished when light flooded out and then further astonished to see every surface of the forgotten closet meticulously covered with aluminum foil. A large heat lamp, suspended in the middle by an intricate web of fluorescent green string, was shining down on three white Styrofoam cups, inside each of which was a small green plant.

Leif, it would appear, had taken an interest in horticulture.

I closed the door, pondering what to do. I went back upstairs, got a piece of paper, a black pen, and some tape. Then I went back down and taped the paper to the door of the closet. On it, I'd written just three words:

See me—Mum

About an hour later, I heard the school bus come to a stop up the hill on the road next to our mailbox. I heard its doors open, then listened to my son's footsteps walking down our long driveway. I listened as he opened the large garage doors, then followed the sound of his footsteps as they went over to the closet, where they stopped for a moment. The closet door opened, then closed again. And then I heard his footsteps, slower now, dragging themselves up the wooden stairs to our kitchen where I sat at the table, nursing a cup of coffee.

He walked into the kitchen and glared at me.

"*What!?*" he said, in a not-unusual teenager's surly way of starting a conversation.

What followed was a heated discussion between a now chagrined mother and her entrepreneurial offspring, a discussion that would grow into an ongoing debate off and on for another year, as Leif presented me with Harvard papers and medical research in support of his beliefs that weed was both medicinal and good for writers and critical thinkers. In short, anything he thought might win me over.

One afternoon, weary of the arguments and unable to think of anything clever to say, I finally blurted out the words, "*You don't have my blessing!*"

I still remember exactly where we were when I said that. I'd just picked him up from school and on the drive home, we'd had yet another go-around on the topic. I was following him along the stone pathway that led through my gardens to the front door when I finally said that. To my shock, my blessing seemed to matter.

"But *why?!*" he said, turning around to face me, dark eyes pleading from under his shaggy dark brown hair; frustration apparent in every ounce of his body language.

It wasn't that I was adamantly against weed. But my bottom line was always that it was still illegal and I couldn't risk anything that might result in having my house taken away from me. It was all I had, and I had worked so damn hard for the precious stability we were now enjoying.

"When you have your own place," I said at the end of each argument, "you can do what you want. But for now, it's *my* house and *my* rules."

(Side note: I *was* impressed with his budding botany interest and skills and let him know that, while also making the point that if growing plants interested him so much, why wasn't he helping me out in the gardens?)

Recalling this, as well as other far more stressful moments my teenagers had given me, including a different weed adventure that led to an actual dust-up with the Asheville police, I decided this painting would be my gift to myself for having pulled it all off: for having gotten all three of us to this point in our lives, often by the seat of my threadbare jeans.

Looking at Jane Filer's painting, I turned to the one person I could always count on to say yes to art.

What do you think, do you like it? Should I buy it? I thought.

Of course you should, honeybunch, Karen replied.

This was a useful trick I played on myself to justify buying a piece of art I really wanted. In my imagination, she always said yes. There were more practical and mature things to do with my money but hanging a savings account or monthly investment statement on the wall wouldn't have had the same effect, lighting up my mind and triggering endorphins the way the colors in this painting did.

That painting was—and still is—a daily reward. I don't think I've ever experienced the same magnitude of accomplishment and relief as I did when both Zoë and Leif had graduated safely and successfully from high school and went on to university.

Despite his side adventure, Leif applied to and was accepted at SCAD. As if foreshadowing his freshman (and only) year there, I was already working on a series for public television called *Farmer's Almanac TV,* headquartered—as sweet luck would have it—in Savannah.

FATV was a mouth-wateringly beautiful farm-to-table agricultural and lifestyle series. The whole crew, including Bill Chisholm, Renee Bishop, and Mickey Younas, was a delight to work with and very supportive of my efforts to get their shows on the air. As a thank you gift to PBS programmers for their support, we hosted an amazing bonfire party on the beach at Amelia Island, where they'd gathered for an annual public television conference.

The production team trucked in dozens of hay bales, built a bonfire for toasting s'mores and brought in a charming band of young farmer musicians from New England. Special red flannel blankets with the series' logo embroidered on them were given to everyone as thank you gifts they could take with them and be reminded of the series each time they curled up with one at home.

Thanks to our collective efforts, *Farmers' Almanac TV* went on to have more than sixty-two thousand airdates in all states, covering 92 percent of the U.S.

As an added bonus, it was nice to have a reason to justify trips to Savannah without appearing to be a hovering mama, to keep an eye on my budding botanist.

My Next Film Idea: The Mountains'll Gitcha

Morning journal, October 27, 2006—This afternoon, while making my usual calls, I phoned a PBS programmer I try to avoid, if possible, as he can be unpredictably temperamental. But I'm working on another film for WNET—this time about the Virgin Mary in art around the world—and I needed to see if his station would air it. He seemed quite astonished I called at that moment, as he'd just been speaking about me with a retired doctor—someone he'd asked to screen Picturing Mary *for him. (How often did programmers ask other people to screen films for them instead of doing it themselves, I wondered.) After watching the film, the doctor had asked to speak with me, as my name was on the copy of the film. The programmer gave me his number and so I called him. We had a pleasant chat, discussed the film briefly, then travel and other things. He ended the call by telling me to breathe. He told me to do one thing at a time, take care to exercise, walk, play, socialize. . . .*

How funny, this advice from a complete

stranger, and on Karen's birthday eve—as if she was giving me advice through someone else. At least, that's what I like to think.

While speaking with him, I walked into my living room and saw how beautiful it was to look down my mountainside and across the valley to the other mountainside with the fall leaves on the cloudy misty day, and wondered why I didn't spend more time just gazing at the mountains through my windows.

THAT YEAR FOR Christmas, I'd ordered a T-shirt for Leif from Slightly Stoopid, a California rock band. Inspired by Mötley Crüe, Guns N' Roses, Metallica, and Def Leppard, Slightly Stoopid describes their music as nothing less than "a fusion of folk, rock, reggae, and blues with hip-hop, funk, metal, and punk."

At the time, Slightly Stoopid was one of his favorite bands. I liked their music, too. "Girl U So Fine," released in August 2007, was one of my favorite songs ever. I loved the guitar work of Miles Doughty and Kyle McDonald.

When the T-shirt arrived, however, I felt slightly stoopid myself when I realized I'd inadvertently ordered a child's size. Luckily, there were still a few weeks left before Christmas, and I had an idea.

Just down the road that connected Asheville to my neighborhood by the lake, there was a little business in a little building over a little wine shop that was called Mary's Magic. After a steep climb up the long flight of stairs on the left of the building, you entered into a warren of rickety old rooms housing Mary herself, and the seamstresses she employed "from the counties"—mountain women who liked to sew and gossip with one another with pauses for a cigarette in between projects.

Still needing one last gift for Leif, I brought the black T-shirt to Mary to see if she could make it into a pillow. She took it into her hands, turned it over and over, then laughed and said, well sure, why not.

With her graying hair and kind dark eyes behind her glasses, I don't know how old Mary was; she'd reached that age known vaguely as "ageless." What I did know, however, was that she was an excellent seamstress and full of piss and vinegar once she felt comfortable talking to you. Mary considered herself "mountain folk" and as an outsider, and a *Northerner* at that, it took her a while to warm up to me.

But once she saw I was a repeat customer, one who was genuinely interested in hearing her stories, if she wasn't too busy she would entertain me with a tale or two of mountain life and culture. I took to calling her "Magic Mary," an affectionate inversion of her business name.

Fortunately, I'd arrived with my slightly stupid T-shirt-to-pillow project on a not very busy day, and so I took the opportunity to ask Magic Mary about something I'd overheard not long before.

"Have you ever heard an expression, *'The mountains'll git ya?'*" I said, in my best imitation of a Southern accent. She looked surprised.

"Ho, yes!" she said laughing. (That's not a typo. Around these parts, it's not unusual to hear the word "oh" pronounced backwards. I think this is for emphasis.)

I told her I'd recently wandered into the outfitters store in Weaverville, not more than a few miles up the road. While there, I'd overheard a group of men man-gossiping about something somebody had done—clearly something they didn't apparently approve of. While I couldn't make out the exact nature of the crime from the other side of the display of fishing and hunting gear I was hiding behind, I did hear the verdict:

"The mountains'll git 'im!," one man said, a statement that was received with a chorus of approving grunts from the others.

I was taken with the idea that the ancient mountains we lived in, some of the world's oldest, could inflict justice or revenge upon those who deserved it and had made a mental note to ask Magic Mary about it. If anyone knew, she would.

"Is that really a thing?" I asked after we'd finished with the T-shirt details and I'd told her the story.

"Ho yes," she said again, this time with a serious expression on her face. "The stories I could tell you!"

"Like what?" I asked, always up for good stories and already thinking what a cool idea this might be for a documentary.

"Well, I could tell you a *lot* of them!" she said. "Like the time I had a customer who brought me a whole bunch of clothes to alter, but then never came back to pick 'em up! And then, many months later, out of the blue, she finally stopped by. I asked her why it had taken her so long. And she told me her husband, who had *a lot* of money, had put in a contract to buy up someone's family land for development."

Here Mary paused for dramatic effect. Knowing the subject of outsiders coming in and buying up mountain folks' lands, especially if they were unable to pay their taxes on it, was a touchy one, I leaned in to listen even more closely.

"And . . . ?" I said, prompting her.

"He died *on the morning* they was supposed to close on the deal!" she said triumphantly. "He had a heart attack—*jesht like that!*"

She nodded her head for emphasis, satisfied with the justice the mountains had meted out. I was genuinely surprised, both by the story as well as her apparent glee in the outcome.

"Tell me another one!" I said, setting up film shoots and interviews in my mind, starting with Mary herself.

Over the next twenty minutes or so, Mary unspooled a few more tales, enough to get me mentally drafting out a grant request for production funds, while hoping there wasn't anything I myself was doing to upset the mountains I'd come to love. I envisioned the documentary as a cautionary tale for those who came to take advantage of the natural beauty of the Blue Ridge Mountains and try to profit from them.

Not long after that conversation, I saw a billboard along the I-26 highway on my way into Asheville. It was an advertisement for a

795-acre parcel of mountain land just east of the city that offered a golf course, designed by Tiger Woods, surrounded by a community of one thousand luxury homes. On the billboard, Woods appeared to gaze off in the distance at the mountains with the words "Come see what *I* see!" representing his thoughts.

That was in 2008.

And we all know what happened to him the following year: a high-profile marital scandal followed by the loss of millions of dollars in endorsement deals. By 2012, seven years after the project was announced and all the trees on the mountainside had been chopped down by the developers, fewer than 50 of the estimated 1000 homes had been sold, and the development project went into bankruptcy.

I don't have any proof, but I like to think the mountains got 'em.

INKED!

IT WASN'T LONG after I moved to Asheville that I decided to get my first tattoo. In a town inhabited by many, many inked individuals, the idea of having art not only on my walls, but also on my body, was irresistible.

I chose Kitty Love, Asheville's very first female tattoo artist. I felt at home in the inner recesses of her studio, which at the time was inside Liquid Dragon Tattoo, Asheville's oldest tattoo studio.

Located at the back of an alley in between two of our favorite restaurants, Bouchon (French) and Mela (Indian), both owned by friends, Kitty's room had shelves of art books, which gave me an added degree of comfort before I went under the needle.

Kitty was an interesting individual. Depending upon which day you saw her, her long hair could be brown or perhaps magenta. She began tattooing in 1991, not long after she graduated from the Maryland Institute College of Art with a BFA in illustration and graphic design— part of a wave of art school grads and other enthusiasts who embraced this intriguing and social art form at the turn of the millennium. Decades later, she still feels that tattooing holds a unique cultural posi- tion and role in contemporary identity.

At the age of 52, I was ready for mine. Zoë was home from university and insisted on coming with me. I was pleased she wanted to be the boss of this new experience, both to look out for me as well as to watch over me.

"So, what do you want?" Kitty asked me when we met.

I'd given this some thought for the past several years. What would I like that really expressed *me* and my worldview, something I could live with for the rest of my life?

And what I kept coming back to was very simple: the Danish word *tak,* which means "thank you." It made a little statement about being half Danish. I also liked that it expressed gratitude because that's important to me. I called it my "grati-tat."

But then, worried it might be misconstrued as someone's initials, like an old boyfriend, I expanded it to *Tusind Tak—A Thousand Thanks.* Even better.

I also decided I wanted it on the center of my back.

"Across the backbone?" Kitty asked. "That's going to hurt."

"I'll be okay," I assured her. I pulled off my T-shirt and she examined my skin.

"Your back has had sun exposure," she said. "It would be better off if I put it a little lower down." She pointed to the tramp stamp vicinity.

Zoë erupted in laughter.

I told Kitty what *tusind tak* meant in Danish, and that having a message that said "a thousand thank yous" inked just above my ass was probably not the best idea.

When Zoë and I got back home, Leif appeared from the dark downstairs recesses of his lair.

"Show him your new tattoo!" Zoë said.

Leif's dark eyebrows shot up. "You got a *tattoo?!*" he said.

"Yup!" I said. I twirled around and lifted up my T-shirt.

"What do you think?" I asked as he studied it.

"You only have a thousand things to be grateful for?" he said, laughing.

As many will agree, getting tattooed can be a slippery slope. One leads to another. And another. It's an artful addiction.

And so, it wasn't long after that mere words were not enough. I wanted images. And I wanted them to represent two passions in my life—my people and my travels—tied together in a botanical theme.

I went back to see Kitty and soon thereafter, colorful flowers began to bloom on my leg.

Clutching a piece of Danish china in a traditional pattern called *Blå Blomst*, I first asked her to copy the blue flowers onto my leg. They would represent my mother, my Danish heritage, and our road trips together in Denmark.

Not long after, I noticed some purple azaleas for sale at the Biltmore Estate's greenhouse. I looked at the tag and discovered they were called "Karen azaleas."

That was just too coincidental—purple had been my sister's favorite color. I bought them. And, as I'd done with Dad's azaleas, I bought not just one, but all they had. I planted them on my hillside overlooking the bird sanctuary.

I brought a photograph of them over to Kitty and asked her to tattoo images of them—representing my sister, my father, and Asheville—around the Danish blue flowers.

Now that my own body was forever inked, it wasn't long before a documentary film came to me on that particular art form. Artists, musicians, and other creatives aren't the only ones to get tattooed. Soldiers like them, too.

In 2009, Emmy Award-winning film director Nancy Schiesari finished a visceral and raw documentary that offered an unusual window into the minds and hearts of U.S. soldiers.

Shot primarily at River City Tattoo Parlor in Killeen, Texas, male and female soldiers revealed aspects of themselves they would likely never have shared had someone sat them down under the lights for a standard interview.

Instead, these soldiers, against the background hum and buzz of the tattoo guns, shared stories about the ink on their bodies and why they'd chosen what they did—while they were getting inked. Their stories (and their tattoos) were mind-opening and heartbreaking; each in their own way inspired respect.

Nancy and I were introduced to one another by Maria Rodriguez, the senior vice president of broadcasting at KLRU in Austin, and Sreedevi Sripathy, associate director of broadcast and distribution at ITVS, a San Francisco-based organization funded by the Corporation for Public Broadcasting (CPB) to help filmmakers bring interesting and untold stories into the world. *Tattooed Under Fire* would be the first of more than a dozen films that would come my way from ITVS throughout the coming years.

Shot on location in Killeen, Texas, home to Fort Hood, America's largest military base, *Tattooed Under Fire* more than qualified as "interesting and untold."

Lying on a tattooist's table or sitting in a chair, under the unique discomfort of having tattoo machines permanently piercing ink into your skin, the soldiers Nancy spoke to opened up with heart-expanding and heart-wrenching stories.

One particular interview was with a young man who had the image of a baby in a blender inked on his upper bicep. Viewers would react viscerally to that, I realized, because in their mind they would imagine what would happen were someone to push the button on that blender. And that was exactly the point.

The soldier's story is told in two parts. At first you hate him for having that tattoo. But in the second part of his time on screen, in between deployments, we see a different side of him as he tells the story of what happened to a child in Iraq, how she jumped into his arms when her family was killed by American soldiers, and how they clung to each other, even though he was the enemy. The impact that little girl had on this soldier, and perhaps even on us as viewers, will last a lifetime.

Moved to tears by this documentary and the windows it gave

into the minds of soldiers, I pitched it for a Veterans Day broadcast. Many programmers responded with prime-time airdates on or close to November 10th.

Five days before *Tattooed Under Fire* was to premiere on PBS nationally, satisfied I had everything under control, I took the afternoon off and went out for a short hike.

And then the unthinkable happened.

When I came back home and checked my email, I was startled to see my inbox flooded with messages.

What on earth?!

While I was out hiking, a mass shooting had taken place at Fort Hood, exactly where Nancy's documentary had been filmed. Nidal Hasan, a US Army major and psychiatrist, opened fire, killing 13 individuals and injuring 32 others. It was the deadliest shooting on an American military base and the deadliest terrorist attack in the U.S. since 9/11.

It takes a long time to make a documentary. As a result, apart from PBS NewsHour and FRONTLINE, a lot of what is seen on public television has been months, if not years, in the making. But *Tattooed Under Fire* was one of those rare moments where we had exactly the right film to respond to the breaking news headlines.

The soldiers killed and injured in the attack were not the same soldiers as those profiled in Nancy's film. But they were *like* those soldiers and their stories provided a great deal of insight into the kinds of individuals America lost in that attack.

One after another, PBS programmers shared their thoughts with me:

I thought about it all the way home from work tonight. Really stays with you . . .

I'm a wreck, this film totally blew me away. [It] is one of the most powerful documentaries I have seen this year . . . a compassionate portrait of America's children in the military . . . and their personal need to arm themselves with body art to help process their reality . . . A very good reason to give peace a chance.

[This tattoo parlor] reminds me of the old local barbershop, where the community would gather for gossip and camaraderie. . . . I don't really like tattoos but now I get why these kids get them.

Sharing stories matters. I love what I do.

DANNY BOYLE AND THE NIGHT BEFORE CHRISTMAS

NOW THAT WE lived in the beautiful mountains of Western North Carolina, Leif and I both started hiking with friends.

I loved and supported this, but it also gave me something new to worry about. Would he hike prepared? Would he know what to do should something unexpected happen? Did he know what to do—and, more importantly, what *not* to do—if he saw a black bear? Black bears prefer forests and mountainous regions and our area was a perfect habitat for them. Almost everyone we know has had at least one or two black bears in their own garden. Driving around Asheville, it's easy to see the neighborhoods bears like best—their trash bins have chains and locks on them. One time, while out walking my dog, I came across a FedEx box left by the road, instead of on the front porch of its intended destination. On it were scrawled the words, "Big Black Bear At Your House!"

Black bears are more timid than brown bears, generally not interested in humans and will often flee an unexpected encounter. Brown bears tend to stand their ground and be more aggressive.

I had seen *Grizzly Man* at SILVERDOCS

Film Festival a few years earlier, Werner Herzog's non-fiction film about the life and horrific death of bear enthusiast Timothy Treadwell and his girlfriend, Amie, at Katmai National Park in Alaska. Treadwell recorded his bear encounters obsessively, which made it possible to make a documentary of his life. Mindful that their parents would likely see the film, Herzog told us afterwards in the Q&A he was careful which clips he included. Even so, the audio at the end of that film is something I'll never get out of my head.

That incident involved a brown bear, not a black bear, but I took that documentary as a nudge to be mindful.

When Danny Boyle's film *127 Hours* came to the Fine Arts Theater, I decided to take Leif to see it. After *Slumdog Millionaire,* I was keen to see any film Danny Boyle made. And for anyone who hikes, I was pretty sure it might teach us both important lessons. I also thought it might be a more effective scare tactic for Leif than hearing advice from his own mama bear.

Based upon Aron Ralston's 2004 memoir *Between a Rock and a Hard Place, 127 Hours* is billed as a vivid "hallucinogenic survival film" based on the true story of the five days Ralston, an avid mountaineer played by James Franco, spent in Utah's Canyonlands National Park after falling and getting his arm pinned under an 800-pound boulder.

In the film, Ralston, an experienced mountaineer, goes hiking without thinking to tell anyone. After his fall, nobody knows where he is. Realizing he is completely on his own, he begins recording a video diary with his camcorder to help keep his spirits up as he tries to chip away at the boulder with his pocketknife. For five days, Ralston rations his precious remaining food and water as he loses all sensation in his trapped arm. Increasingly depressed and desperate, he begins hallucinating about escape and past experiences. On the sixth day, inspired by a hallucinatory vision of his future son, he fashions a tourniquet, methodically breaks the bones in his arm, then slowly amputates it to free himself and find help.

It was a real head trip watching it. I worried Leif might have lost interest, but he surprised me when he said he really liked it. The hallucinogenic interior story of Ralston's mental and emotional journey appealed to him. On the way home, he appeared lost in thought as I yattered away about safety issues.

I slept peacefully that night, happy my point had been made. Another item off the list of the potential perils of raising kids in the mountains of Appalachia, I thought.

We saw *127 Hours* approximately 127 hours before Christmas. Not long after the sun set on Christmas Eve, Leif found me in the kitchen.

"C'mon, Mom," he said with a smile. "Let's open presents!"

"You want to already?" I asked. Now that the kids were older, we opened our presents, in the Danish tradition, by candlelight on Christmas Eve.

"Yup," he insisted cheerfully.

"Okay!" I said.

I went into the living room and turned on the Christmas tree lights. The colors sparkled in the softly lit room, reflecting in the windows overlooking the bird sanctuary. I lit the candles and poured myself a glass of red wine. Together, Leif and I pulled presents from underneath the tree and set them on the floor between the sofa and coffee table for easy opening. Our dogs, Bandit the Schnoodle and Klejne, a large, white GoldenDoodle, wandered in to see what was happening and if it included food.

"Start with your stocking!" Leif said to me as soon as I was settled.

"Why?" I asked, unable to remember the last time anything had been put into it—not that it stopped me from hanging it up each year, if for no other reason than decoration.

"Just do it!" he said, grinning.

Going over to the mantel, I was surprised to see the stocking bulging slightly. I reached inside and to my surprise, found several small packages.

Leif watched me carefully, not taking his eyes off me, not even to tear into his own presents.

I opened the first package and found an emergency lightweight poncho with a hood.

"That's really thoughtful, thank you!" I said, kind of surprised such a practical gift would occur to Leif. I set it aside to put in my hiking backpack.

"Open the others!" he commanded.

And so, I did. One by one, I discovered a magnesium fire-starter, an emergency mylar blanket, and a bear bell—all useful things for hiking and camping.

I was super impressed by his thoughtfulness and started to tell him so.

"Wait!" he said. "There's one more!"

Curious, I undid the wrapping. Inside, there was a small commando pocket wire saw, capable, I noticed, of cutting through bone. I looked up at my son.

"In case you're ever stuck between rocks," Leif said, cheerfully. "Now you'll be able to saw your arm off!"

James Franco was nominated for an Academy Award for Best Actor for his portrayal of Ralston.

The following spring or summer, Leif was back in Asheville after his freshman year at the Savannah College of Art and Design. One evening, while hanging out with friends at the Thirsty Monk downtown, he felt a tap on his shoulder. He turned around and there was James Franco.

Franco smiled, held up a disposable camera and asked if he could take Leif's picture.

"Okay," Leif said, shrugging good naturedly.

When he told me about this later, I thought Leif might now be the one hallucinating.

"Are you sure it was him?" I asked skeptically.

"Yup," said Leif.

I checked it out and learned Franco was, in fact, taking classes at nearby Warren Wilson College. He'd already earned an MFA in poetry and was now working on his MFA in fiction.

He was apparently often seen in downtown Asheville and Leif just happened to be in the same place at the same time. Leif thought it was pretty cool that a famous actor was not fending off selfie requests but instead, asking if he could take photos of others.

As for Aron Ralston, years later he got married and had that son he'd seen in his hallucinations. He also continues to hike and climb, and always leaves a note telling his family where he has gone.

FINDING PROMETHEUS— LIFE ON THE OTHER SIDE OF 52

AS THERE WAS nowhere to advertise my work as a self-styled, free-lance PBS station wrangler, I was completely dependent upon word of mouth. Fortunately, new film projects and referrals now came in steadily enough that I could finally relax somewhat about staying afloat and paying the bills.

Despite that, I still had another balance-threatening fear. There was an unseen clock—no less scary for being intangible—ticking in my head. I wanted to outlive my sister, to be older than Karen was when she died. We were ten years apart in age. If I could make it past 52, I thought, then I might be okay and could breathe a little easier. But that silent countdown haunted me until I reached what I'd come to think of as "the other side of 52."

Well-intentioned friends often sent me stories and articles about breast cancer. While I appreciated their thoughtfulness, I found the association very stressful. To have my only sister, an amazing artist, associated with and remembered, not for her art, but for having died of breast cancer? That was *not* how I wanted to remember her, nor how I wanted her to be remembered by others.

And the other problem—one I'd not anticipated—was that there was now no older sister to show me what 53 looked like if you had the same genetic combination. Or 54, or 55, and on and on for the rest of my life. Did those of us with strawberry blonde hair go gray or straight to white? Did we gain weight after 55? How quickly would our fair Scandinavian skin wrinkle up? (Quickly, it turns out.) Karen would have shown me but here I was, navigating the future on my own.

When I turned 52 in 2008, I thought I'd be relieved by surpassing that milestone which, in my darker moods, looked like a gravestone. But then, there was also my adventurous grandmother, my father's mother, to worry about. I was writing a book about her and the years she'd lived in Ethiopia. She'd died of breast cancer at 57, two years before I was born, and so my focus turned to another gloomy milepost, another tombstone in my mental cemetery of relatives.

In January 2011, while pondering a New Year's resolution, I remembered the question Howard Hanger had asked that dark Christmas Eve six years ago: *What if you were not afraid?*

In four months, I would turn 55. And so, I decided to test myself, pushing beyond any limits I'd previously experienced. I signed up for a 12-day REI Adventures hiking expedition to Iceland. It would be just extreme enough to feel I was testing myself without a reasonable expectation of dying in the process. I didn't know anyone in Iceland or on the trip, and I don't speak Icelandic. I would definitely *not* be in control. Of anything.

After signing the paperwork and sending in my deposit, I then spent a ridiculous amount of time worrying that I might not be able to keep up with the others on the trip, fit as I was from hiking and yoga. I'd spent a week hiking and camping in Yellowstone National Park with my high school boyfriend when I was in my twenties. But that was three decades ago.

And even though I was hiking regularly in the Blue Ridge

Mountains in my mid-fifties, I had visions of twenty-somethings scaling the landscape in athletic leaps and bounds with me slowly trudging through ice and volcanic ash, some distance behind them. What if I ended up a middle-aged *den mother* to a bunch of adventuring young jocks?

And then, just in time, I remembered—*Be not afraid.*

The trick was, how to *not* to be afraid? And so began a mental dialogue inside my brain as the logical, rational part of me tried to calm the freaked out, irrational part of me by framing the trip as a photography assignment. By appealing to my creative, storyteller side, the ruse worked. Which is a good thing, for had I succumbed to my fears, I would have missed out on ten days of astonishing adventures, sights, and new friendships.

A few months before leaving on the trip, I was contacted by John Kaplan, a photographer who'd documented his personal journey with cancer in a one-hour film, *Not As I Pictured: A Pulitzer Prize-Winning Photographer's Journey Through Lymphoma.*

John was at the top of his game professionally when he was diagnosed with a rare case of potentially deadly lymphoma. Despite his shock, John had the presence of mind to turn his lens on himself. Over time, he created a visual journey that documented his determination and the support he received from his family, musician Philip Anselmo of the heavy metal group Pantera, and even Mother Teresa. David Bowie donated the use of his iconic song, "Heroes," for the film's soundtrack.

This journey was what he wanted to put into my hands. Would I consider representing his film, John asked, and help him get it on PBS stations throughout the country? He wanted to use his broadcasts to spread the word that he was giving away free DVDs of his documentary. It was an incredibly generous offer to help anyone dealing with lymphoma. He wanted to give them hope.

I was scared to watch it. Twelve years after Karen died, I was still worried that what had happened to her would also happen to me. Even though the sculpture class had helped channel some of my sadness into that little *pietá*, it hadn't taken away the fear that I, too, would get breast cancer and die too young, just as she had.

I took the film on anyway because I liked John, because he wanted to help others, and because it was a powerful and well-told story.

But first, there was the trip to Iceland. It ended up being the trip of a lifetime. Each morning began with a new adventure I could never have imagined—soaking in warm thermal waters after long hours of strenuous hiking through a landscape of rainbow-colored peaks; walking along black sand beaches; photographing colonies of puffins perched on grassy slopes high above the sea; boating through a frigid glacier lagoon; watching a herd of wild Icelandic horses run by; exploring a waterfall rumored to have a chest of gold hidden behind it; camping in the highlands; and drinking cold Icelandic beer bathed in the light of a midnight rainbow. These and all the other adventures filled the more than twenty hours of daylight each day.

Much to my surprise, I was out-hiked every single day, not by twenty-somethings (there were none on the trip) but by a trio of sixty-somethings. *How inspiring was that!?*

There was also the flat-out exhilaration of being with a group of intrepid souls hiking up and down the slopes of an active volcano—each of us hoping we would be able to make the two-and-a-half-hour descent through fields of snow and razor-sharp lava rocks in a breath-takingly inadequate thirty-minute window should it happen to erupt, which it was actually scheduled to do "any day now," the seismologists told us.

Even in Iceland, though, films didn't leave me alone. As if to mess with me, the dirt road through the highlands was unexpectedly closed and our driver had to figure out an alternative route to the base of the mountain through the highland tundra. It turned out Ridley Scott's production team was there ahead of us, filming the opening to his film, *Prometheus.*

While in Iceland, a mind-twist happened when it dawned on me John's film was actually the story of a *survivor.* John was still here!

I came back and got to work on *Not As I Pictured,* securing almost fifteen hundred airdates across close to 85 percent of the U.S.

After hiking for ten days in Iceland and working on John's film, I changed my mantra. An ad I saw that summer from The North Face outerwear company reminded me of what I had gained from being not afraid—*that the truest version of ourselves stands well beyond comfort's perimeter.*

Slaying Inner Dragons with Joseph Campbell and a French Gypsy

THE CAMERAS WERE rolling in the late 1980s when Bill Moyers sat down for a series of conversations with Joseph Campbell, the foremost interpreter of the world's mythologies and the fascinating stories humans have told one another to explain the mysteries of the universe.

That this happened in the library of Campbell's good pal, film director George Lucas, at his Skywalker Ranch, made it all the more intriguing to me.

Despite nearly four decades as a highly regarded professor and writer, and for having collaborated with Lucas on the *Star Wars* trilogy, Campbell was relatively unknown at the time.

"If it hadn't been for him," George Lucas told a New York City crowd gathered to honor Campbell at the National Arts Club in 1986, "it's possible I would *still* be trying to write *Star Wars*."

Theirs was a mutual admiration society.

"*Star Wars* is a valid mythological perspective,"

said Campbell. "It shows the state as a machine and asks: Is the machine going to *crush* humanity, or *serve* humanity? Humanity comes *not* from the machine, but from the heart!

"I think it was in *The Return of the Jedi* when Skywalker unmasks his father," Campbell said. "The father had been playing one of these machine roles, a state role. He was the uniform, you know? And the removal of that mask, there was an undeveloped man there, there was a kind of a worm. By being executive of a system, one is not developing one's humanity. I think George Lucas really did a beautiful thing there."

Campbell's status as a relative unknown changed when *Joseph Campbell and the Power of Myth with Bill Moyers* aired nationally on PBS in 1987—the year Zoë was born.

Described as "a vibrant collection of extraordinary stories spun by a great storyteller," the series fired the imaginations of millions of viewers and became one of the most popular series in the history of public television.

Even the critics loved it.

"(Campbell) skips nimbly from one culture to another, from one concept of God to another, pointing out the differences and deftly drawing together the similarities . . . between peak experiences and epiphanies, between the beautiful and the sublime," commented *The New York Times*.

"If you crave exhilaration," wrote *The Los Angeles Times*, "here's your fix!"

In the spring of 2012, twenty-five years after its premiere, PBS was rereleasing *The Power of Myth*. And luckily for me, I was asked by Al Perlmutter—the producer husband of Joan Konner, the journalist/filmmaker who'd once compared me to a sheepdog—to promote the most popular PBS series ever to stations across the country.

In the series, Moyers and Campbell compare creation myths and discuss how religions and mythologies need to change and evolve in order to maintain relevance in peoples' lives.

"Joseph Campbell's most profound teaching was that each of us can slay the inner dragons that imprison us," said Moyers, "so that we might experience fully the rapture of being alive."

The rapture of being alive was *not* something I was feeling at the time.

Much as I loved the house I'd bought when we moved to Asheville, a 100-year-old Dutch barn-style house closer to town had just caught my eye. It was an architectural mash-up with crazy appendages and porches added on, like an aging dowager who can't decide which jewelry *not* to wear to the party.

Located next door to a women's homeless shelter, there had been a For Sale sign in the front yard off and on for the better part of a year. It was now being offered at a price significantly lower than what I thought I could sell my house for. I realized I could use the difference to pay off what I still owed for both kids' college tuitions.

Slightly tipsy on visions of the transformation I could make, my infatuation turned me into a house-stalker. Every drive into town was calculated to detour me past her so I could slow down, gaze longingly at her, making sure she hadn't yet been sold. At night I dreamed about how I would someday walk through her rooms—even though I had yet to see them—and how I would decorate those rooms. How I would create gardens around her stone walls and give her a colorful facelift.

Around the corner, there were ruins of an old house that had burned down when squatting crackheads accidentally set it on fire. And only a few blocks away, neighbors complained that a former lawyer was now dealing drugs out of her vintage two-story wooden house, causing all manner of annoying traffic at night.

But I didn't know any of that yet. All I thought was what a great walking neighborhood it was for me and the dogs.

Before I could buy my lovely old dowager, however, I had to sell the house I was living in; my realtor informed me I couldn't make an offer on her until I did.

Asheville in 2012 was still mired in the contrails from the

2007–2008 financial crisis, the most severe worldwide economic crisis since the 1929 Wall Street crash and the Great Depression. The previous year, statistics showed that median household wealth in the U.S. had fallen 35 percent since 2005—the year we moved to Asheville.

One day, after a particularly hot and physical yoga class, I decided to ignore my realtor's advice and approach the owner of the house myself. *I really wanted it.* This strategy had worked back in my married days when I bought the *Money Pit* house, that little wreck of a mid-century modern. So, why not?

I rolled up my mat and, still in a slightly post-yogic trance, drove over to the house without stopping to change out of my sweaty clothes or tidy my appearance.

Moments later, I was standing on the old wooden porch. Up close, there was a faded linen aura of weariness about the blue-gray paint with black trim, but it was still magical to me. I hesitated only a minute before knocking on the front door. It wasn't long before I heard footsteps.

The door opened slowly, revealing a man perhaps in his mid 40s. His slender but muscular body was clad in a dark T-shirt and jeans. He had dark hair, a neatly trimmed mustache and short beard. Tattoos covered his arms, and the word "Gypsy" was inked in large flowing script across his throat.

"Yes?" he said, scowling at me.

"Hello," I said politely. "I would like to buy your house."

His dark eyes, devoid of any expression, regarded me for what felt like a very long moment.

I waited nervously for him to speak, counting his tattoos, pondering their meaning.

"Would you like to come in and see it?" he asked finally. I thought I detected a slight French accent. He opened the door perhaps an inch wider.

"Thank you," I replied. "I would."

And with that, I followed the tattooed French Gypsy inside, leaving the sunshine and safety of the outside world behind me.

Campbell's life mission was to understand the power of stories and legends, especially the common themes and deep principles that had energized the human imagination throughout the ages.

"Basically, myths serve four functions," Campbell told Moyers. "The first is mystical . . . realizing what a wonder the universe is and what a wonder you are. . . .

"The second is a cosmological dimension with which science is concerned—showing you what shape the universe is but showing it in such a way that the mystery again comes through.

"The third function is supporting and validating a certain social order," he said. "The sociological function of myth that has taken over in our world and is out-of-date.

"But there is a *fourth* function of myth—and this is the one that I think everyone must try today to relate to. It is the pedagogical function of *how to live a human lifetime* under *any* circumstances."

What I found inside the French Gypsy's house astonished me. I stepped into a book lover's dreamscape—a romantic living room lined with floor-to-ceiling, built-in bookcases on one wall reaching all the way up the 11-foot-high walls. Cozy furniture had been arranged to encourage conversation in front of a patterned brick fireplace decorated with a strand of twinkling fairy lights. A Persian rug covered part of the old hardwood floor. Dark antique wooden furniture accented the room. Family furniture from France, the Gypsy told me, pointing to each piece.

Dazed with delight, I followed him through the large sliding pocket door that separated the living room from the dining room, the walls of which had been painted an attractive dark olive green. More strings of small lights danced along the tops of the walls. There was a little pyramid of brightly wrapped presents piled up on two chairs.

"Today is my two-year-old daughter's birthday," he said, seeing me looking at them.

"And see that table?" he asked, pointing to a beautifully hand-crafted long table made of finely sanded and polished wooden planks at the center of the room. I nodded.

"I built that so my wife and I could dance on top of it the night we got married." He said this with a wry smile that I couldn't quite decipher.

We moved through a small hallway, and I think I may have gasped out loud as I walked into the light-filled kitchen with its large window overlooking a small deck, where I glimpsed a child's colorful tea service set up on a small round table. A piece of pretty blue and white batik fabric was strung above the window and blue and white teacups hung in a row underneath old glass-fronted pine cupboards. There were contemporary cement countertops, a hidden pantry, and a light-filled back room with its walls of windows overlooking more gardens. The French Gypsy pointed out a small Fisher & Paykel dish drawer, or dishwasher, cleverly tucked into one of the pine cupboards, making sure I saw it.

I followed him back into the living room through a different door and up a broad set of wooden stairs to a landing decorated with hanging plants and a large piece of stained glass over the window, then on up to the second floor.

Upstairs, under the eaves of the Dutch barn roof, there were three light-filled bedrooms with high ceilings. The French Gypsy led me into the master bedroom where a four-poster bed crafted of slender, finely wrought pieces of dark wood dominated the space.

"People say that what we're seeking is a meaning for life," said Joseph Campbell. "(But) I don't think that *is* what we're really seeking.

"I think what we're seeking is an experience of being *alive*, so that the life experiences we have on the purely physical plane will resonate with those of our own innermost being and reality.

"So that we actually *feel* the rapture of being alive. That's what it's all finally about, and that's what these clues help us to find *within* ourselves. That's what people want, that's what the soul asks for."

Back in the master bedroom, the French Gypsy pointed to the ceiling. With its luminescent blue background and hand painted golden stars of various sizes, it could have been in a chapel in Ravenna, Italy.

"I painted that for my wife, as a surprise when she was away one weekend," he said. "It was a reminder of the night I met her, which was also the first time in my life I saw a shooting star."

A former sleeping porch on the back of the house and adjoining the bedroom had been converted into a bathroom, complete with jacuzzi. Three sides of the room had small-paned windows that opened up over the gardens. In the distance, I could see downtown Asheville. I felt like I was in a treehouse.

Room after room, I followed him, listening to his stories. I had fallen hard in love—not with him, of course, but with this house, its amazing architectural details and, most of all, its stories. This wasn't just a house, this was *a home.*

I'd never before responded with such physical sensations to a house—but then, I'd never experienced a house quite like this. This was a house that made me feel alive, rapturously alive. I knew I had to live here.

But first I had to sell the house we were already living in.

"Eternity isn't some later time; eternity isn't a long time; eternity has nothing to do with time," Campbell told Moyers. "Eternity is that dimension of here and now which thinking in time cuts out. The experience of eternity *right here and now* is the function of life.

"It's a wonderful, wonderful opera," he said, "except that it hurts."

What followed next was the eternity and the opera of selling my house—six long months of frustrations with more than sixty showings and multiple offers that, for a variety of reasons, failed to go through.

Each month, I paid the French Gypsy not to sell the house to someone else. If I was able to buy it, those payments—eventually six of them—would be deducted from the sales price of the house. If not, I would *not* get that $9000 back. That's the deal we cut. That's how in love I was. It seemed to take forever.

"I think of (mythology) as the homeland of the Muses, the inspirers of poetry," Campbell said. "And to see life as a poem, and yourself participating in a poem, is what the myth does for you."

"What do you mean by a poem?" Moyers asked.

"I mean a vocabulary in the form, not of words," said Campbell, "but of acts and adventures."

Perhaps the Muses conspired to help me out, for the 66th showing resulted in the fourth offer which finally resulted in the sale of my house. A few weeks later, I was clutching the keys to the house of my dreams tightly in my hand.

Of course, there were a few things the French Gypsy *didn't* tell me about—like the headstone of a little girl from the 1920s I would soon discover in the garden (a story for another day and another book), an upstairs closet with its secret past (too upsetting to discuss), and the realities of living next door to a homeless shelter with all its inherent drama. All this, and much more, would be mine to discover over time.

Working on *The Power of Myth* was yet another documentary experience that rearranged my mind. For years, I had internalized the social issues of many of the projects I'd worked on. As a moderate progressive, I often felt it my responsibility to worry about them.

That changed when, not long after, I happened to see a purple bumper sticker at an incense boutique in downtown Asheville. I stared at it in amazement, for here was the answer I didn't know I'd been seeking. And, as if fate had placed it right in my path, it was a quote from Joseph Campbell.

You cannot cure the world of sorrows,
but you can choose to live in joy.

Reading it, I finally realized my harboring of the world's problems was not helping anyone—least of all me—and that I could make a better contribution to the world by trying to live in joy. It was *permission* to be happy. Tears filled my eyes. I hadn't understood how much I'd needed that.

I bought it and stuck it on the back of my Subaru, where I would be sure to see it each time I put my dogs or groceries into the rear compartment and be reminded to live in joy. That it was *okay* to live in joy.

Because joy, it turns out, is just as contagious as fear—and a much better contribution to the lives of everyone around me.

My Under the Appalachian Sun House

THIS WILL BE my very own *Under the Tuscan Sun* house, I thought, standing on the sidewalk looking at the weary old house that was now mine. But then, it's often about a film's influence, isn't it?

That it was in Asheville—and not Italy—didn't matter to me. This was my very own Diane Lane moment. This is where Zoë and Leif, once grown, will come for the holidays. This is where friends will visit, I thought, as happy scenes from the film played out in my head. There will be parties and gatherings, with wine and delicious food in the gardens. And maybe this is where I will find love.

The amazing thing is that *all of it* came true.

It wasn't a ruin like the one Frances Mayes purchased, but once it was mine, I began seeing ways it could be improved. Then I saw some more. And then a few others. Just as in the children's book, *Give a Mouse a Cookie*—or, in my case, a house—and one thing led to another, and then another.

In the coming months and years, every room would be freshly painted. All of the wooden floors throughout the house would be sanded and sealed. The front porch would be sanded, repaired, stained, and sealed. The 100-year-old interior wooden doors would be taken down, stripped and refinished, then rehung. A simple but glorious outside shower would be installed on the back deck. A half bath would be gutted, then revisioned into a full Euro-style bath by my visionary artist friend, David Joerling.

The floor-to-ceiling living room bookcases would all be hand-sanded, then painted white. Broken windows would be replaced. Appliances would be upgraded. The chimney, ignored for years, would be repaired and a Norwegian Jøtul wood burning stove installed in the fireplace. An unnecessary back porch bathroom would be ripped out and transformed into a yoga and meditation space.

Fences would be installed between my house and the homeless shelter next door. The exterior of the house would be painted in bright colors, turning her from an old dowager to a "painted lady." The tired gray wooden siding would become Wedgewood blue trimmed in French blue, accented by window trim painted aqua. The front porch would soon glow in a rich yellow, its blue wooden railings punctuated by coral-colored posts, like a set of earrings at both entrances to the deck. Soon, people would tell me how happy it made them feel just to look at it.

The gardens surrounding the house would be redesigned and trans-formed with an abundance of new plants, wood chips, and flowers. It took a few years, but with help, I pulled it off. Finished phases were celebrated with parties as I filled the house with hiking friends, artist friends, and neighbors.

Both Leif and Zoë were by now living more or less independently. And so, for most of the first year, it was just me and our two dogs, Klejne and Bandit, living there.

One day, while working in my front garden, I got into conversation with Joachim, a German architect and gardener who was pruning some bushes across the street. Somewhere in that 20-minute chat, I asked if he had any single friends. He eventually introduced me to Tom and an unexpected and unlikely tale of romance unfolded that included beers on the front deck after a day of hiking, candlelight dinners in the back gardens and lazy Sunday mornings with hot coffee, making breakfast in the kitchen together to the soothing sounds of jazz. After many years of post-marriage singledom, I was delighted to be in this new phase of life. We had the house to ourselves.

And then the phone rang. It was Leif. After a year at SCAD, he'd returned to Asheville to figure out what to do next.

"Mom, my roommate situation's not working out," he said. "Can I move back in for a while?"

"OK," I said.

A couple of months later, the phone rang again. This time it was Zoë calling from Seattle, where she'd moved after graduating from university and spending a gap year in Geneva.

"Mama, I think I might like to move back to Asheville," she said. "Can I live with you until I find a job and a place of my own?"

"Of course," I said.

The third call was from my mother, now 92 years old and still living in her condo in Alexandria, Virginia, not far from the old documentary workshop.

"Honey, I don't think I can live on my own anymore," she said. "Can I move in with you?"

Well, why not?

As I was renovating the house, family was coming and going, staying, cooking, and eating. The house filled up with love and laughter, food, dogs, and moments together. There were dinners on the deck and more gatherings of friends.

"What are you thinking?" Frances (Diane Lane) asks Martini, the handsome Italian realtor, during a gathering at her home at the end of the film, *Under the Tuscan Sun.*

"I think you got your wish," Martini replies.

"You're right," Frances says, looking around at the people laughing and chattering, eating, and drinking. "I got my wish. I got everything I asked for."

What are four walls, anyway? They are what they contain. The house protects the dreamer. Unthinkably good things can happen, even late in the game. It's such a surprise.

FRANCES MAYES

A Prophetic Scrapbook, Hidden in a 100-Year-Old Cellar

Morning journal, May 13, 2011—There have probably been a hundred moments—words said, observed behavior, snatches of conversation, a thousand impressions perhaps, like confetti sparkling in the air all around me as I walk through time. Some good, some not so good, these tiny memory photos, each one patiently waiting til they reach critical mass, and I begin to see the path they've created.

IN THE MIDST of my Under the Appalachian Sun house renovations, I decided to tackle some of the boxes of old papers and ephemera I'd hastily stashed in the cellar when I moved into the house. I didn't love the cellar. One hundred years old, it had a dirt floor, cobwebs, and a lot of dust. Once upon a time, black, dusty coal had been stored in one corner of it.

With its massive stones, low ceilings, and very little daylight, I thought the main area could be turned into an amazing wine cellar with small bistro tables, candles, and checkered tablecloths.

But I had neither the money nor the energy to realize this vision. Besides, there was always so much else to do upstairs.

Looking at a pile of boxes the movers had stashed on some old shelves, I was tempted to toss everything into the bin and just be done with it. But then I thought, what if there's something hidden in all these boxes that I haven't looked at in decades, something I might actually want? That thought had derailed progress before. But seriously, *what if?*

And so it began, the process of putting on gloves and opening up box after box of old papers, letters, magazines, photographs and *stuff*—as in the stuffing, the inner guts of what filled the belly of my cellar.

I hauled a few boxes out onto my front porch where I might (hopefully) be distracted by people passing by. Much went right into the bin. But when I came across an old scrapbook of postcards I had put together when I was just eight or nine years old, I paused. The last time I'd looked inside it, I was a teenager. Old and musty now, I thought—one quick look, then I'll toss it.

Between sips of tea, I turned the pages. Childish handwriting labeled where the postcards had come from—*Denmark, Africa, Italy, Switzerland, Spane, Floridia, Greece, and America.*

They were glued down so I couldn't see the writing on the back. I didn't remember many of them, much less who'd sent them, but coming from a multigenerational family of travelers, the collection was not a surprise.

The postcards from Denmark were likely from my Danish grandparents who lived in Copenhagen. When I was seven, we visited them there before spending a few days on Skagen, a very cold beach in northern Denmark. Mom and I returned to that same beach together many years later on one of our three around-the-country road trips. And in my twenties, I'd worked for a Danish textiles company, fallen in love with a Danish guy, and traveled there often.

Then there were a couple from Paris, where I would live as an *au pair*, or nanny, for a long hot French summer just ten years after putting together that scrapbook. I whizzed around the *Arc de Triomphe*, beautifully lit up, very late one night, clinging to a friend on the back of his motorcycle. And here was a postcard of it.

I kept turning the pages.

There were postcards from Zurich, which I explored briefly in my twenties, on my way to that week of skiing in the French Alps with my Danish boyfriend. And some from Italy, where I would travel for two different careers—initially to Venice for textile design in the 80s, and then again, a decade later, to other parts of Italy to shoot *American Byzantine.*

There was a long-forgotten postcard from my sister, written the summer she was hitchhiking in Greece. I'd just been in Athens with Zoë and Leif the previous year, for my nephew Jon's wedding.

The more pages I turned, the stranger it got. I caught my breath, slowly realizing that I had been to *almost every single place* (with the exception of Ireland and the Philippines) that I had received a postcard from as a little girl. Despite sitting in the darkest corners of my homes for so many years, neglected, it was eerie how prophetic this scrapbook had turned out to be, as if it had been just quietly waiting.

I kept going. There were even postcards from Mount Vernon in the collection that I didn't remember at all. As a nine-year-old child living in London, I would not yet have known what Mount Vernon was. And yet I ended up living there for five of my married-with-children-years.

And the postcard of the pounding surf in Coastal Carolina? The kids and I enjoyed a number of holidays on the beaches of North Carolina when they were small. And Zoë spent four university years there.

There was also a postcard from Geneva, where I would visit her the year after she graduated.

And then there were postcards of exotic birds and animals from Africa where my grandparents lived at the time, and where I would spend a few weeks researching a book on my grandmother's adventures, many years later.

How very strange that this simple postcard collection became a child's vision board—an illustrated map of so many of the very places that would become meaningful to me over the coming decades.

Pondering this, I took a break from the mustiness and memories and went inside for a bite to eat.

Later that afternoon, I returned to the porch to tackle one last box. As I pulled out yet another handful of papers, a torn fragment of newspaper slipped out and fell to the floor. I picked it up to see a clipping from a book review—not the whole thing, just a fragment of it. And on it, these words were underlined:

"The dreams of a child become the journeys of a woman."

BREAKING BAD IN AUSTIN WITH VINCE GILLIGAN

IN 2013, IT felt like I was the only person in Asheville to have seen just one episode of *Breaking Bad*, the crime drama television series by Vince Gilligan. It's not that I hadn't heard about it. *Everyone* was watching it. *Everyone* was talking about it. Even down at Greenlife, our local organic market, people were talking about it.

"Hey, did you see *Breaking Bad* last night?!" my checker asked as he carefully packed up my groceries. This kind of conversation happened back in the days before streaming and on-demand television, back when what we called "appointment viewing" was still pretty much the norm. Which gave rise to the so-called water cooler conversations and spontaneous chatter, even from checkers who *didn't* work at Trader Joe's.

"No," I said politely, hoping he wouldn't ask me anything else.

He was touching on two things that make me uncomfortable: 1) not being *au courant* with what's going on in film and television; and 2) checkers who make small talk with me. (I once wrote a letter to Trader Joe's, asking if they could add a checkout line for introverts and have yet to receive a response.)

"Dude!" my checker exclaimed, cheerfully rearranging the yogurt and kale in my carrier bag.

I glanced around, thinking he'd recognized someone behind me. But no, his remark appeared to be aimed at me. He tucked a stray blonde dreadlock back up into the arrangement piled on his head, the head he was shaking in disbelief as he thought back on the previous night's episode of *Breaking Bad.*

On a side note, this guy had the most amazing long blonde dreadlocks I'd ever seen. I think he was also a musician in his nocturnal, not-for-the-paycheck hours. Once upon a time, I used to cue up to check out in his line intentionally because he was such a sweet-natured guy. That was before I'd overheard him talking to the customer in front of me about the enormous pile of dreads on top of his head. She asked him how long it had taken to amass such volume.

"Oh wow, yeah, like a crazy amount of time!" he responded cheerfully.

"Are they heavy?" the customer asked. "Do they bother you?"

"No, not really," cheerful checker dude responded with a laugh. "But one time, a little spider actually came out of them and hung down in front of my face!"

After that, I watched carefully for any tiny escapees whenever I found myself in his line.

Getting back to *Breaking Bad,* the reason I was so woefully behind in my viewing is that I was scared to watch the series, scared it might depress me. Back in the 80s, it had taken me months to get scenes from *Apocalypse Now* and *Deerhunter* out of my head. Life was precarious enough as it was for a freelancing single parent—I didn't need anything else to keep me awake at night. I admitted I'd only seen the first hour so far.

"I'm going to binge on it soon and catch up," I lied, grabbing my bags to beat a quick retreat. "Don't tell me anything—no spoilers please!"

That year, I was promoting a television series about writers and writing on behalf of KLRU, the PBS station in Austin, Texas. Called *On Story*, it featured segments and interviews from the Austin Film Festival, billed as the only film and television festival just for writers. A perfect blend of my two passions, I thought, and was delighted when the festival director invited me to fly down to Texas to attend.

This wasn't my first visit to Austin and I was happy to be back. As the festival takes place in multiple venues, every cabbie had a script they wanted to talk about or recite, even to someone who likely couldn't do anything to help them. I had three pitched to me during the few days I was there.

Upon arrival, I checked into the press area and greeted Barbara Morgan, the festival's co-founder and executive director. It was the first time we'd met in person. Understandably distracted by press, guests, and attendees, she took only a quick moment to greet me between conversations.

"Hey, Vince Gilligan is here this week!" she said. "Make sure you see him wherever he's speaking!"

Vince Gilligan, the writer, producer, and director of *Breaking Bad*, was the star attraction of the Austin Film Festival that year. Able to come and go pretty much as I pleased, I dutifully consulted the festival guide and circled all the sessions with him, along with other breakout sessions and films I wanted to see.

Check-in complete, I headed over to the theater showing *A Birder's Guide to Everything*, a coming-of-age film by Rob Meyer starring Ben Kingsley. I'm not a birder but that didn't matter; the film was charming.

Waiting in line to get in, I got into conversation with a pleasant man who worked in computers and intelligence somewhere in Colorado. In the course of explaining what he did for a living and what he knew, he cautioned me to cover up the camera on my computer. He also reiterated that Vince Gilligan was here at the film festival.

"Be sure to see him!" he said.

"Who?" I asked, having momentarily forgotten his name. His eyes opened wide.

"*Vince Gilligan!*" he said a little louder this time, like I was an idiot, or a foreigner. "The director of *Breaking Bad!*"

"Oh, right, I'll be sure to do that," I said, fully intending to do so. Because I *am* the kind of person who often takes suggestions from people I've only just met, because sometimes I think the universe is nudging me through these random strangers. (It still surprises me how often that seems to work out.)

That afternoon, I went over to KLRU's studios to watch a taping of *Overheard with Evan Smith,* another series I was promoting. Seeing KLRU's general manager, Bill Stotesbery, in the audience mingling outside the studio before the taping, I went over to say hello. We chatted briefly and then he said, "Hey, did you see that Vince Gilligan is in town for the festival?!"

I nodded. *Ok, that's three,* I thought. *I'd better find him.*

Next on my list, however, was a feature film that was premiering here at the festival, *Nebraska*—a dark comedy drama shot in black-and-white starring Bruce Dern, June Squibb, and Will Forte. I loved it.

Consulting the festival guide as the lights came up, I saw "The Alpha & Omega of *Breaking Bad*" was starting in just a few moments at the venue next door.

Breaking Bad tells the story of Walter White, a chemistry teacher played by Bryan Cranston, who discovers he has cancer and gets into the meth-making business to pay his medical debts and sock away money for his family after he's gone. Vince Gilligan himself would be speaking. Perfect, I thought. I had just enough time to get there before it started.

The theater was filled nearly to capacity, but seeing my press pass, the gatekeepers waved me in just as the lights were dimming and told me to go upstairs. Whispering apologies for disturbing those already seated, I made my way past a very long row of knees in the darkened theater to the last remaining seat in the balcony's front row.

The stage lights came up and there was Vince Gilligan sitting in a director's chair next to the festival interviewer, a bearded young guy in blue jeans and a baseball cap. After a few words of introduction, the stage went dark. *Breaking Bad,* episode one came up on the screen.

Seriously?! I thought in disbelief. *I've only seen one episode, and this is the one they're showing?*

I was quickly swept up in the story, however. Knowing what was coming, I could sit back and admire the writing, the acting, and the scene setting, so it wasn't a waste of time. In fact, I liked it even better the second time and made a mental note to watch the full series when I got back home.

As the episode came to a close, I anticipated the lights coming back up and a Q&A with Vince Gilligan. Instead, a second episode began.

Wow, I thought, a few moments in—the character of Walter White looked so haggard; he'd really aged between the first and second episodes! A few minutes passed before it dawned on me, much to my dismay, that I was watching the series *finale.*

Talk about spoilers. Having only just decided to watch the full series, I realized how pointless that would be now that I would soon know how everything ended. I was crushed. Like a fabulous first date that doesn't end with him asking for your number. Like being asked to leave the restaurant after the appetizer. Not wanting to disturb the long row of knees a second time, I decided to stay.

To my surprise, it turned out to be an amazing way to admire what Vince Gilligan and his team had done. By the time the episode reached its conclusion and the soundtrack of "Baby Blue" by Badfinger began playing, I was sobbing in the dark recesses of the upper balcony. How ridiculous to be so emotionally grabbed by the final episode of a series I hadn't even seen. *Guess I got what I deserved.* But wow, what a testament to the show's writing.

When the lights came back up after the final credits, Vince Gilligan returned to the stage and a thunderous round of applause. He couldn't have been nicer or more patient with the questions from all the students and aspiring writers in the audience. He explained how the inspiration for the series came from a want ad he saw in a New York City newspaper for an old RV. He told us the character Jesse was originally going to be done away with after the first season, but Aaron Paul turned in such an incredible performance they rewrote the script in order to keep him in it. Gilligan gave credit to everyone else in the series' green room telling us what a tight team they'd become; throughout all five seasons and 62 episodes they'd only made two changes to the original writers. They worked so well as a team, he said, that watching it now he often can't remember who wrote which lines. Classy guy.

After the film festival, I returned home filled with admiration for what a genuinely nice guy Vince Gilligan is—as well as a head full of inspiration. I still haven't watched the rest of *Breaking Bad*, not because I now know how it ends, but because I wanted to stay in awe of the unique alpha and omega experience I'd had.

I did, however, put a Band-Aid over the little camera eye on my computer.

STRANGER WITH A CAMERA: LOST IN APPALACHIA

CELTIC DRUIDS THOUGHT mistletoe represented the oak tree's heart or soul. Greeks considered it a symbol of sexuality and fertility. Thinking it would be nice to hang in my big old house during Christmas, I went out to buy some. I soon discovered, however, when you live in the southern Appalachian Mountains, you don't buy mistletoe in a store. You search for it in the woods then blast it out of the treetops with a shotgun.

"*Seriously?!*" I asked my Appalachian-born boyfriend, Tom, when he told me this.

"Yes," he said, seriously. "It's called harvesting. It grows high up in the treetops. Beyond the reach of ladders."

Mistletoe is a lazy and opportunistic plant, most often found in the top branches of apple and oak trees. While it's capable of creating its own food through photosynthesis, it prefers to wriggle its roots down into the bark of a host tree and freeload nutrients, often harming or killing the tree in the process.

Once I learned this, I didn't feel so bad to hear that it sometimes gets shot.

"Oh, *please* take me with you to find some!" I begged him.

This was exactly the kind of Appalachian adventure I was looking to capture in photographs, so the hunt for mistletoe was on.

By now I had lived in these mountains long enough to know that life in Appalachia can be a tease—any time you assume you are in control of your own adventures, you may quickly find out how very wrong you can be.

Tom began looking for mistletoe each day as he drove around for work. On the weekends, he told me he scanned the trees in the mountains surrounding his parents' farm. But no mistletoe; the upper branches held nothing but the occasional squirrel's nest.

And so, with Christmas only a few days away, I decided to drive out into the mountains myself. Asheville is a popular tourist town— but surrounded by bucolic areas, it takes only a few moments to find yourself in a completely different world. I ended up driving somewhat aimlessly around a 66-square-mile area once known as Turkey Creek. It's said that in 1859, a frontiersman by the name of Leicester Chapman renamed the area Leicester for the Earl of Leicester. Most likely, he named it after himself.

While no longer a frontier, it's still a very rural area. A world where road signs are pulled down at night to confuse outsiders looking to buy land cheap. A world where you still see skinny metal mailboxes in a row alongside the road, their little red flags hanging down listlessly, their doors hanging open like baby birds waiting to be fed. A world where everyone knows everyone else's kin, but not you or yours. A world where you might have to be a little careful if you are an outsider who happens to wander onto someone's property.

Tom had cautioned me about driving around by myself out in the mountains and hollers, but I was determined to find some mistletoe.

I was about thirty minutes away from the relative safety of town when, just as I was rounding a curve on a rural country road, I spotted a bundle of green hanging on a nearby porch. *Was it mistletoe,* I wondered? I pulled my car over and got out to take a closer look.

Camera in hand, I was walking around the edges of what looked to be someone's front yard when I heard a door creak open. A gruff voice said grudgingly, almost menacingly, "Can I help you?"

I froze, then slowly turned around.

The man attached to the voice was perhaps in his early 70s. His piercing gray eyes looked at me from underneath a worn cap, sizing me up.

In a heartbeat, scenes from *Stranger with a Camera*—the 2000 documentary film by Elizabeth Barrett about the 1967 killing of filmmaker Hugh O'Connor—flashed through my mind.

Being a documentary, it was, of course, a true story. O'Connor, a Scottish Canadian filmmaker, had been hired to direct a film about President Johnson's War on Poverty. His film was largely focused on Letcher County in the eastern Kentucky region, which with its poor coal-mining areas had become a metaphor for the parts of the U.S. the "American Dream" had never reached.

Reporters, journalists, and film crews had been coming to this impoverished region of Appalachia for years, which made some residents hopeful for change. But others felt exploited and embarrassed by the media's spotlight on them which had yet to result in any improvement or change to their circumstances.

On his last day in the area, O'Connor was filming a conversation with a weary miner sitting on the front porch of a shack he rented from Hobart Ison, the Appalachian version of a slum lord. Word of the outsider film crew had quickly made it around town. When the news reached Ison, he grabbed his Smith & Wesson and, as the story goes, drove over to the location where he shot the crew, killing O'Connor.

I'd first heard about the film at the Grove Park Inn in Asheville. My mother and I were having a glass of wine near the roaring fireplace at a table we shared with an older gentleman from Kentucky and his wife. When he heard I worked with documentary films, he told me the story of *Stranger with a Camera.* As strange circumstance would have it, he'd been part of the legal team *defending* Ison—and in so doing, at least in their own minds, defending a way of life in Eastern Kentucky.

Ison was convicted of involuntary manslaughter. *Involuntary!?*

"Did he go to jail?" I'd asked the lawyer.

"For about a minute!" he laughed. "Ison served just one year of his ten-year sentence. That's just how things worked around there."

And now here I was, trespassing on this man's property, also a stranger with a camera, *and* in Appalachia. Was I willing to risk my life for mistletoe? Hell, no.

The old man was quiet for a moment, looking me up and down, judging me. From my side of the face off, I was trying—as discreetly as possible—to see if he was carrying a gun.

Slowly and quietly, I introduced myself, apologizing for stepping onto his property and identifying that I lived in Asheville. When I mentioned I lived in the old Giezentanner house, I was in luck. The old man had known the Giezentanners; he'd shopped in their store, as had many, back in the day. He even knew some of them personally.

"I'm just looking for mistletoe to hang in my house for Christmas," I explained, hoping I sounded innocent and unthreatening. "Can you tell me where I might be able to find some?"

Those old and canny Appalachian eyes gave me another long, hard stare.

"Charlie might have some up the road," he said, after some thought. This man's house was at the intersection of several rural roads, so I had no idea where exactly "up the road" was, much less who Charlie was.

"Up Bear Creek Road," he added helpfully.

One comment slowly led to another, and we got to talking. He invited me to come inside the large cinderblock garage next to his old house so we could sit down and have a proper talk. Heart in my mouth but uncertain how to make a graceful exit, I followed him inside.

It was his tire business and there were tires piled up in stacks everywhere. He looked around, then gestured for me to sit on a stool at the service counter while he did the same. Soon, he was telling me stories about Asheville in the old days. He told me about his grown son and two daughters, which ones were a disappointment and which one he was proud of. Gradually, I realized he just wanted someone to talk to. After an hour or so, the stories began tapering to an end, and I got up to leave.

"About that mistletoe," he said, remembering. "Take a left up Bear Creek and look for the end of the fence. See if there's any up around there."

I nodded, thanked him and with incredible relief, got back into my car. I found Bear Creek Road, not far from Good Intentions Road, and I found many fences. I didn't, however, find any mistletoe.

Even though it turned out fine in the end, after this run-in I gave up my search and the adventure of seeing it being "harvested."

The day after Christmas, Tom and I decided to work off our holiday excesses by hiking the Kitsuma Peak Trail in Pisgah National Forest with a group of friends. About an hour into our climb, he turned around.

"Look up!" he said with a smile.

I looked skyward. And there, high up in the trees, was a lovely lacing of green leaves.

Mistletoe.

ABOUT EFFING TIME!

Morning journal, October 1, 2015—I woke up, turned on the computer and, as I was making myself a cup of coffee, opened a message informing me a photograph of mine had been picked by National Geographic *as one of their Photos of the Day.*

It was a photograph I'd taken at sunset at the Mountain State Fair—a silhouette of a little boy jumping into the sky on a harness as cable cars passed by in the air above him. I titled it Skywalker. I am super pleased and excited about this.

But I'm not the type to feel "humbled and honored and blessed"—I've seen those words so often, they feel disingenuous, the clichéd, go-to phrase, used so often they've lost their power.

I've worked too long and too hard to get to this moment. Instead of being someone picked at random to receive a dose of good luck, I picture myself, a little stick figure standing on top of a mountain with hands clenched into tight little balls at her sides as she shouts up to the stars in the night sky—

"IT'S ABOUT EFFING TIME!"

WORKING ON OTHER people's

documentary films now provided enough financial security that I was able to spend time on my own storytelling through travel writing and street photography.

In 2008, I spent nearly two weeks solo traveling in Africa, photographing, researching, and writing a book about my grandmother's adventures there. In 2011, after getting a certificate from Álfaskólinn, the Icelandic Elf School in Reykjavik, I wrote a travel article, "Hiking with Trolls and Elves in Iceland." In 2013, I spent a week in Barcelona wandering the streets with my camera, not photographing Gaudi architecture as planned, but instead photographing the stories of love I saw all around me. Although I'd been paid for my feature story in Asheville's Mountain XPress, I was not compensated for any of the travel essays.

In the coming years, I'd write stories based upon my travels and street photography in Athens, Lisbon, Finland, San Miguel de Allende, Austin, Salt Lake City, Rome, Southern Italy, Poland, and Paris. In 2016, a travel feature I'd written about "Getting Naked with a Dragon in Helsinki" was published in Finland. And in 2019, I'd be a semifinalist in an international *Atlas Obscura* competition with a $15,000 prize—*to travel and write!*

And of course, there were always plenty of stories to tell and photographs to take in Asheville.

Although I'd helped create a couple of documentaries that had my name on them, this little seal of approval from National Geographic along with the feature article in *Mountain Xpress* about Moni's photography, were the much-needed affirmations and self-confidence boosts I craved.

I internalized this moment so much it even infiltrated my dreams—dreams that within days materialized into a paid professional photography gig.

Morning journal entry . . . October 7, 2015—Last night I dreamed I'd become recognized as a professional photographer, finally! I remember walking through a hallway, wearing blue and purple, and being congratulated by people. I don't know what the exact situation was. All I know is that it felt completely natural to me.

Morning journal entry . . . October 19, 2015—I just spent two hours talking with Stacy L. at Dobra Tea House in Asheville this evening, discussing her vision for her wedding day over cups of "Memories of Prague" tea. She wants me to be her photographer!

I told her I wasn't a wedding photographer, that I was more a street photographer, more journalistic in capturing stories and people, not ceremonies.

"That's why I want you to do it," she said.

I'd met Stacy two years earlier on a purple party bus tour of Asheville with Sirius.B—a self-described Absurdist Gypsy Folk Funk Punk band based in town.

Halfway through the tour, the bus stopped for refreshments at the Double Crown bar in West Asheville. As Stacy got off the bus in front of me, I could see colorful tattoos on her back peeking out around the edges of her white yoga top. When I asked her about them, she told me she had an entire back piece.

"Would you like to see it?" she asked.

"Absolutely!" I said.

She turned her back to me and pulled her top up to her shoulders, revealing a colorful and detailed tattoo.

"It's a story of survival," she said.

When I told her I had a growing collection of photographs of body art, she said it was fine to take photos of hers, if I wanted to. Which, of course, I did.

And that's how we first became acquainted with one another. I love meeting people that way. Tattoos have started many conversations.

Asking people tactfully about their body art is a great way to hear interesting stories about them. Since then, we'd run into one another several times on hiking adventures in the Blue Ridge Mountains.

October 19, 2015—When I asked her why she was asking me to photograph her wedding, Stacey said she'd picked me for three reasons: 1) I hike; 2) she likes my photography; and 3) I'm "unconventional." This made me extremely happy. She gets me.

She's planning to have the ceremony on top of a mountain at Max Patch—a favorite spot for both of us—and on Leap Day. If I don't get this right, we'll have to wait another four years to try again. No pressure!

So, my first professional shoot will be on the top of a mountain in winter. Ignoring my qualms, I was so excited about the gig, I said yes.

Finally, I am now a for-real, professional, hired, and paid photographer.

PART IV

SAVING ROOM FOR THE UNIMAGINABLE

"Keep some room in your heart for the unimaginable."

MARY OLIVER

My Side of the Mountains— Appalachian Poetry

AFTER A FEW years in Asheville, I noticed a shift taking place in the films coming my way. It was as if I'd caught up with the story frames and we were now working through issues, ideas, and healing side by side—instead of me simply following their lead. I loved this surprising new sense of interplay.

Looking back, I think it began when I was asked to help launch a new PBS series, *Appalachia: A History of Mountains and People*.

The title brought back memories of one of my favorite childhood books, *My Side of the Mountain* by Jean Craighead George. It won a lot of awards and even made the Hans Christian Andersen Award honor list in 1969, which may be why my mother was inspired to get a copy for me.

My Side of the Mountain tells the story of Sam, a 12-year-old boy who so dislikes living in his parents' cramped New York City apartment with his eight siblings, he runs away to the Catskill

Mountains to live in the wilderness. Using survival skills learned from a book he borrowed from the New York Public Library, Sam traps animals for food and forages for edible plants. He lives in a hollowed-out tree with his pets—a Peregrine falcon and a weasel. When his clothes wear out, he fashions deerskin clothing from animal hides. And as winter approaches, he makes storage spaces in other hollowed-out tree trunks for the fruits, nuts, wild grains, tubers, and smoked fish and meat he has gathered.

Sam was my hero, and his story has always stayed with me. During the city years of my childhood, I would sometimes daydream about escaping to a life in the mountains.

That dream finally came true in 2005. By then I was 49, and old enough to appreciate that I could live in the mountains without living in a tree or catching my own food.

And now that I was living in some of the oldest mountains in the world, one of the smartest and luckiest things I did early on was to join the Asheville Hiking Group. Headed up by two new friends, Chris and Tracey, joining this group opened up a world of friendships and adventures I'd never imagined possible.

Weekends were soon filled with hikes through the mountains, along streams and rivers with picnics by some of Western North Carolina's more than 150 waterfalls. Sometimes I brought my dogs and sometimes even Zoë and Leif when they were home. Soon, I had strong legs and a big and diverse bunch of friends.

My parents were not hikers, but they were both walkers and some of my favorite memories of both of them were the talks we had on our weekend walks—in cities, along rivers, near beaches, and in the countryside. Living the advice of Søren Kierkegaard, the Danish father of existentialism, I have been a walker all my life.

"Above all, do not lose your desire to walk," Kirkegaard once wrote. "Every day, I walk myself into a state of well-being. I have walked myself into my best thoughts, and I know of no thought so burdensome that one cannot walk away from it . . . if one just keeps on walking, everything will be all right."

I loved the idea of walking myself into my best thoughts.

It was through hiking that I started becoming someone I hadn't been before. To my surprise, it was someone I liked. Someone who was fit. Someone who hiked *mountains*. Someone who *could* hike mountains. Someone who was happier when hiking in the mountains. And the more I hiked, the more I healed.

Documentaries like *Stranger with a Camera* as well as other news stories and films, with their negative images of the Appalachian poor, have only told part of the story. While there is some truth to them, it's certainly not the whole story, nor the *only* story.

Ten years in the making, *Appalachia: A History of Mountains and People* was touted as the first environmental series about a region. Getting it on the air gave me the opportunity to share with viewers all over the country the stories of those who live in Appalachia, and an opportunity to give back something positive in return for what living in these mountains had done for me.

Narrated by Sissy Spacek, famous for her role playing Loretta Lynn in *The Coal Miner's Daughter*, the series begins with the deep and surprising history of Appalachia, exploring the region's unique mosaic of plant, animal, and early human life. From there, it goes on to tell stories about people who made the Appalachians home, stories of people struggling to find a true and proper relationship to the natural world, along with stories about the mountains themselves, which are treated as characters in the narrative.

Appalachia reveals that coal, so valuable to the region's economy, was created by tropical jungles compacted over millions of years. Deep underground, ghostly outlines of these ancient, petrified plants still glow on the black coal. Miners called them flowers of darkness. One acre of cove forest in the Great Smoky Mountains can support more species of trees than are found in all of Europe.

Author Barbara Kingsolver, Pulitzer Prize-winning scientist E.O. Wilson, and many others weave colorful personal stories with scientific anecdotes about the region's complex ecosystem, explaining the dynamic interaction—both positive and negative—of natural history with human history. I could hardly think of anything I'd enjoy working on more than the story of what was all around me. And I wasn't the only one. We ended up with close to fifteen thousand airdates on PBS stations all over the country.

Whenever a new feature was released that had been filmed in North Carolina, like *The Hunger Games* in 2012 which was partly shot on location in DuPont State Forest, dozens of us piled into the movie theater together, each trying to be the first to identify a trail, tree, or waterfall. The beers we'd had beforehand helped (or maybe didn't help) our efforts.

Every so often, friends also organized hikes around mountain areas used in film shoots. There was my friend Glenn's infamous *Last of the Mohicans* hike, an all-day hunt up and down Walker Knob (elevation 5497 feet) in search of Daniel Day-Lewis. Or rather, the actual twigs and leaves he might have run through half naked.

According to Glenn, we covered the opening scene from the film, taking Elk Pen across a wide shin-deep stream, then up through an old stand of oak and poplar and across another wide stream. Following that, a trek up to and along Upper Corner Rock that involved a steep ¾-mile ascent. Then we hiked through Laurel Gap, stopping to admire one waterfall, a tiny swimming hole, and the nice views, before finishing the afternoon with a rocky descent on Perkins and Walker Creek Trails to end up back at the trailhead. I can still picture the entire trail in my mind, as I can with just about every other hike I did in these mountains.

Two years after *Appalachia*, Catherine Tatge and Dominique Lasseur from Global Village Media in New York City contacted me about working with them on their American Masters special, *John Muir in the New World*. As it was a PBS national broadcast, they didn't need my help getting it on the air. What they *did* want was outreach: How could they get it into classrooms and encourage kids to interact with and develop an appreciation for nature and the natural world?

I was one of just two entities they'd reached out to for a proposal. The other one suggested a full color poster that could be hung up in classrooms with getting-out-in-nature suggestions on its back side. (I didn't understand this; if the poster was hung up on the wall, how would the kids see the activities written on the other side?)

One day, driving into the parking lot at Greenlife—the natural foods grocery store where the *Breaking Bad* dude with the long blonde dreads worked—I saw a card table set up just outside the front door. An enthusiastic young woman was standing behind a banner that read Muddy Sneakers.

I'd never seen them there before but was delighted that the non-profit's entire mission was to get kids out in nature. If I just paid attention, Asheville provided me with the inspiration and answers I needed.

Through Muddy Sneakers, I discovered the Children & Nature Network, founded by Richard Louv, an American journalist and author of several books about family, community, and nature. It was Louv who coined the term Nature-Deficit Disorder—which was just what I felt I had been suffering from while living in the Washington, DC suburbs.

I wanted to share my passion for being in nature with kids all over the country—not with a poster on a classroom wall, but with actual experiences, as John Muir surely would have done. Together, the team at C&NN and I crafted an education packet of resources and ideas, partnered with the U.S. Forest Service, and set up simultaneous screening parties in living rooms all over the country.

As Muir himself said, "When one tugs at a single thing in nature, he finds it attached to the rest of the world."

As if there was some sort of geological pull in effect, more nature-themed documentaries began coming my way. I intertwined my weekday work on them with weekend adventures hiking to places in the mountains with storytelling names like Rainbow Falls, Bridalveil, Turtleback and Linville Falls, Rattlesnake Lodge, Panthertown, Max Patch, Turkey Pen Gap, Bearwallow Mountain, Black Balsom, Unaka and Tanawah, Slate Rock and Looking Glass Rock. Just saying their names sounded like Appalachian poetry to me.

The films themselves seemed almost to be responding to what was going on in my world. There was a new harmony and balance in my life, a sense of symmetry and wholeness I'd never before experienced.

THE BEST CONVERSATIONS

IN 2013, NOT long after I moved into my Under the Appalachian Sun house, Robin Melanie Leacock contacted me to see if I would help get her film about her mother—*Stella is 95!*—on the air on PBS stations around the country.

Robin is the daughter-in-law of *cinéma vérité* pioneer Richard Leacock. Her husband is documentary filmmaker Robert Leacock. I had already worked with her on an earlier film, *A Passion for Giving,* and knew whatever film she had created would have a big heart.

This time Robin had turned her lens on her mother, Estelle Craig, a lively character who'd lived a remarkable life. At 95, she still had stories to tell, an active social life, and was in the middle of writing a play.

Robin's documentary foreshadowed and gave me insight into dealing with my own mother's final years. Mom was 92 at the time. I remember watching *Stella is 95!* and wondering how many years together we had left.

Throughout my life, I'd had a complicated relationship with her. Sometimes it was good, sometimes it wasn't.

My mother had already raised two children, a boy and a girl—the perfect family. I was the straggler, that awkward third child—born unexpectedly a decade after my sister and eight years after my brother—who held her back from having the unencumbered adult life she hankered after.

A child of Danish immigrants, she'd grown up during the Great Depression. She was the kind of girl who married her college sweetheart before he went off to serve in World War II.

By contrast, I was a child of the sixties. I came of age during Woodstock, Haight Ashbury, Carnaby Street, rock 'n roll, miniskirts, and Vietnam protests.

She was a world traveler, but I am more open-minded than she was, and even more adventurous. In retrospect, I think it was my free and creative spirit that worried her. I can't even count the number of times I made one of my pronouncements to her, like the time I said, a mere twenty minutes after arriving in town—"This is it, I'm moving to Asheville"—and she looked at me as if I was from another planet.

Over the years, we knocked heads many times over many things. Her criticisms never failed to highlight the ways in which we were two very different people. Infuriating as they could be, I think these criticisms were rooted in her desire to protect me—both from others and from myself. In retrospect, I wonder if she was scared of, and perhaps just a little bit intrigued by, the freedoms of my era.

In many other ways, however, she was a good mother—positive and upbeat, with a passion for art galleries and museums, interested in seeing films (especially if Jeremy Irons was in them) and talking about geopolitics. She was good about staying in touch with family and always sent everyone postcards when she traveled. She loved chatting over meals out, welcoming people to her place for cocktails and dinner, and was always up for a travel adventure.

She was a mother who couldn't say "I love you," so she expressed it in other ways. Throughout my childhood, she'd kept me supplied with a steady stream of thought-provoking books—*The Chronicles of*

Narnia, Little House on the Prairie, The Hobbit, A Wrinkle in Time, My Side of the Mountain, and so many others. Books that got inside my head and sparked my imagination.

Growing up, I had a lot of freedom. At just eight years old, I was walking a mile each way through the streets of Chelsea all by myself to school. By eleven, I was riding a combination of buses and trains by myself back and forth from one side of London to the other each day to school.

When I was a high school senior in London and she noticed me spending hours listening to Joni Mitchell and writing poetry up in my bedroom, she took me to see classical guitarist Christopher Parkening in concert. Then she bought me a guitar, which I still have.

A few months later, she and dad gave their approval for me to spend two weeks traveling around Russia with some of my classmates and one of our teachers. After high school graduation, I went off to college in a different country. At nineteen, I moved to Paris for the summer to be a nanny.

These freedoms she encouraged and never seemed to think twice about or doubt my ability to pull off.

But "mumsy"—in the words of Michael Caine in the film *Alfie*—she was not.

Like a fine wine, however, my mother improved with age. She turned out to be a better grandmother than she had been mother—warmer, more enthusiastic, more interested, more hugging and loving than she had ever been with me. And so, when she asked if she could live with me in my Under the Appalachian Sun home in Asheville, I said okay.

She was 93 when she moved in and 93.5 when she moved out. Living together at this point in our lives turned out not to be easy for either of us.

She moved into a garden flat in a retirement village in the nearby town of Black Mountain. The separation established a peace and acceptance between us. It was here that we finally learned to live together—as long as we were 20 miles apart. We continued to do many small adventures in and around Asheville, which we limited to just a few hours, given her age.

I took her out to small, local art galleries and cafés for coffee or wine. Sometimes we just stayed in Black Mountain and had reubens and beer at the Dark City Tavern. Some evenings we went to Asheville to listen to big band music at 5 Walnut Wine Bar.

Unfortunately, she soon made up for her 93 years of good health with a rapid-fire streak of health disasters. A stroke was followed by a heart attack, then a bad case of shingles. She went from living independently in her own little garden apartment, to assisted living, to skilled nursing, to hospice care—punctuated by two more trips to the emergency room and another unexpected surgery. I found myself living in a state of suspended animation, with peeled back awareness of her imminent loss, holding my breath in anticipation of the next emergency, the next phone call with more bad news.

She never lost her sense of humor, however. Just weeks before she slipped away, I wheeled her into one of the living rooms at her retirement village, positioning her in front of a large television set so she could watch the men's finals of her beloved Wimbledon Championships. Roger Federer, her favorite, was playing Marin Čilić of Croatia. Federer won his eighth Wimbledon singles title that afternoon, which made her very happy. After the presentation of trophies, I turned to her and said, "He has a nice smile, doesn't he?"

"He has a nice *everything!*" she replied, a sparkle in her eyes. She was definitely *still there.*

Mom died a few weeks later, three days shy of her 96th birthday.

In the months after my mother's death, fragments from our chats kept popping into my head, often when least expected.

She had her favorite places in Asheville—Malaprop's Bookstore and 5 Walnut Wine Bar among them. But I think her favorite of them all was Battery Park Book Exchange & Champagne Bar.

There, over a glass of wine and a cheeseboard, she and I would have long discussions about the affairs of the world, my kids, and good adventures from days gone by—hers, mine, and ours. We could (and did) talk for hours.

Each week I joined her for lunch or dinner in the dining room at her place to listen once again to the stories. Often, we were there, still talking, after everyone else had left. She loved that.

"We have the *best* conversations!" she would exclaim when I eventually walked her down the hall to her little flat—even if she had (as usual) done most of the talking.

She'd call a few days later to thank me for coming over and tell me how much she'd enjoyed our visit, often ending with the same words, "We have the *best* conversations!"

In February, I offered to take her out for a glass of wine in celebration of Karen's life. She started automatically to demur, but when I suggested we go to Battery Park Book Exchange & Champagne Bar, she couldn't resist. And so we celebrated Valentine's Day with memories of my sister there together in the usual way: a glass of wine, some cheese, and of course—stories.

"We have the *best* conversations!" she remarked happily as I drove her back to her place in Black Mountain.

It was to be our last visit to BPX together. In the weeks that followed, she became increasingly reluctant to leave her little garden flat.

She did admit, one time, that she would love to have one more trip there. A mischievous little-girl-smile of hopefulness and delight lit up her face at the very thought of it. But somehow, I either didn't have or didn't make the time. I also wasn't sure she could manage it. It bothered me that I didn't work that out for her. Second guesses and regrets are part of the pain of dealing with death, but I've realized that trying to mentally outwit the sharper edges of remorse is pointless.

Rather, the best antidote to the relentless head tricks and mind games we put ourselves through in the wake of loss might just be an unexpected little piece of magic.

And so it was one night, several months after she died, that a painting almost hidden in a dark corner of the old Wedge building in Asheville's River Arts District happened to catch my eye.

I was wandering around the Mark Bettis Gallery during a reception called "Accidentally on Purpose" that was showcasing the work of mixedmedia artist Jacqui Fehl. Jacqui who has large gray eyes and long ropes of platinum and black dreads, describes her paintings as "a blend of grunge, whimsy, and outsider."

Influenced by music, lyrics, feelings, and *stories*, Jacqui's art is unpredictable—playful, colorful and humorous with an appealing edge of darkness. "It is a dance of layering on, removing, covering up, and revealing," her artist statement reads. "I like my work to be loose, a bit flawed, and not too precise or perfect."

That sounds like my life, I thought.

Even though it was not part of the show, I felt there was something very compelling about the painting I saw in the dark corner. The colors and the mood—it had a storytelling aura and lovely intimacy about it.

Another gallery artist caught me staring at it.

"You like that one?" she asked.

"Yes, I do," I replied. Once again, there I was, standing in front of another painting, unable to tear myself away. This time, it was not a colorful landscape that reminded me of Italy.

This time I was drawn to the random appearance of places to sit throughout the canvas. Aware that Jacqui always gives her paintings interesting titles, I asked her colleague if she knew what Jacqui called it. She picked it up from the easel and in the low light of the darkened corner, squinted at the writing on the back of it.

The Best Conversations, she said.

I stood there, speechless. So, she said it again, a little louder this time, as if she thought I might be hard of hearing.

"It's called The Best Conversations."

My head flooded with delight—and relief. Finding this painting felt like love.

Accidentally on purpose, indeed!

The Best Conversations came home with me that night. I hung it up in the little writing/breakfast room behind the kitchen that looked over the gardens of my Under the Appalachian Sun house—just one of the many places where Mom and I often had our best conversations.

A year later, we'd all moved on—Zoë to a new life in Seattle and Leif to Finland for university.

After five years, despite the many good gatherings and memories, I was more than weary of living next to the homeless shelter's seemingly endless drama. Sad as I was to leave it, I sold my Under the Appalachian Sun house.

I bought a little mid-century modern home, the design of which brought back memories—mostly good—of both the "New House" of my childhood as well as the old *Money Pit* house Steve and I had renovated back in the late 80s. Fortunately, this one was in much better condition. I could move in without fear of toxic poisoning, cat shit, smoke damage, and broken shards of glass, and take my time fixing it up and revisioning it. The profit from my Under the Appalachian Sun house paid off all remaining university debts for both kids, just one of the many gifts from that house.

Fate delivered me the perfect buyers—a former international director of Save the Children and her husband, a former nightly news editor for NPR and retired war correspondent for *The LA Times*. They'd fallen for each other, they told me, because one thing they had in common was that they were both the only ones running *towards* international crises to help or report on them, when everyone else was running *away* from them.

A homeless women's shelter next door? *Not a problem!* they said cheerfully.

SWEET HOME ALABAMA

YOU'RE NOT LIKELY to miss the moment you cross the state line from Tennessee to Alabama. Large green signs by the side of the highway welcome travelers to "Sweet Home Alabama." That a state uses Lynyrd Skynyrd lyrics on their signs to welcome visitors was the first indication of interesting things to come.

In February of 2020, Tom and I were on the highway, driving southwest from Asheville towards Birmingham for the film premiere of *Dreams of Hope*—a documentary I'd done the PBS station wrangling for.

I was worried visiting Birmingham would make me sad, angry and upset, given America's civil rights history. Instead, my time there was an inspiration.

We got into town early enough to explore the downtown area before the premiere. After checking into our hotel, we walked over to Linn Park, a quiet green space surrounded by impressive buildings, including Birmingham's Museum of Art and the Jefferson County Courthouse. Designed by the Chicago architectural firm Holabird & Root, the courthouse's Art Deco facade was so lovely, I pulled out my camera to take some photographs.

That attracted the attention of a large, burly, white guard who came over and asked what I was doing. Knowing I was within my rights to take exterior shots without permission, I told him how much I admired the architecture.

"Want to see something *really* interesting?" he asked.

"Sure!" I said, having no idea what to expect but hoping his uniform meant he would do me no harm. He turned his back to me, waving an arm to follow him.

A short distance away, Tom watched the conversation unfolding, a little concerned. Seeing me follow the burly man into the courthouse, he quickly caught up to us.

Inside, the guard proudly pointed to the large-scale murals on the lobby walls painted by John W. Norton, WPA-commissioned works of art contrasting the Old South to the New South. They were astonishing. My grandfather, Perry Fellows, had been the Chief Engineer of the Works Progress Administration (WPA) between 1935 and 1947, during which time he was responsible for five thousand projects all over the country. So, I was always interested in seeing WPA projects.

But the guard had something else in mind.

"Want to see something that's not open to the public yet?" he asked.

What the hell could this be? I thought, nervously. But by now, Tom was by my side, so I nodded yes—if Tom could come with me.

The big guard smiled, then led us both over to an elevator with a sign on it that said, 'closed to the public.' Entranced by the beautiful Art Deco brass decorations around it, I stepped inside. Tom followed, the doors closed, and the guard pushed the button for the seventh floor.

When the doors opened, we stepped out of the elevator—and into jail.

Specifically, the jail cell where Dr. Martin Luther King Jr. had been held for an act of civil disobedience—parading without a permit. In a few months it would be open to the public, the guard told us, but we were welcome to see the actual jail cell and take photographs of displays, including a telegram to King from boxing legend Muhammad Ali. He was clearly proud of it and enjoying showing off what Birmingham was doing to preserve its unique and educational Civil Rights history.

The documentary *Dreams of Hope* featured a violin solo performed by Caitlin Edwards on one of the Violins of Hope—musical instruments that belonged to Jews before and during the Holocaust and have since been lovingly restored by violin maker Amnon Weinstein and his son, Avshalom. In the heart and mind of Weinstein, these Violins of Hope represent the victory of the human spirit over evil and hatred.

After seeing a Violins of Hope concert in another city, Birmingham resident Sallie Downs thought the violins could also bring hope to Birmingham if used in a concert to pay tribute to the American Civil Rights movement and the four African American girls killed by the 1963 Ku Klux Klan bombing of the 16th Street Baptist Church.

Sallie pestered composer Dr. Henry Panion III, Director of Music Technology at the University of Alabama at Birmingham, until he agreed to help her pull together the event. Best known for his work as conductor and arranger for his friend, Stevie Wonder, Panion has led many of the world's most notable orchestras and was, in Sallie's mind, the perfect person to create a unique piece of music for the Birmingham concert.

As excitement grew around the idea, filmmaker Mike Edwards was invited to weave together in documentary form the history of the violins, Henry's composition, and the concert at the 16th Street Baptist Church. The result was a celebration of the resilience of those who have faced hate, discrimination and racism.

Once the film was finished, I was brought in to do the national PBS station wrangling. The documentary captured my heart with its story and Henry's soaring music.

The film premiere was held at the Alabama Theater, a charming and unique 1920s combination of Spanish Colonial Revival and Mission Revival architecture, and the sold-out crowd of nearly 2000 responded enthusiastically to the film.

It has since been recognized with dozens of awards, including Los

Angeles Film Awards, Spotlight Documentary Film Awards, New York Movie Awards, and Near Nazareth International Film Festival, as well as the unusual feat of winning 13 Telly Awards.

Although none of us could have known it at the time, the entire world was about to explode into the confusion and fears of a full-scale global pandemic. And we would need some dreams of hope ourselves in the coming days, months, and years. With Zoë living and working on the west coast in Seattle, Leif at university in Finland, and me in the middle in Asheville, I sketched a cartoon of me standing on top of one of the Blue Ridge Mountains. It showed a sad and frightened little stick figure with impossibly long arms stretching in opposite directions, reaching out to try and hold them both.

WORKING FROM WHEREVER

Morning journal, March 7, 2020—Panicked emails from Stephen, who'd flown from DC to Los Angeles, only to be told his 8-9 days paid production gig was cancelled. He was told to take an immediate flight back to the east coast. Thousands of dollars of work evaporated for him.

It's surreal. Everything is cancelled. Amazon and Google are both closed, everyone has been told to work from home. SXSW in Austin is cancelled. The PBS Annual Meeting in Seattle is cancelled, and with it, my trip to see Zoë and spend our first Mother's Day together in at least a decade. Normalcy is cancelled. Enter an eerie and weird limbo.

WITH THE EMERGENCE of a global pandemic, the world suddenly lurched into uncharted territory. We were individually isolated, but united in our confusion and frightening lack of understanding about what on earth was going on.

Despite this unforeseen plot twist, however, it felt like the films and story frames once again had my back, as I found myself in what was a highly unusual position for me—I was in *advance* of a work trend. After parting ways from the documentary workshop back in 2000, I had already had twenty years of experience as a remote or freelance worker under my belt.

March 8, 2020—I rearranged some of the art on my walls today because for some reason it felt important to get that right. Who does that in the face of an impending pandemic?! Today I'll clean the house and, if it's not too windy, work in the gardens for a bit. And try to wrap my head around the sudden weirdness of life these days.

As the daughter of a computer guru, I was also lucky to be in the right era for technology.

I was still in high school when NASA physicist and engineer Jack Nilles laid the foundation for modern remote working in 1973, coining the term "telecommuting" nearly 50 years before the COVID pandemic.

March 10, 2020—I bought some hunker-down food supplies yesterday: lots of Indian food, rice, quinoa, plus tins of sardines, tuna, and mussels from Spain and Portugal. And chai. The latest case of this COVID flu was just reported in Spartanburg, South Carolina. It's getting closer to Asheville.

By 1983, what had started with a handful of remote workers rose to two thousand as IBM's call center staff—who conducted their work via phone anyway—had the option of doing so from home.

The first website came into being in 1990, the year Leif was born.

March 11, 2020—Friends just bailed on plans to join us at the White Horse over in Black Mountain for an evening of music this coming Friday. They'd been exposed to someone who'd been with someone who since tested positive for COVID after attending a conference in New Orleans. The National Guard has been called out in New York City. Who knows what today will bring.

In 1998, Jack Nilles reappeared on the scene with a book on remote working. *Managing Telework* offered "a step-by-step guide to managing a successful, efficient, and happy virtual workforce."

Skype, created by two Scandinavians—Niklas Zennström from Sweden and Janus Friis from Denmark, along with four developers in Estonia—was released in August 2003. Zoom came along in 2011.

March 12, 2020—Tom and I had a lovely dinner out last night at Mela Indian Restaurant downtown with my Indian yoga teacher Venita, and her husband, Darshan. It may be our last night out for . . . who knows how long? This virus is taking over everything. The NBA has cancelled games until further notice and the World Health Organization has officially declared it a world pandemic. All flights from Europe to the U.S. are being cancelled, which means Leif can't come home from Finland. So, no Zoë or Leif visits for the indefinite future. I still have that cartoon image of myself in my head, the one with two very long arms stretching from Asheville to Seattle, and from Asheville to Finland, where Leif is now in his fourth year of university. How on earth do I "mother" in times like these?

Working remotely has boomed in the last decade and is predicted to keep growing in the post-pandemic world. I felt lucky to have parted ways with Martin, even if it hadn't been my idea.

Altogether, I promoted 18 documentaries in 2020—films about the lives of professional female chefs, the history of women's emancipation, vertical greenhouses that trained and employed workers with Down syndrome, a global Lego robotics competition, American farmers, Afro-Latino culture in South America, the 1942 internment of Japanese Americans, the future of energy, the need for living wages, slavery, breast cancer, music, and a pioneering village of small houses for the homeless in Austin, Texas.

These films kept me connected to filmmakers all over the country.

They kept me connected to ideas, issues and, most importantly, to people and the world.

Because documentaries can often take years to make, I had a robust pipeline of projects in place. These were all films that had been dreamed up, financed, shot, edited, and produced in the years leading up to the pandemic.

But with people and crews suddenly unable to be together on location for new and ongoing work, how long that pipeline would last was anyone's guess.

HOLY SILENCE: SLEEPING IN A CONVENT IN ROME

WHEN I STARTED working as a PBS station wrangler in 2000, there were only a handful of people who did this kind of consulting. These days there are likely dozens. And so, you might be wondering, how do I convince a filmmaker *I* am the right person to represent their film?

I begin by looking for a personal connection or way into their documentary. But sometimes it just boils to what Bob Dylan might call a simple twist of fate—like when a non-religious half Dane and an American Jewish documentary filmmaker realize they were both inside the same small Catholic church in Rome, within weeks of one another. There are around 900 churches in Rome, so what were the chances of *that* happening?

In May 2020, two months into the pandemic, I was contacted by author and filmmaker Steven Pressman (*50 Children: The Rescue Mission of Mr & Mrs Kraus*) to discuss representing his latest documentary, *Holy Silence,* to PBS stations nationally. He'd heard about me from our mutual friends, filmmaker Abby Ginzberg, with whom I'd worked on her films *And Then They Came for Us* and *Waging Change*, and editor Ken Schneider, with whom I'd first connected a decade earlier with his wife Marcia when representing their 2009 ITVS film, *Speaking in Tongues.*

Steve's film was an emotionally charged examination of the thinking and actions of key individuals who'd played a crucial role in shaping the Vatican's controversial response to the rising Nazi threat across Europe. They included a leading American industrialist dispatched on a mission by President Franklin Roosevelt, along with high-ranking officials within the Vatican determined to carry out their own agenda, Pope Pius XI and Pope Pius XII, as well as a humble Jesuit priest from New England.

Holy Silence was strategically targeted to release in conjunction with the opening of the long-secret Vatican archives from that period.

Emotionally charged? Controversial? Secret archives? I was instantly interested.

The Vatican and Mussolini worked out a treaty in 1929 that established the Holy See as a sovereign city-state. As the Nazi Party's anti-Semitic rhetoric spread across Europe, what did the Catholic Church, one of the world's most influential institutions, do to confront the persecution of Jews? Did Pope Pius XII warn the Jews, especially those in Rome, of deportation after the Nazis took control of Italy? Did he order churches and other Catholic institutions to provide shelter to those persecuted? Or did he keep quiet, hoping the Germans would not bomb Rome and the Vatican with its many invaluable art treasures and its religious significance to Catholics all over the world?

As I screened *Holy Silence*, I liked that it refrained from drawing hard conclusions about Pius XII's actions during his papacy, leaving viewers to decide for themselves. It was intelligent, compelling, thought-provoking, well researched, and beautifully produced. For once, I had no suggestions. I just wanted to work with it—and Steve.

Serendipitously, I had spent a week in Rome the previous year researching and tracking down my grandmother's footsteps there for my book *Lions, Peacocks & Lemon Trees.*

In my walks around the city, I wandered, quite by chance, into the historic Jewish Quarter where I noticed a scattering of little brass cobblestones on the sidewalk outside certain doorways.

These *Stolpersteine* or "stumbling stones"—in Italian, *Pietri d'inciampo*—are the vision of Gunter Demning, a German artist, whose mission has been to draw attention to the fate of each *individual* stolen away from their everyday lives.

Each little brass square begins with the words, *Hier Wohnte*— in Italian, *Qui Abitava*—meaning "here lived," followed by the name of the individual who had been seized from his or her home, their date of birth, the date of the arrest and deportation—as well as that individual's date of death, if known. In a nod to the desecration of Jewish cemeteries by the Nazis who repurposed grave markers as sidewalk paving stones, the *Stolpersteine* are embedded into the pavement and are now considered the world's largest decentralized memorial.

Demning laid his first stone in 1992. There are more than 200 little stumbling stones in Rome, more than 100,000 worldwide—each one a quiet memorial to someone who was stolen from their life over that very doorstep and never seen again. Having noticed and felt the power of them set the stage for working with a film set in Rome about the Holocaust.

Not long after leaving the documentary workshop, I'd read two books about the Resistance to the Nazis during WWII, one about resistance efforts in rural France and another, *Darkness over Denmark,* which told the story of how the Danes helped Jews escape the Nazis and the Holocaust.

Being half Danish, I felt proud of this. I reached out to the book's agent to see about optioning the rights to make a documentary from the book about the French resistance thinking, in a moment of grand delusion, I actually had the skills to do that. Fortunately, they'd already been optioned so I was saved not only the expense but also the potential professional embarrassment.

When Steve and I jumped on our first phone call, I revealed my Danish roots to him.

"As you know, the Danes helped the Jews during WWII," I told him, hoping to impress him that I was a genetically empathetic person to represent his film.

"Oh, I know," he said. "In fact, there is a wonderful bit about that in the film festival version of the documentary. Unfortunately, it got cut when we edited the film down to the one-hour length for PBS broadcast."

"*The part about the Danes was cut?!*" I yelped.

"Sorry, it happens," he replied, good-naturedly. "But if you'd like to see it, I'll send you the full-length version."

The longer version of the film included several minutes of what was happening to the Jews in Rome after the Nazis occupied the city in 1943. Susan Zuccotti, one of the historians who appears in the film, contrasts the silence of Pius XII to the situation in Denmark, "where the local citizenry went out of their way to protect Jews."

Interested in what else might have been cut out, I let the film run after the bit about the Danes. The action moved back to Rome and an interview with a nun. It took me a moment, but then I reached for the controller to pause it. Unbelievably, I recognized the chapel behind the nun. I phoned Steve back.

"Your interview with the nun . . ." I started to say.

"Mother Superior," he corrected me.

"Whatever," I said, impatient to ask him about the church. "I recognize that chapel. It's the Sisters of the Seven Sorrows, isn't it?"

"It is!" he said, sounding surprised. "How did you know that?"

"*I slept there* when I was in Rome last year," I told him. "The convent attached to that chapel is now a hotel. There was even a larger-than-life statue of Jesus *pointing* to the chapel as I walked into the hotel, as if he wanted to be sure I saw it. And one of the bellboys there showed me the subterranean grotto where the nuns hid Jews."

I think we were equally speechless. How strange, I thought. Were my own actions now *triggering* the films that came to me?

Steve and I exchanged photographs from the chapel, the convent, and its subterranean grotto. He responded right away with how amazed he was by the small-world coincidence, and I got the gig.

Holy Silence premiered in November that year in conjunction with the PBS release of a three-part series, *The Rise of the Nazis*. The title was perfect, and the pairing worked well. Since its launch, *Holy Silence* has aired close to four thousand times on PBS stations all over the country.

As long as I had now been working with films, it was likely inevitable there would be moments of foreshadowing for what might soon cross my path in terms of projects.

Still, it caught me by surprise when this happened in—of all places—a convent in Rome.

MUST LOVE DOGS

March 13, 2020—Leif is isolated in his little flat in Finland. He sent me a photo of the empty grocery store shelves over there.

March 14, 2020 —Zoë called from Edmonds, Washington, sounding calm and fine even though she and her boyfriend are living close to the epicenter of the virus in the U.S. from what they tell me. And so, we live in our bubbles of uncertainty, not sure what is coming, not knowing what to expect, only that it will likely be bad, possibly very bad.

March 15, 2020 —The turkey buzzards are circling high up in the air over our neighborhood this morning, making ominous and silent black circles in the sky. What if this is it? What if this is how it ends for me —the victim of a pandemic? That plot twist had never occurred to me. I also never thought daydreams about travels would suddenly evaporate and all travel become impossible. I never thought of a world I couldn't travel in. I've always existed in a state of "where to next?" It was never a thought that I might not be able to travel for years! When will I see my kids again?

March 16, 2020—The Fine Arts Theater

downtown is closed until further notice. I'm strangely, morbidly fascinated by the news these days and listen to NPR almost nonstop. Like a scary thriller you can't put down, each hour brings another unbelievable and unexpected cliff-hanger and I nervously can't wait to turn the page and see or hear what will happen to the characters next. Only, we're the characters in this book.

March 18, 2020—Hoping to avoid people, I made a late-night run to Publix to get butter, coffee, disinfectant wipes, bananas, and dog food—along with their <u>last</u> bottle of Tylenol and their <u>last</u> bag of rice. There are signs on bread, milk, toilet paper, and bleach to not take more than two per family, due to "the times." Lacking the right gear, I wore kayaking gloves on my hands and a bright hiking scarf over my nose and mouth—face masks and gloves are hard to come by and it was the best I could do to stave off potential germs. A father pushing a cart with two small kids with curly mops of brown hair passed by me as I was hunting down dog food. One of the kids looked at me with eyes of wonder and as they walked away, I heard him say, "Daddy, why is that woman . . ."

Because in just four days, that's what I've become—that woman who lives alone with her dog and wears strange things when she shops for food late at night.

IN ADDITION TO the documentaries I worked with, some of the story frames of my life were influenced by feature films. *The Money Pit* had inspired Steve and me to renovate a pretty terrible fixer-upper. *Under the Tuscan Sun* foreshadowed my adventures with my own Under the Appalachian Sun house.

And then there was *Must Love Dogs*, another film starring Diane Lane. Released in 2005, the year we moved to Asheville, it also tied in thematically with my life. Although I didn't care for the film (neither did the critics), I loved the title. Three simple words that summed up one of my key priorities in raising my kids. Looking back over the single mom years, despite all the chaos and uncertainties, one thing I *know* I did right was to bring up my kids with dogs.

Despite years of pleading, neither of my parents would allow a dog in the house. I never had that companionship, which would have been good for a child constantly uprooted and put in a variety of different schools and cultures due to her father's work.

Steve was aware of this, and in the waning years of our marriage, surprised me with a little Yorkie puppy for my birthday. I named her Zydeco for the music we both loved. She was great for the kids and they included her in whatever they did. Zoë took ownership of my birthday present immediately.

After we parted ways, Steve got a puppy to keep Leif company when he stayed at his apartment. Leif named him Bandit and it wasn't long before Steve gave me that puppy, as well.

By the time we moved to Asheville, little Zydeco was old and frail. One sunny winter afternoon, she slipped away from us out in the gardens. The four of us held a somber *Three Lives of Thomasina*-style burial for her on the hillside overlooking the lake and bird sanctuary. The following Christmas, I surprised the kids with a Golden Doodle puppy with a red bow around her neck, just like in *Lady and the Tramp*. They named her Klejne after their favorite Danish Christmas cookies.

When Bandit died several years later, he was buried in the garden of our big old Under the Appalachian Sun house. Three years later, our big beautiful Klejne died unexpectedly of cancer.

Tom's cousin's dog had just had a new litter of puppies and he suggested I get one. Fortunately, I took him up on the idea and had Kiitos (meaning "thank you" in Finnish) by my side a few months before the pandemic started.

March 21, 2020—I find myself watching and reading the news too much—afraid to look away and not see something, and also afraid of what I will see and read. I follow the news of Italy compulsively: 726 deaths just yesterday. Or was it the day before? More than 9000 have died so far. Their economy is in ruins. Hospitals, doctors, nurses, and morgues are stretched beyond capacity. The doctors themselves are dying.

Yesterday I lost my first gig because of the pandemic. It was not unexpected, but Sun Studio in Memphis has been a client of mine with their music series for eleven years! That takes away $9000 in income this year. I may continue to help them anyway, in a reduced way, as John Schorr, owner of Sun Studio, and Jeff Davidson, the series producer, have both been very good to me over the years.

The kids and I kept in touch with phone calls, text messages, and Skype. I was grateful for the technology. Despite the pandemic, those years brought life partners—and dogs—to both Leif and Zoë. Leif met Maria in Prague and soon after, they acquired a puppy they called Bambi.

When Zoë called one day in the spring of 2021, I was surprised to hear her boyfriend, Brian, was also on the line. They'd met the year before the pandemic and now they were calling with the delightful news that they were engaged. Love in the middle of a global pandemic, how incredibly uplifting and romantic.

That fall, they visited me in Asheville. Brian had not grown up with dogs and was initially a little uneasy around Kiitos, who now weighed 75 pounds. But two days into their visit, I found him lying on the bed between Zoë and Brian, his head on Brian's chest. Looking up, Zoë smiled at me. *Must Love Dogs.*

When she and Brian got married two months later, Tom and I gave them a puppy—another one from his cousin—for their wedding present. They called her Islay in memory of a trip to Scotland they'd taken together a few years earlier.

By coincidence I'd just taken on a new documentary called *The*

Water of Life. Produced by Blacksmith & Jones, the film tells the story of the resurrection and creative explosion within the world of single malt whisky in Scotland, and was filmed primarily in Islay. Once again, my life was now foreshadowing a story frame.

STORY FRAME 78

THE LAST PIG

*After ten years of staring into thousands of pig
eyes, I've come to understand they're never vacant.
There's always somebody looking back at me.
I've taken two thousand pigs to the slaughterhouse, and I've
become haunted by the ghosts of those pigs. I don't want to have
the power to decide whether someone lives or dies anymore.*

BOB COMIS, FARMER AND POET

THERE WAS NO end in sight to the pandemic. But as the
world lurched from one variation of the virus to another one,
films that had already been made continued to come in and
filmmakers were still asking me to help them get them on
the air across the country.

One of them was *The Last Pig* by filmmaker Allison
Argo. Known for her intimate portraits of endangered
animals, many of Allison's films have been broadcast
by PBS and National Geographic and have reached
audiences worldwide. Altogether, her films have
won over 100 awards internationally, including
six national Emmys; a duPont-Columbia Award;
and awards at Jackson Hole, Banff, and dozens

410

of other film festivals from New Zealand to Japan. Hundreds of thousands of people have seen her work.

Seen through the eyes and words of one small farmer, Bob Comis, as he questions his own beliefs and the value of life, the film offers a glimpse into how animal agriculture in America may be changing. Comis finds each individual pig so intelligent and compelling that having them killed feels like an act of betrayal.

Musician Moby, a well-known vegan, described *The Last Pig* as, "startling, honest and deeply beautiful."

The two-minute trailer for *The Last Pig* brought me to tears. It was a hero's journey of a different sort and one I couldn't resist.

The Last Pig especially resonated with me as one of my favorite adventures in the Blue Ridge Mountains each year was Farm Tour, when many of the farms in the mountains surrounding Asheville opened to the public for a weekend. Grown-ups and kids were able to see where our food comes from, learn how animals are cared for, and find out about other agricultural splendors such as raising Alpaca goats for their wool, growing flowers for weddings and other occasions, and cultivating hops for craft beers. Many of Asheville's restaurants proudly display their farm-to-table credentials on their menus.

When the world stopped for the pandemic, grocery store shelves were empty, and everything shut down—including restaurants—it was our local farmers who came to our rescue. Actually, we rescued each other.

Founded a decade earlier by Andrea and Graham Duvall, an organization called Mother Earth Food swung into action as a bridge between area farmers and the community. Soon they were making weekly home deliveries of bins filled with fresh produce, dairy, eggs, baked goods, hummus, chocolate, meat and veggie proteins, coffee, and more—much of it regionally sourced.

"When restaurants in Western North Carolina closed March 17," wrote *Mountain XPress,* "a window of opportunity opened for Mother Earth Food. The Asheville-based produce and grocery delivery service suddenly found itself able to fold more partners and customers into its mission: making it easier for people to eat local, organic food while supporting the businesses that provide it."

March 22, 2020—Solid sleep for once last night—there was no Coronavirus in my dreamscape and for that, I am grateful. I took a drive out into the mountains west of Asheville in search of an organization that is selling boxes of produce from the farmers, produce they can no longer sell to restaurants because they've all closed.

It took me a while to find the distribution point, hidden away as it was behind a bunch of scary-looking abandoned greenhouses with broken glass and trees growing inside of them—nothing to do with the pandemic, but still creepy. I drove down the dirt road to an open building surrounded by still more old greenhouses. Three people stood outside. As I pulled up in my car (they ask you not to get out), a tall, attractive, slender guy in blue jeans and a work shirt, his long gray hair pulled back in a ponytail, peered in my open passenger side window.

He had friendly blue eyes. He smiled at me.

"You're in luck!" he said. "You got the last box!"

I was close to tears at this point. Tears of exhaustion and tears of appreciation for what these lovely people are doing as the go-betweens between local farmers and the people in the community who need food.

"We LOVE what we do!" he said when I thanked him and handed him the $20. "Thank YOU for coming out to get our fresh produce!"

I was never so thankful that I was living in a mountain town surrounded by farms, farmers, and a plentiful supply of fresh water. Each week, I drove out to the Mother Earth greenhouses to collect a produce box. Whatever was in the box determined what I would cook or bake that week. Some things were not familiar to me and I had to ask friends what they were and how to prepare them. When I think back on those farm boxes, it's *good* feelings I remember—not the frightening atmosphere of the pandemic.

Allowing yet another film to direct my life, *The Last Pig* was a reminder that it wasn't hard to go back to a meatless routine. When the kids were younger, I'd stopped eating meat for seventeen years but then drifted back into it sometime after moving to Asheville.

Moved by Bob Comis's thoughts and emotions, as well as the beautiful camerawork of Joseph Brunette, an award-winning National Geographic cinematographer, I once again stopped eating meat (although I still eat fish).

Allison has gently pointed out to me that fish are sentient beings, too. I like Allison and wanted to make her happy, so I made an inner bargain with myself: If I am ever pitched a beautiful film about fish, I'll take that as a sign and give them up, too.

LEARNING TO SKATEBOARD IN A WARZONE (IF YOU'RE A GIRL)

"AND THE WINNER of the 2020 Best Documentary Short Subject is . . ." and here, actor Mark Ruffalo paused for dramatic effect.

"*Learning to Skateboard in a Warzone (If You're a Girl)* by Carol Dysinger and Elena Andreicheva!" he yelled out to the audience.

I was so excited on Carol's behalf. It was exhilarating to see a filmmaker I'd worked with win an Oscar!

I wasn't there, of course. It was Sunday, the ninth of February 2021, and I was watching the 92nd Academy Awards on television at home, curled up on the sofa with my puppy, Kiitos, and a glass of prosecco.

Carol Dysinger has been a feature film and documentary editor for decades and she gets the art of story. Her editing credits include a number of films accepted into the Sundance Film Festival. She is also a tenured Professor of Graduate Film and New Media at NYU Film School in the Tisch School of the Arts and a Guggenheim Fellowship recipient. *Learning to Skateboard in a Warzone (If You're a Girl)* also won Best Documentary Short at New York's Tribeca Film Festival in 2019.

I'd met Carol through ITVS, public media's independent film incubator, when they hired me in the spring of 2010 to pitch Carol's earlier film to PBS stations nationally. *Camp Victory, Afghanistan* is a fascinating documentary that looks at the stark realities of the U.S. and NATO "exit strategy" from Afghanistan.

The U.S. arrived in Afghanistan after 9/11 to train the Afghan National Army to fight terrorism. Using nearly 300 hours of *verité* footage shot between 2005 and 2008, Carol's film was the first to examine the boots-on-the-ground story of trying to build a functioning Afghan military there.

Camp Victory, Afghanistan follows a battle-hardened but endearing Afghan general as he tries to work with an ever-changing stream of U.S. National Guard members deployed to train his soldiers. Carol's film highlights the daunting challenges of creating a modern Afghan army when in her words, "Eighty percent of the enlistees are illiterate, all are impoverished, the weaponry is second-rate, and the enemy is elusive, dangerous, and lawless."

Despite heavy military aid from the U.S., Carol's film demonstrated that money alone does not produce an army—people do. *Camp Victory, Afghanistan* was also a story about friendship and the unlikely bonds that form in war, showing that Afghans and Americans have more in common than anyone would expect.

The critics got it.

"The film crackles with the emotional energy and intelligence of its subjects," raved *The New York Times.*

"Excellent, thought-provoking . . . a clear-eyed look at an irretrievably messy situation," *VARIETY*'s reviewer commented, praising the film for showing how "the war to win the hearts and minds of Afghan soldiers carries its own perils and paradoxes."

New York Magazine called it "Excellent . . . heartbreaking . . . the new face of war documentaries."

I watched Carol make her way to the podium, then stand in the floodlights, beaming. I would have given an Academy Award to her just for the title of her film.

"*Oh my god!*" she said, turning around to look at Elena.

"Frank Capra handed me a student academy award in 1977, and I thought I'd skipped the hard part. I thought I would go on to make movies," she continued. "And if I hadn't had that encouragement at my back, back then, I wouldn't have been able to withstand the last four decades in this business!"

Carol paused to nod in affirmation to the clapping and hoots from the audience. She then went on to thank a short list of backers, her editor, her cinematographer, and many others.

For anyone who has ever yawned through these moments, please try to understand how amazing and surreal it is to hear your name called, to be acknowledged and thanked in front of a global audience.

[Sidenote: For anyone who has ever yawned through these moments, please try to understand how amazing and surreal it is to hear your name called, to be acknowledged and thanked in front of a global audience.]

When President Biden unexpectedly announced the American withdrawal from Afghanistan on August 30, 2021, my first thought was to call Carol for her thoughts. I wasn't the only one.

"*Everyone's* calling me!" she laughed when I got her on the phone.

It was good to catch up and hear her latest news. I told her I still had the beautiful and evocative photograph she'd taken of three young girls on location in Afghanistan on a wall in my studio.

It's the only time a filmmaker has gifted me with a location still from their documentary and it's one of my most cherished souvenirs from this unexpected career of mine.

THE MAN WHO FELL TO EARTH FROM A PLANE

I AM SITTING on the edge of the open door in the plane, staring at the tiny landscape far below, about to skydive for the first time in my life with the knowledge that 15,000 feet separate me from the earth.

Falling through the air, I will be tethered to Nick, a guy with "Adrenaline Junkie" tattooed on his chest, a guy whose legs have been amputated below the knees.

"Go ahead, *jump!*" he says, laughing.

I hesitate. This situation is completely counterintuitive for me. I'm a Taurus, an earth sign. I have spent a lifetime trying *not* to be separated from whatever plane I happened to be flying in.

"*Go ahead!*" he says again, nudging me ever so slightly.

And so, I do, tumbling from the plane out into the sky with Nick on my back.

Did this actually happen?

No. But this scene played over and over on a continuous loop in my imagination while I was working with a documentary called *Get Busy Living*.

It was the fall of 2020, and I had just received another email from Keith Ochwat, the Los

Angeles-based documentary filmmaker and film consultant with whom I'd teamed up on several films, including one of my favorites—the tongue-in-cheekily titled *Thank You for Coming* by Sara Lamm, about the search for the sperm donor who had fathered her.

Would I like to represent a film about a man who fell out of a plane? he asked.

You've got to be kidding me, I thought. *Do you even know my history with flying?*

But I like Keith, so I agreed to watch the film.

Get Busy Living tells the story of Nick Fener, a veteran skydiver who somehow managed to not only survive a fall when his parachute failed to open properly, but also resume skydiving, despite the amputation of both of his legs below the knees.

The film's title was based on a line from the Academy Award-winning film based on a 1982 novella by Stephen King, *The Shawshank Redemption*.

"Get busy living or get busy dying," is a line said by actor Morgan Freeman, who plays a contraband smuggler, to his fellow inmate played by Tim Robbins. It became Nick's favorite mantra and the one his wife Lindsay used to pull him through his grueling, eighteen-month, post-freefall rehab.

When *The Shawshank Redemption* was released in 1994, I saw it with Martin and Burch, our gaffer (a film term for lighting guy or electrician) at the Old Town Theatre, located just up the street from the documentary workshop. It wasn't my idea, prison films not being at all my thing, but Burch had already seen it once and wanted both of us to see it, too. He persuaded me with the promise of a pint of Guinness at Murphy's Pub before—*and after*—the film.

I hate being afraid of anything and, much as it pained me to admit, I was still a nervous flyer. When flying home to London from the U.S. during Christmas break from college back in the 70s, the turbulence was so bad a man near me had a heart attack. The pilots turned the plane around and flew back to Boston to get him into a hospital. The rest of us spent the night in the airport hotel and were put on another flight the following day.

Then there was the 747 with the gaping hole in its wing.

And then I remembered something else. Somewhere deep in the dark tissue of brain memory, something was stirring, and I realized my problems with flying began when I was eight years old, and we moved from the U.S. to London.

My father was already living and working there and my mother, having fallen for the romance of a transatlantic crossing, decided that she, my brother, and I would travel to England by boat. In those days of transatlantic travel, there was nothing much to do. I was eight, Pip was fifteen and while my mother wrapped herself up in blankets on a deckchair, read books and sipped *consommé*, just as she'd fantasized, Pip and I were bored out of our minds.

The only entertainment *Holland America* offered was a movie shown once a night and so Pip and I saw all of them. Disney's *Three Lives of Thomasina, The Girl with Green Eyes,* The Beatles' *A Hard Day's Night* and, in what can only be thought of as a completely self-serving and sadistic choice for an ocean-crossing boat company, *Fate is the Hunter*—a dramatic black and white film about, of all things, a plane crash.

Although it starred Glenn Ford, Wally Cox, and a very young Suzanne Pleshette, the only character I remember to this day was the airplane's sole black passenger—a little girl in a party dress, traveling on her own, and clutching a rag doll. After the crash, only the stewardess survives. The rag doll is shown among the wreckage without the little girl.

The critics hated it as much as I did. Writing for *The New York Times,* Bosley Crowther called it a "stupid, annoying film" and wrote that "it might be better for airline travelers if they never see it."

So, when Keith called to ask me to take on a film about a skydiving accident, I needed a moment to get up the nerve to sit down and watch it.

Once I did, however, I found to my relief that I could turn it down. The storyline was a bit unclear, and I felt overall it had the feel and production values of a home movie. While that can sometimes be effective, I didn't feel it suited this particular film. In its present form, it wasn't ready for broadcast. I also didn't like the title which I thought sounded more like a PBS pledge special than a riveting story of survival. It wasn't a clickbait film title, which is important given the many options viewers have these days.

Keith, however, was persistent.

"What would it take for you to work with us on this film?" he asked.

"A better title," I said. "Seriously, who's going to remember a line from a film from the 90s?" *Get Busy Living* sounded finger-wagging to me.

"Suggest something," he said.

"Okay, say you're going out with your wife to the movies on a Friday night," I said to Keith. "Which film would you rather see—*Get Busy Living* or *The Man Who Fell to Earth from a Plane*? With the second title, people will want to know—and then what happened?! That's just human nature."

I also pointed out, as tactfully as I could, that the film's production values were not broadcast quality.

"It looks like a home movie," I said. I guessed a good portion of it was shot on an iPad.

Keith laughed good-naturedly, said he took my points and promised to run them past the film's director, who was a close friend of Nick Fener, the self-described "adrenaline junkie" skydiver.

To my surprise, I won one of those battles. Rather than change the title—words that had carried Nick and Lindsay through Nick's eighteen-month rehabilitation—the team chose to have the entire documentary reedited.

They took my recommendation and hired my good friend Tal Skloot, the talented director, writer, and editor of *4 Wheel Bob,* for which I'd done the national broadcast wrangling. Tal put together a new edit plan for them with a changed point of view. It was Tal who realized the film was not just a survival story but, at its heart, a love story. And everyone was on board with that.

The results of the re-edit were so astonishing and the story so powerful, I gave up my quest to have the name of the film changed.

Get Busy Living premiered nationally in 2021 in conjunction with the anniversary of the Americans with Disabilities Act, receiving nearly one thousand airdates throughout 83 percent of the U.S.

I still think it could have done even better with a different title. It's an unusual and very compelling action-adventure story with two interesting characters. A love story and a hero's journey.

Even *The Shawshank Redemption* suffered from its title. While it received a lot of acclaim, it earned a paltry $16 million during its premiere theatrical run. One of the reasons cited for this box-office disappointment was the title, which critics considered "confusing" for audiences.

It was also up against *Pulp Fiction* and *Forrest Gump* that same year, very tough competition for audience attention. After it secured seven Academy Award nominations, however, it got a lot of publicity and people had a better understanding of what it was about. *The Shawshank Redemption* was re-released, and the box office grew to over $73 million.

So, how did working with this film affect my life?

For a while, I was tempted to face up to my own fear of flying by asking Nick Fener to dive with me. I gave it serious thought, thinking if I could jump *out* of a plane, it might make it easier for me to fly *inside* of one.

I haven't done that yet, but I also haven't given up on the idea completely. Oddly enough, after spending four months with this film, I find I'm much more at ease flying these days and no longer grab that pre-flight beer.

FROM ASHEVILLE TO ANYWHERE

NOT LONG AFTER we moved to Asheville in 2005, I heard about a new film in the making—*Asheville: The Movie* by Venezuelan director Chusy Haney-Jardine and his wife, Jennifer MacDonald.

Curious, I decided to check out a screening of it down at the Fine Arts Theater. It was shot entirely in the Asheville area using mostly non-professional actors.

In 2007, Haney-Jardine changed the film's title to *Anywhere, U.S.A.* Writing for *Indy Week,* Marc Maximov writes that Haney-Jardine renamed the movie "for artistic reasons"—to reflect the universality of the American experience. But he also acknowledged some Asheville residents had complained of overexposure. (There was a lot of overexposure going on—*Rolling Stone* magazine had just named Asheville "the new freak capital of the U.S.")

Anywhere U.S.A. went on to premiere at Sundance, one of 121 films selected from a field of 3,624 feature-length submissions. It won a Spirit of Independence Special Jury Prize for its originality and "willingness to take risks on a limited budget."

Maximov called it "a sprawling, three-part

examination of a bunch of small-town eccentrics who collide in a series of determinedly random events."

"Audience reaction was mixed," he noted. "The jokey tone and fanciful plot keep the viewer at arm's length, but in its best moments there are flashes of real style and tenderness, and Haney-Jardine's unabashed love of his adopted hometown and its residents gives the movie its soul. . . . Haney-Jardine slyly accommodates the title change by bleeping out the names of area towns and neighborhoods: It's a surprisingly funny gimmick that also lets locals feel like they're in on an inside joke."

In retrospect, the title change from *Asheville: The Movie* to *Anywhere, U.S.A.* foreshadowed the creeping encroachment from developers, corporate interests, and wealthy vacation home hunters—a sellout that was threatening to obliterate much of what was unique and original about the town.

During my eighteen years in Asheville, as I watched it become more like, well, anywhere in the U.S., I realized—with a breaking heart—that it might be time to move on.

Remember those five index cards on which I wrote my goals in the middle of the night, after parting ways with Martin? Over the years, I had diligently ticked off almost everything—including getting the kids through college, writing a book, being able to work from wherever, and—once I sold my house—becoming debt free.

There was only one goal left on the list—and that was to live in Europe (at least part of the year).

PART V

WHEREVER YOU ARE

In a sense, no creative act is ever finished . . .
creativity lies not in the done, but in the doing.

JULIA CAMERON, *THE ARTIST'S WAY*

THE UNSEEN CARTOONIST

January 1, 2021—Writing this date, it suddenly feels quite the accomplishment to have made it through 2020 alive. In tough times especially, it really is a brilliant invention to be able to call it quits—in the middle of winter no less—and say, here's a brand-new start and it begins today!

January 21, 2021—Zoë called yesterday to point out today will be the 21st day of the 21st year of the twenty-first century. Here's hoping that's a good omen. . . .

LOOKING BACK OVER the past nearly 30 years, I can see the storyboard frames moving me along in the right direction, as if there was an unseen cartoonist always just a step ahead of me, sketching out where I should go and what I should do next.

It's been a career with amazing highs, and I love the euphoria that comes with being upbeat and genuinely happy. But there were also times when it felt more like a game of snakes and ladders as hidden serpents seemed to jump out at me when I attempted to move up a rung. During the time of snakes, I was often tempted to cave to the stresses, pressures, disappointments, frustrations, and all-out weariness that comes with having spent three decades in film and television.

I understand how some older women become so fierce. Now that I'm in my sixties, I'm finally letting all that fierceness and creativity shine through without fear of rejection and criticism—*and how freeing is that?*

I've come too far and been through too much to be anything other than what I am—a world-wise, compassionate, creative, complicated, and opinionated older woman. It's liberating and exhilarating to be and feel this way—making full use of decades of work, people encounters, travels, storytelling, and life experiences.

At this point, I can look back and laugh at some of the moments that once upset me. Like the time a PBS station general manager once asked me to speak with someone on his staff for an hour or so and tell her "Everything you know."

Everything I know?

He didn't offer any compensation for this, mind you, but did offer to "toss a few airdates" my way if I helped him out. I know it's just part of the stressful and competitive television ecosystem, but I suspect it's unlikely he would have asked a man to tell someone on his staff everything he knew for free. The request was so preposterous to me, I may actually have laughed out loud on the phone. (At least, I really hope I did.)

"An hour?" I said in astonishment.

"Yes," he said.

"Sum up everything I know *in one hour*!?" I repeated because I just couldn't help myself. "She would have to have lived *my entire life* to have *any* understanding of how and why I do what I do!"

But that was lost on him. Of course, I said no.

For better or worse, those *what if* seeds of curiosity have always been inside me.

When I was in first grade, the school principal—a large man with a pleasant disposition—paid a visit to our classroom to remind us that whistling was not permitted in school. My teacher listened respectfully as he spoke, then resumed whatever it was she was teaching us after he left.

I waited a moment. And then I whistled. It was just a low whistle, not as loud as when I used two fingers in my mouth. But it was heard. My teacher turned around from the blackboard and scanned her flock of six-year-olds in astonishment.

"Did someone just whistle?" she asked.

Silence.

"Who was it?!" she demanded.

I raised my hand. My teacher appeared genuinely shocked. Normally a quiet and well-behaved student, I may have been the last one she would have suspected.

She shook her head in disbelief, then promptly sent me to the principal's office where I spent a lifetime—for a six-year-old—cooling my heels in the outer office, imagining there was a special machine for disobedient children inside, a sort of conveyer belt with paddles extending downwards to spank the bottoms of bad children. I was the kid of an airline executive, so maybe that's where that image came from. I can still see it in my mind—my little body just another piece of wayward baggage going around in circles on a moving black surface, getting the disobedience spanked out of her.

To make matters worse, my mother was a teacher at the same school. I was sure she'd hear about this very soon.

There was no spanking machine inside the principal's office, to my great relief. And there were no repercussions at home that night, either. Just surprised looks and suppressed laughter around the dinner table when the story came out that I'd whistled mere moments after the principal told us it was against the rules.

"*Why* did you do that?!" my brother asked, laughing.

"I wanted to see what would happen," I said.

Looking back, that little six-year old's curiosity is still within me.

It has, I realize, *always* been with me. What would happen, I once wondered, if I called a PBS station and offered to help them, even though I had no experience working in television? What would happen if I reached out to a stranger wearing nice shoes? What would happen if I asked to cowrite and coproduce a half-million-dollar documentary no one else wanted to work on? What would happen if I insisted a particular film be shot on location in Italy? What would happen if I lost my job and went into business for myself? What would happen if I took on one film project after another, despite qualms I was not qualified, or qualified enough? What would happen if I uprooted my kids and moved the three of us to Asheville? What would happen if I took them to Belize?

In his popular book *Save the Cat,* screenwriter Blake Snyder wrote that films are "intricately made, emotional machines"—and I have responded to them as such, choosing to tease out ideas and suggestions I thought I saw in the films and documentaries that came my way in order to shape my own life. As a result, many problems and life issues were solved or resolved, often in surprising ways.

A Baryshnikov special opened the door to freelance work, which in turn led to working at the documentary workshop, which led to an education in making documentaries along with unexpected international adventures and my name in the credits. There have been scary times when I rode my fears and anger like rocket fuel, but mostly I followed the path the films seemed to lay out before me.

Had it not been for working at the documentary workshop, I wouldn't have met my good friend Stephen, who uttered those famous words "What about Asheville?" and thereby changed my life's direction in a hundred unimaginable ways. I would have missed lessons on the craft of writing from Madeleine L'Engle. Had it not been for working as a freelancer for WNET in New York, I wouldn't have worked on the Bill Moyers specials and would never have met the mystical monk of Capitol Hill, who helped make my IRS troubles go away. Had it not been for working with documentary films, I wouldn't have met Bruce Norfleet and found the inspiration for my father's last wonderful year. I was able to make peace with my sister's untimely death from breast cancer thanks to John Kaplan and his uplifting film *Not As I Pictured,* and Patrick Norman's *Full Circle.* Thanks to the storyboard of documentary films I'd worked on, I was already a digital nomad two decades before the global pandemic hit and work patterns changed. Most importantly, the Joseph Campbell series gave me permission to live in joy.

There have been hundreds of "what would happen if" moments throughout the past three decades. Not all of them have worked out, but a surprising and encouraging amount of them have.

And now, a positive, emboldened change in tense—a switch from conditional to future tense—has blossomed inside my head. My thoughts are no longer what *would* happen if. . . . They have become what *will* happen if. . . ? What will happen if I leave the world of documentary films and PBS station wrangling behind me and try something new?

Ever curious about the "what ifs," it feels like a good time to move on, both to a new location and to working for myself.

Letting Go of the Monkey Bars, Again (This Bird Has Flown)

THE MORNING OF November 30, 2001, Zoë came into my bedroom, sat on my bed and stared at me until I awoke. I sensed her presence but resisted for a few moments, lingering in subconsciousness.

"I've got sad news for you, Mama," she said when I eventually gave in and opened my eyes. All kinds of things came into my mind, but not what she had to tell me.

"What is it?" I asked. "*Are you okay?*"

She paused a beat before saying, "George Harrison died."

Knowing he was my favorite Beatle, Zoë had wanted to be the first to give me the news.

I had always associated George Harrison with "Norwegian Wood," the first Beatles song on which he played the sitar. Being part Danish and having spent most of my twenties in the Scandinavian furniture industry, I often thought of this as my theme song.

When the album *Rubber Soul* was released in December 1965, my sister Karen bought a copy. She brought it home and played it for Mom and Dad. I remember her laughing at the lyrics of

"Norwegian Wood," which my ten-year-old self thought a bit shocking. It was about a man and a woman spending the night together and there she was, playing it and laughing about it *in front of our parents.*

In an interview with *Rolling Stone* magazine about his seeming lack of contributions to the Beatles' output of songs, Harrison said the breakup of the Beatles was the best thing that could have happened to him as a creative person.

Being a part of the Beatles, he said, "was like having diarrhea and not being allowed to go to the toilet. I think a lot of people were surprised to see 'Oh, *he* writes songs, too.'"

I've never forgotten that quote—it resonated with me.

For decades I've been working with all kinds of creative people, helping them get *their* work out there, and I've loved it. But ever since I can remember, I've had this longing inside me to work and create *just* for myself—books, photography, illustrations, whatever. *My* ideas, *my* stories.

In 2006, five years after George Harrison's death, colleagues at Oregon Public Broadcasting sent me a copy of a new documentary to see if I would be interested in working with them to represent it to PBS stations nationally. *Out of the Shadow* told the very personal story of filmmaker Susan Smiley's mother, Millie, and her struggles to raise her two small daughters while navigating schizophrenia's bizarre behaviors and the tangle of her own personal mental jungle.

This sounded frightening to me. Worried that watching it might torpedo my hard-earned positive spirits, the DVD sat on my desk untouched for almost two weeks. Eventually the nudges from Selena and Nimmi in Portland grew more persistent until I could no longer avoid getting back to them with my thoughts on the film.

One evening, glass of wine in hand, I finally watched it. Empathy grew inside of me as I watched Millie, a beautiful young blonde with movie star radiance, in faded and jittery home movies as she alternated between loving mother and lost soul.

To my surprise, sad as the story was, it didn't depress me. It was a warm and loving portrayal of what was often a difficult and bewildering childhood. I took on the film and became friends with Susan throughout the process.

It wouldn't be accurate to say the film foreshadowed or changed my life in any way. At least not in the usual way. In this case, it was just the title.

As I neared the end of writing this memoir, I decided to reread *The Artist's Way* by Julia Cameron. I still had my original, dog-eared, highlighted copy on the shelf among other books I have accumulated on writing and creativity. It had been twenty-five years since I'd first read it (not long after the interview with Madeleine L'Engle) and Cameron's tools of "morning pages" and "artist dates" were both well ingrained in my daily and weekly routines.

Reading it again, however, I noticed two words I'd highlighted, then apparently forgotten about: shadow artists.

> *Shadow artists are to be found shadowing declared artists. . . Artists love artists. Shadow artists are gravitating to their rightful tribe but cannot yet claim their birthright. . . Shadow artists often choose shadow careers, those close to the desired art, even parallel to it, but not the art itself.*

A shadow artist. I must have realized that's what I was when I first read *The Artist's Way* so many years ago. But I also knew I had to earn a living—and I chose to do that by helping other people with their own stories.

I decided it was time to take one last cue from the many films I've worked with, step out of the shadow, and focus on my own storytelling.

I've loved writing since I was nine years old. At the time, we were living in London and *Bunty*—my favorite weekly comic book for girls—had just announced a poetry competition. Immediately, I knew I wanted to enter.

"But what should I write about?" I asked my mother.

"Well, they always say to write about something you know," she replied.

I looked around my bedroom and decided to write a poem about my Danish troll. I sent the resulting eight lines off to the editors of *Bunty*, then waited impatiently to see my name in print.

Several weeks later, a small envelope addressed to me in beautiful handwriting came through the letter slot in our flat. Inside I found a very polite rejection letter. I was shocked. Certain they had made a mistake—and against the better judgment of my mother—I sent them my poem *again*. This time, they didn't bother to reply.

It makes me smile each time I remember this—not because I was rejected, but because that little nine-year-old had such confidence in her writing. Where did that come from, I've often wondered—and where did it go?

At 14, I began writing an illustrated newspaper for my family about all the mundane little nature events that happened in our two-acre garden outside Philadelphia. It had a grand distribution of six and featured a contributing column from a *New York Times* foreign correspondent, Lawrence Fellows (my uncle).

By the time I was 17, we were once again living in London. I kept writing, crafting somewhat off-the-wall short homework assignments in my senior year English class. My teacher, Linda Riebel, liked them.

"Kris is a natural language arts student," she wrote in my quarterly report. "I hope she pursues literature and writing in the future."

It was my favorite report card ever, my north star. I rediscovered it in a box of old papers a few years ago and now keep it taped to my computer as a reminder of her confidence in me.

I think in stories. They are always telling themselves to me in my head. And I am always listening. That's why the world of documentary film has been so appealing to me. What's always held me back from telling my own stories, however, was letting go of my hard-won financial safety net. Now, nearly two hundred film projects later, I am challenging myself once again to "be not afraid" and jettison myself from my safety perch, out into the void. As C.S. Lewis wrote, it's like crossing monkey bars—you have to let go at some point in order to move forward.

With Susan Smiley's *Out of the Shadow*, it wasn't the substance of the documentary that inspired or changed my life. It was just the title, a gentle suggestion to let go of the monkey bar and reach ahead for the next one.

The first time I saw the house I would eventually buy in Portugal, I knew which room would be my writing studio. And now it is.

My father's old English pine cupboard and bookshelves are on one wall. His colorful, antique Persian rug lies on top of the tiled floor. There's a black drafting table with art supplies against another wall. My computer sits on a second black drafting table with another old English pine chest of drawers close by filled with paints, brushes, and my old marble carving tools.

The walls are hung with posters and artwork from my storyboard years, including a poster I bought during one of the *American Byzantine* shoots in Italy. Copies of articles I've written and writing awards I've won are taped on a door—a new vision board for this next stage of my life. Instead of index cards, I'm four-walling my entire studio with my dreams.

Many years after we parted ways, I got an email from Martin. It was in response to an email I'd sent him congratulating him on an award I saw he'd won for one of his films. Along with my congratulations, I wrote a few words about the films I was working on, as well as a note about the book I was writing on my grandmother's life in Ethiopia. I ended with a few words of appreciation for all I'd learned from my years working with him, expressing the hope that my work would be a credit to his mentoring and support.

To my surprise, I received a response from him that afternoon telling me about a film he was making on the topic of forgiveness. He ended with a few words of encouragement.

"The work you are involved in sounds terrific," he wrote, "and very much you. The book is something I think you wanted to get under your belt . . . now maybe it will be two or three. You don't need mentoring, just a chance to show your stuff."

WHEREVER YOU ARE IS ALWAYS THE RIGHT PLACE

There is never a need to fix anything,
to hitch up the bootstraps of the soul
and start at some higher place.

Start right where you are.

JULIA CAMERON, *THE ARTIST'S WAY*

DO YOU REMEMBER that young woman, the one who was sitting alone and shivering in the cold on a park bench in the middle of Washington, DC?

When we began these adventures, it was the week before Christmas, she was six months pregnant, and she was crying because she had just lost her job in a career she loved. She had absolutely no idea what lay ahead and if you'd told her the adventures that would unfold over the coming years, it's likely she would not have believed you.

She had not yet heard of Julia Cameron—it would be another four years before *The Artist's Way* would be published.

Nevertheless, she started from the right place, which was right there, in that moment, on that park bench. After she'd had a good cry, she wiped her eyes with her reddened hands and pulled herself together.

In the coming days, she perused the employment section of the *Washington Post,* looking for architecture firms hiring project architects. Not that she was trained as an architect. She wasn't. But having worked—albeit it tangentially—in corporate interior design, she thought it sounded like an interesting field.

She called a few firms successful enough to be hiring staff, getting past the receptionist each time by asking for the principal's name mentioned in the ad. When she was put through, she immediately explained to the principal that she was *not* an architect. However, she had worked in commercial design and perhaps she could help them on the business development side?

To her surprise, her non-linear thinking got her in the door. Several interviews resulted in two jobs and she earned enough to get through the next two years, but just barely.

It would be that same sideways thinking that would prompt her to call her local PBS station the morning after seeing Baryshnikov's *Nutcracker* and offer to help them raise money—the first frame in her very own storyboard.

None of it would be easy.

But in retrospect, that is what has made it better.

CLOSING CREDITS

At the risk of coming across like an Academy Award-winner at the microphone with a long list of names in hand, there are many people to thank.

There are different kinds of mentors. If you're lucky, they appear when you least expect it. It's up to you to notice them.

Mentor of the Mind

Alan von Eggers Rudd taught me how to think, gave me confidence, told me I was the purple bead, then kicked me from the nest so that I could free fall, find my own wings and fly into a new and even better career, using the ideas I learned from him as fuel.

Mentor of the Craft

Julia Cameron, whose advice about morning pages and artist dates changed everything.

Martin Doblmeier, who has now produced dozens of films on religion and spirituality, for wearing a nice pair of shoes to a town hall meeting and for giving me my start in art research and documentary film production. I will be forever grateful for the insight and perspective his film *Final Blessing* gave me on how to handle my sister's cancer diagnosis and eventual death. In retrospect, I'm very appreciative he had a change of heart about our future together. He was right.

Door-Opening Mentors

William F Baker—teasingly nicknamed "The Doctors Bill" for the multiple PhDs he's been awarded for his work (I think it's close to a dozen now)—for believing in me and for jump-starting my career with his religious art films, *The Face: Jesus in Art* and *Picturing Mary,* and for guiding other film projects my way, including *Jerzy Popieluszko: Messenger of the Truth.*

Joseph Braddock, PhD—noted nuclear physicist, businessman and Catholic philanthropist, who left us in 2021 at the age of 91. During his long career, Joe was recognized for his contributions in national security, healthcare, education, and information technologies. An intelligent, kind, and generous man, he left his mark on the world—and on me, the night he told me to "Let go and let God."

Bill Moyers, for giving me the opportunity to help get the word out internationally about many important programs he created.

Paul Peckar, MD, without whom my life would be entirely different.

Congressman Jim Moran—had he not hosted a town hall meeting one evening in the early 1990s, my whole career might never have happened.

And, of course, thanks to **Mikhail Baryshnikov,** whose ballet on PBS started everything for me.

Filmmaker and Storyteller Friends

Stephen Ames for his friendship throughout the past three decades of upheavals and plot twists and for his life-changing suggestion, "What about Asheville?"

Keith Ochwat for creating Show&Tell, a wonderful community for documentarians, and for sending dozens of filmmakers my way. And for always being a cheerful, can-do, positive, and generally delightful guy to work with.

Bruce Norfleet for (unbeknownst to him) inspiring me through his film *The Price of Freedom* to find the perfect environment for my father's adventurous last year of life at the Old Soldiers' Home in Washington, DC.

Bob Olive, former Chief Operating Officer of Georgia Public Broadcasting, for suggesting about twenty years ago that I quit my day job and write (I still have that email, Bob!)

Heartfelt thanks to the following filmmakers, producers, visionaries, and professional friends
You have helped me in ways you may or may
not be aware of, and you each deserve your
own special shoutout. Thank you!

Andy Abrahams Wilson • Andy @ WNVT • Mike Abrams • Claire Adamsick • Allison Argo • Hannah Lillith Assadi • Ned Augustenborg • Ron Bachman • Robin Baker Leacock • Judy Barlow • Rob Beemer • Sky Bergman • Thomas Bertch Jr • Hülya Biren • Renee Bishop • Layton Blaylock • Jack Bogdanovich • Paul Bonesteel • Regan Brashear • Peter Broderick • Steve Budlong • Bruce Bucklin • Ken Burns • Katie Cadigan • Molly Casteloe • Frances Causey • Melody Cavanary • Liz Cheng • Bill Chisholm • Richard Chisolm • Carrie Corbin • Kim Christiansen • Nan Davis • Jeff Davidson • James Davie • Robyn De Shields • Nancy Dobbs • Judy Doctoroff • Beth Dolan • Joe Dorman • Reilly Dowd • Bob Dreyfuss • Tom Dunkle • Carole Dysinger • Scott Dwyer • Mike Edwards • Michael Ehrenzweig • Regina Eisenberg • Galia Farber • Cynthia Fenneman • Dan Ford • Mark Fortney • Ruth Friendly • Brian Gadinsky • Dave Gallagher • Juan Garcia • Mary Gardner • Nathan Gebhard • Stella Giammasi • Abby Ginzberg • Eric Gnezda • Gillian Gonda • Amy Green • Kate Sullivan Green • Peter Gregutt • Jamie Haines • Kim Haas • Shawn Halford • Dan Hamby • Mat Hames • Donna Hardwick • Megan Harrington • Aundrea Hart • Steve Heflin • Aine Henderson • Christie Herring • Ulf Herrmann • Sheila Higgins • Beverly Himm • Rich Homberg • Gale Anne Hurd • Feriha Ishtar • Marcia Jarmel • Aimee Jones • J.R. Jones • Trevor Jones • Gabriella Jones-Litchfield • John Kaplan • Devin Karambelas • Lisa Kaselak • Annisa Kau • Nancy Kelly • Fiona Kennedy • Richard Kilberg • Kris Koenig • Joan Konner • Katie Koskenmaki • Diana Kushner • Sara Lamm • Lisa Landi • Shara Lange • Darren LaShelle • Dominique Lasseur • Selena Lauterer • Jennifer Lawson • Chuck

Leavell • Roland Legiardi-Laura • Joan Lence • James Lewis • Gayle
Loeber • Eric Luskin • Craig MacGowan • Mickela Mallozzi • Barbara
Margolis • Roselynn Marra • Mike Marriner • Harry Mavromichalis
• Matt Mayers • Ryan Mayers • Brian McAllister • Jordana Meade •
Miles Merritt & Gail Kempler • Segundo Mercado-Llorens • Linda
Midgett • Julia Mintz • Ed Moore • Barbara Morgan • Douglas
Muchoney • Michael Murphy • Tom Neal • Sara Needham • Lesley
Norman • Patrick Norman • Stephen Olsson • Charles Oppmann
• Christina Pagones • Henry Panion III PhD • Al Perlmutter • Bob
Petts • Rosemary Plum • Steve Pressman • Salvatore Rassa • Valerie
Red-Horse Mohl • Neal Reed • Debi Robertson • Robin Rodriguez •
Kristen Rolf • Frank Romeo • Jamie Ross • David Rubinsohn • Mikol
von Eggers Rudd • Tom Salmon • Donna Sanford • Chris Sariego •
Nancy Schiesari • Ken Schneider • John Schorr of Sun Studio • Joseph
Schroeder • Greg Schwartz • Nina Gilden Seavey • Stephen Segaller •
Tom Shepard • Zvi Shoubin • John Siceloff • Jonathan Silvers • Angee
Simmons • Lisa Simon • Andrea Sims • Nimmi Singh • Tal Skloot •
Susan Smiley • Stephen Smith • Marc Smolowitz • Nancy Southgate
• Ed Spier • Sreedevi Sripathy • Kellie Castruita Specter • Ross Spears
• Robert Sproul-Cran • Kai Statts • Rick Steves • Anne Stonehill •
Bill Stotesbery • Jean Strauss • Paul Sutter • Michael Tang • Catherine
Tatge • Moni Taylor • Ellen Temple • Jennifer Tennican • Bill Thrash
• Chris Tomlinson • Barbara Valentino • Tina Apellaniz Waganer •
Vera Wagman • Bruce Ward • Suzannah Warlick • Leah Warshawski
• Morrie Warshawski • David Washburn • Gary Waxler • Michael
Webber • Ernest White II • Kenji Yamamoto • Mickey Youmans •
Chris Zaluski • Stuart Zuckerman

Thank you for trusting me with your films, dreams, and friendship.

Most of all, more gratitude than I can express to all of my PBS friends
and colleagues, without whom I could not have pulled any of this off.

Lastly, I am so appreciative to my talented and supportive global publishing team. In Portugal, Leslie Hinson, whose line-editing sessions were not only fun but somewhat magical. In Baltimore, Kathryn Goldman, who made a legal review surprisingly interesting and not nearly as scary as I'd anticipated. In Switzerland, Caroline Smrstik painstakingly polished the rough edges of this manuscript into an acceptable Chicago standard and did it with kindness. And in New Zealand, special thanks to the team at Damonza who dreamed up the book's unique cover and gave the book's interior a distinctive layout.

Dammit, I hear that music playing, which means it's time for me to leave the microphone even though there are so many more filmmakers, colleagues, and friends yet to thank. My heartfelt apologies to anyone I have not included, I know there are many of you. . . .